Screen Presence

Screen Presence
Cinema Culture and the Art of Warhol, Rauschenberg, Hatoum and Gordon

Stephen Monteiro

EDINBURGH
University Press

For Manisha and Dhruv

Edinburgh University Press is one of the leading university presses in the UK. We publish academic books and journals in our selected subject areas across the humanities and social sciences, combining cutting-edge scholarship with high editorial and production values to produce academic works of lasting importance. For more information visit our website: www.edinburghuniversitypress.com

Edinburgh University Press Ltd
The Tun – Holyrood Road
12 (2f) Jackson's Entry
Edinburgh EH8 8PJ

First published in hardback by Edinburgh University Press 2016

Typeset in Garamond MT Pro by
Servis Filmsetting Ltd, Stockport, Cheshire,
and printed and bound in Great Britain by
CPI Group (UK) Ltd, Croydon CR0 4YY

A CIP record for this book is available from the British Library

ISBN 978 1 4744 0337 5 (hardback)
ISBN 978 1 4744 2597 1 (paperback)
ISBN 978 1 4744 0338 2 (webready PDF)
ISBN 978 1 4744 1180 6 (epub)

Contents

Figures

Acknowledgements

I have benefited from the support and encouragement of many as I researched and wrote this book. I would like to thank Amy Freund, Ellen McBreen, Jennifer Olmsted, Tania Ruiz and John Tain for their responses to early versions of this work. My colleagues – past and present – at the American University of Paris have provided an environment conducive to exploring the ideas posited here. Among them, I would thank particularly Kathleen Chevalier, Waddick Doyle, Jérôme Game, Jayson Harsin, Mark Hayward, Justin McGuinness, Robert Payne, Charles Talcott, Julie Thomas and Hervé Vanel. This book has been enriched by conversations over the years with Valérie Berty, Nicholas Mirzoeff, Richard Misek, Laura Mulvey, Brenda Murphy, Thomas Ort, Surajit Sarkar, Nanna Verhoeff and Gregory Zinman. I am grateful to all of them for their insights. Parts of this book were presented at New York University, Jawaharlal Nehru University and the annual meetings of the Society of Cinema and Media Studies and the Association of Art Historians. My thanks go to the organisers and audiences of these events for their interest and feedback. In the final year of writing, I benefited from a visiting professorship in the Department of Art History and Communication Studies at McGill University, and I thank Christine Ross and Jenny Burman for organising this opportunity, as well as Jonathan Sterne and Tamar Tembeck for welcoming me into the sphere of Media@McGill. Grants from the Terra Foundation for American Art, the Canadian Centre for Architecture and the Faculty Development Fund of the American University of Paris have supported this research at key moments and I appreciate the generosity of those institutions. I am indebted as well to Bob Adelman, Lucinda Devlin, Douglas Gordon and Mona Hatoum for granting me permission to reproduce their work here. I am particularly appreciative of Mona Hatoum's decision to waive fees for images of her works. Hannah van den Wijngaard at White Cube and Miriam Perez at Gagosian Gallery were helpful in researching and securing images for Chapters 3 and 4. I owe my editors at Edinburgh – Gillian Leslie and Richard Strachan, and series editors Martine Beugnet and Kriss Ravetto – my gratitude for their enthusiasm for this project and guidance in getting the manuscript to print.

My parents, Lois Ann Hodgins Monteiro and George Monteiro, and sisters, Emily and Katherine, have inspired and challenged me in innumerable ways over the years, and for that I will always be grateful. Manisha Iyer and Dhruv Iyer Monteiro have made my life more joyous, exciting and rewarding than I could ever have hoped. My love for them is much greater than the book's dedication can attest.

Introduction: Cinema's Grey Spaces

Moving images inhabit the spaces of contemporary art. We regularly find them glowing on screens at exhibitions, fairs, festivals and performances. They form a part – sometimes a large part – of public and private collections around the world. As a result, screens and beams of light have become as common to the gallery experience as white walls and track lighting. Despite this ubiquity, however, there has not been adequate reckoning of the diverse historical and aesthetic origins of projected, moving-image art. 'After years of being fixed onto celluloid, gripped by the teeth of the film projector, and confined to the single screen of the cinema auditorium, the moving image has escaped', Catherine Fowler declares in her study of the projected image in the gallery. 'No longer purely celluloid, no longer solely projected, present on multiple screens and in a variety of spaces, "cinema" . . . is everywhere'.[1] Whether it be everywhere today, the historical evidence suggests cinema was already everywhere yesterday. Throughout its history, collective viewing of projected moving images has never been limited to the single screen of the theatre, but has proliferated in a variety of places, institutions and circumstances. This diversity of cinema culture (whether relying on film, magnetic tape or digital supports) has shaped art's appropriation of, and response to, projected moving images since the second half of the twentieth century. However, the intersection of these multiple historical and cultural vectors in projection-based contemporary art has been largely minimised or ignored by critics and historians.

This book attempts to remedy that error by demonstrating the influence of cinema's differing forms on the careers of four highly regarded artists. It asserts the dependence of Andy Warhol, Robert Rauschenberg, Mona Hatoum and Douglas Gordon on a broad range of moving-image practices as they employed the materials, mechanisms and aesthetics of several modalities for making and projecting images. The chapters that follow trace the impact of multiple, popular film and video cultures on artworks instantiating the moving image from the mid-1950s into the 2000s. They reflect the hypothesis that often marginalised non-theatrical forms, such as home movies and pornographic peep shows, or specialised commercial exhibition modes such as CinemaScope and the drive-in, represent variant examples of cinema that are fundamental to such art. Recognising these influences – and that of other historical forms of moving-image production and exhibition – will only enhance our understanding of moving-image works – and contemporary art in general – by opening onto new, competing interpretations that further erode already troubled ontological distinctions between art and mass culture. It also may benefit considerations of present-day media culture, suggesting that our increasing dependence on multiple, interconnected platforms reflects tendencies that extend back through earlier networks of now-obsolete viewing technologies and formats. Within the interpretative frame proposed here, one may consider the artworks examined in this book as important critiques of modern visual regimes, regimes that appear all the more pervasive and powerful when understood as intrinsic to multiple, popular moving-image practices.

The Whole Lot

Interpretations of the origins and significance of projected-image artworks have taken a number of paths, none adequately accounting for film's history as a cultural form marked by multifarious social and material practices. The construction and functioning of these works have sometimes been understood primarily in relation to experimental cinema, or other forms of art, such as painting and sculpture.[2] On other occasions, they have been considered in simple relief against a mythical standard, classical cinema, by concentrating on a false opposition between the movie theatre and the gallery. In all of these instances, projected-image art's particular qualities are cast as radical departures in the history of the projected image even when they stem from identifiable antecedents in the long, variegated past of multiple and often widespread ways of creating and accessing such images. As Haidee Wasson states, 'Film is productively understood as a family of technologies, an assemblage of things and systems that are multiply articulated across its history and its contexts.'[3] While this pluralistic past of the moving image is increasingly important in film and media studies for shaping understandings of contemporary technologies, media ecologies and participatory practices, it has been slow to penetrate scholarly accounts of moving-image art.

The prevailing interpretative modes for explaining such art have routinely invoked the feature film and movie theatre – both already targets of apparatus theory and the historical antagonism between mainstream commercial and experimental (or avant-garde) cinema – as the paradigms against which moving-image artworks should be distinguished and assessed. For example, in his extensive work on moving-image art Raymond Bellour identifies a shift from the 'self-assured cinema that belongs to a specific time in its history . . . of projection in film theatres' to the onset of '"multiple cinemas" inherent in contemporary installations'.[4] The frequently implied antagonism between the movie theatre and the art gallery, often described in terms of the 'black box' and the 'white cube', creates an additional opposition held together by well-worn distinctions between film and art – and film studies and art history – as discreet areas respectively serving mass and elite culture.[5] As Helen Molesworth has described it

> The hygienic isolation of the white cube has slowly, but steadily, been over-taken by an increasingly promiscuous black box. As any turn-of-the-century member of the art public knows, darkened rooms and heavy black curtains signal the omnipresent film and/or video installation . . . One effect of this development is that the stream of moving images that defines contemporary visual culture has seeped into the water table of contemporary art.[6]

Although Molesworth is a curator and advocate of moving-image art, her description of promiscuity and contaminated water supplies manifests fears surrounding the blurring of those cultural distinctions. Limiting the discourse around projection-based moving images in art contexts to comparisons with a monolithic commercial film industry both simplifies the task and clarifies the outcome of interpretation. Under such comparisons, the presence of these works in art spaces must signal either the rejection of commercial cinema (Bellour) or a corrupting force in art (Molesworth). Any other possibility further compromises already contested distinctions between popular media practices and art environments.

Such a historical narrative typically comprises two episodes. The first is the rise of 'expanded cinema' in the 1960s and 1970s, which produced works and events of great diversity seeking to challenge and expose the ideological foundations of the material conditions of both cinema and gallery. From this perspective, movies and commercial media are taken to task by the artist's transformation of the film apparatus into a new form that is no longer transparent or immediately accessible. Aspects of this thinking survive in recent assessments of the function of film-based works in the gallery, as with the claim that 'the progressive integration of film into the gallery and the museum, as it mutates and fractures to take on *a guise very different to any we have seen before*, changes our conception of cinema'.[7] While certain configurations of presenting and viewing moving images may strike twenty-first century art audiences as novel, in truth there are usually significant precedents in modern popular practices, a few of which are considered in this book. The second episode of the inherited narrative begins with the millennial surge in projection-based artworks observed by Molesworth. These works enter the gallery, along with recuperated examples of expanded cinema, as though the space might serve as refuge from digital media's accelerating threat to film-based production and the long-standing, seemingly stable historical conditions of film exhibition. 'The gallery's current default setting is the acknowledged but unanalysed and uncritical acceptance of narrative cinema – replaying it, re-enacting it, duplicating it and fetishizing its modes of address,' A. L. Rees has said of the aftermath of this surge.[8] Recalling the legacy of expanded cinema, Molesworth has commented, 'Given the medium's decidedly oppositional and non-narrative beginnings, this seeming embrace of mass culture and its storytelling devices signals a significant shift in the trajectory of the medium.'[9] Some have feared the cinematisation of the art space itself, as though galleries and museums would become a derivative of the multiplex. As George Baker explained in 2003, 'Film and projection are dominant aesthetic modes for contemporary art institutions and mega-exhibitions [inducing] an intense relativization of the field of the art institution, the art critic and the art historian by film history, cinema history, film theory.'[10] Indeed, in the present century the theory and history of projected-image artworks and their exhibition have been considered with nearly equivalent interest by film journals such as *Screen*, *Cinema Journal* and *The Velvet Light Trap*, and art journals such as *October*, *Grey Room* and *Art Journal*.[11]

Across these opposing views of projected moving-image artwork as a subversion or survival of the theatre-based cinema of the culture industry, there runs a tendency to reduce the entire history of projected moving images to commercial (i.e. Hollywood) and experimental cinema. A few examples may illustrate this point. In 1967, at the height of expanded cinema's penetration into art and performance spaces, Sheldon Renan claimed that the movement

> destroyed the old idea – that the motion picture is a static work, that it is exactly the same work every time it is shown, and that motion pictures should be made to universal specifications on given machines under given and never changing conditions.

Through alternative techniques that 'attack', 'fragment' and 'destroy', cinema was 'liberated from the concept of standardization', according to Renan, a sentiment that corresponds with Fowler's description of film's liberation from both projector and movie theatre.[12] Film-maker Bradley Eros also sustained Renan's assessment nearly forty years after he made it, claiming in 2005

> Since the architectural limitations from which [cinema's] physical parameters derive were often not sufficient to match the new perceptual paradigms of this radical conception of cinema, not engendered from a traditional theatrical model, experiments with other screening environments were demanded. Pioneers of paracinema, with varying degrees of complexity, subtlety, and

effectiveness, created imaginative alternatives to the rigid standard of the popular moviehouse.[13]

As recently as 2009, curator Ian White posited that 'Cinema . . . is a word everyone understands' embodying 'the auditorium [and] narrative films of a certain length, of one genre or another'. White added

> We do not think about the industrial system of production and distribution that generates our assumptions about cinema as just one way amongst others by which things might be organised. This other work – let us say, work made by artists – is remarkably different from the institution that comes to mind when we read the word 'cinema'.[14]

Four years later, Erika Balsom pointed out that 'it is clear that the cinema's ontology has always been diverse and variable'. However, her examples of that diversity are limited to cinema's development 'from a mute technological marvel through the epic spectacles of CinemaScope and the advent of the blockbuster, to the small screens of television broadcasting and VCR platforms'. As such, she concluded that 'for decades, the elements of the cinematic apparatus had been relatively tightly sutured together to form a discernible entity, [but] recent years have seen these elements dispersed across the field of culture.'[15]

In recognising an 'institutional promiscuity' (that word again) in moving-image art, Andrew Uroskie has perceived a problematic relationship between art and film, within the limits of strict black-box/white-cube thinking. Seeing artists' film-making – in 1960s and 1970s expanded cinema above all – as an attempt to either bring the theatre and gallery together or 'discern . . . how one might be approached from the perspective of the other', Uroskie explains that

> the difficulty of locating artist film-making in the aesthetic discourse of the 1960s and in later discourses of art and film criticism is inextricably bound up with the difficulty of locating these practices within the physical, institutional or discursive space of either the art gallery or the cinematic theatre.[16]

Whether expressed by artist, curator, theorist or historian, these statements share a restricted historical vision of cinema reduced almost exclusively to the theatrical releases of national film industries and peripheral experimental work. Experienced against that backdrop, projected-image works in contemporary gallery spaces become 'events', according to film-maker and critic Yann Beauvais. 'They put cinema out on a limb, away from the "general history of cinema" or the history of experimental cinema understood as an experience of theatricality.'[17] While film and cinema have undergone enormous changes since the end of the twentieth century, particularly with the advent of digital recording equipment and networked storage and exhibition platforms, such a limiting vision underestimates the endemic lack of 'universal specifications' and 'rigid standards' that marked film's incarnations in varying film gauges, projection speeds, screen ratios and screening spaces *throughout* its history. It also downplays the sometimes vibrant history of avant-garde cinema, especially in the interwar period. Most important, at least in terms of the study at hand, this exclusionary discourse ignores the diverse terms of film exhibition and consumption that marked everyday life in the twentieth century. Amateur, commercial, industrial and educational movies seen in homes, drive-ins, peep-show booths, Panorams, classrooms, planetaria and in itinerant cinemas, among other examples, represent the 'other' cinema that existed beside, and circulated around, mainstream theatrical and experimental cinema, but that has remained largely outside the purview of criticism and scholarship regarding moving-image art.[18]

There have been occasional, encouraging signs of acknowledging that legacy. In a 2003 *October* roundtable on the projected image in art, Hal Foster asked, 'And what exactly is this common knowledge that we call cinematic? What is its canon? Is it commercial movies only?' Chrissie Iles, film and video curator at the Whitney Museum of American Art, responded in that context 'It's film as a physical medium, and it's also commercial movies.' Even when asked subsequently by Malcolm Turvey 'But, when you say film world, are you talking about commercial entertainment cinema, or film in general, including art cinema, and experimental film?' Iles widened the field only enough to include those categories, replying, 'Mainstream, independent, experimental, the whole lot.' George Baker offered a more inclusive vision in this roundtable, however, when he stated 'One of the most interesting uses of the projected image now is to disidentify with commercial, Hollywood cinema, and to somehow reconnect to and explore legacies within film that are outside of the Hollywood or the mass-cultural.'[19]

Maeve Connolly, in her work on moving-image art environments, has reaffirmed this belief, explaining that 'cinema history (rather than film theory) seems to hold an appeal for some [art] practitioners because it may offer models or prototypes for collectivity'.[20] Giuliana Bruno claims that the contemporary art museum represents a prime site for accessing the collected fragments of that history. Her conception of this diversity is limited to cinema's first years, however, before the establishment of movie theatres. 'There was an actual history of "installations" that took place at the very origin of film', she reasons. 'Today's artists appear to be winking at this very historic moment out of which cinema was born.'[21]

Jonathan Walley has argued the dangers of defining film through medium specificity, although he also regards cinema's historical relationship to art as dominated by Hollywood and art cinema, on the one hand, and the aims of experimental film-makers, on the other. Walley states that the history and theorisation of cinema in art contexts has been fraught by a split between a focus on medium specificity – most noteworthy in structuralist film – and generalisations 'bloated to the point of near meaninglessness' that would include nearly any temporally based media practice or performance.[22] In contrast to the limitations set by Iles, Foster and others, this tendency to broad inclusiveness was already well-represented in 1970 in Gene Youngblood's *Expanded Cinema*. Youngblood's seminal study considers not only film, but also television, software, cybernetics, holography and intermedia. 'Expanded cinema isn't a movie at all,' Youngblood states plainly. Proclaiming the onset of a new 'synaesthetic' cinema language advancing into other modes of communication, he explains that 'When we say expanded cinema we actually mean expanded consciousness.'[23]

Youngblood's call for such an opening of the mind should be heeded by those considering the history of projected-image artworks today. This would not require a descent into relativism, but rather a consideration of the important historical research done by film and media scholars in recent years in assessing the complex cultural applications and technological developments of the moving image in modernity. Outside the white cube and black box, it would recognise the scattered grey spaces of popular moving-image culture and their influence on art involving screens and projected images.

CINEMAS, MAJOR AND MINOR

Erika Balsom justly notes that projection-based artworks since 1990 'may be said to exhibit cinema in a double sense: they move it into the exhibition space of art, certainly, but they also expose it to view, hold it out for examination as a medical patient might exhibit symptoms'.[24] By studying the intersection of cinema with the work of four major artists representing different periods and backgrounds, this book's examination cuts across a large part of this patient's life, taking into account symptoms that may have been detected previously, but that have been misdiagnosed. Through a comparative approach that draws links between the production and exhibition choices of artists, on the one hand, and alternative, vernacular and specialised historical film forms, on the other, this book resituates moving-image based artworks within a spectrum of moving-image practices that may be considered major or minor but would have been familiar to twentieth-century audiences. Emphasising historical circumstances and overlooked relationships across media, environments and practices, such as the rivalry between film and television that spawned or shaped several of the popular and artistic practices studied here, this book affirms the presence of such modes of film making and viewing throughout the history of post-war and contemporary art. As its title suggests, it places particular emphasis on the critical role the screen has played not only in the look, operation and experience of these works, but also in the projected image's history of diverse cultural applications. The adaptability of the screen's material components, form, size and location has made it a pivotal object in the conception, execution and recognition of the projected image's many uses and contexts.

This undertaking relies on theories and approaches drawn from contemporary film and media studies, particularly those based in media archaeology, and brings them to bear on the theory and history of art. Erkki Huhtamo has described media archaeology as the investigation of those recurring phenomena across historical contexts that produce a sense of déjà vu when one confronts contemporary media forms and operations.[25] Unlike traditional historical approaches, media archaeology seeks out objects and applications that might be dismissed as dead-ends or peripheral distractions because they do not readily conform to teleological narratives.[26] What is exceptional about the examples studied in this book is their close, but frequently ignored, ties to relatively contemporaneous and widespread media technologies. That is, while media archaeology usually entails deep digging (as its name implies) this research uncovers artefacts that are still temporally close – film objects and practices of the last fifty to sixty years – that were readily at hand, or at least still extant, at the moment these artworks were produced. Indeed it would be nonsensical to label as 'archaeological' Robert Rauschenberg's insinuations of widescreen formats or Andy Warhol's evocations of home movies, or even Mona Hatoum's formal references to peep-show booths or Douglas Gordon's simulation of a drive-in, when such formats and models were familiar to people experiencing these works when they were first exhibited.

It is in the tendency of art scholarship to claim a 'jamais vu', rather than any sense of a déjà vu, when discussing the characteristics of moving-image based works and their exhibition that an archaeological approach may be the most effective response. This study therefore situates itself within current media archaeological debates not as a customary rereading of the technologies and practices it explores, nor as an explanation of current technologies and practices through exemplary antecedents, but rather as a means of demonstrating how such technologies and practices were read through coeval artistic interventions, and how (and why) those readings may have been lost. This requires delving into contemporaneous accounts, formats and practices, as well as the critical legacy and continuing theorisation of these works, to unearth the extent to which art history and curatorial decisions have undervalued or ignored relationships to diverse cinema practices in casting such works as a revision, subversion or deconstruction of the dominant theatrical model of cinema.

Jay David Bolter and Richard Grusin have considered such ties between media formats, technologies and contexts in relation to contemporary digital culture as processes of remediation, whereby aspects of earlier media forms and practices survive in those that follow.[27] Remediation is a particularly useful concept here. On the one hand, we can identify the perpetuation of such earlier cinema practices through formal and material traces in several of the works examined. Rauschenberg, Warhol, Hatoum and Gordon each formally and materially remediate a specific, popular form of cinema within different temporal and spatial frames of art production, exhibition and reception. However, curatorial and art historical discourse often identifies these formal and material traces as determinant factors in critically distancing these works from cinema (when understood narrowly as the theatrical model). In other words, the process of remediation is compounded in these cases, as the work's initial remediation of film in art contexts passes through the potentially obfuscating remediation of curatorial and critical reception, where ties to specific media forms can be attenuated, dismissed or lost.

Until the current generation of film scholars, studies of cinema's multiple forms and practices mirrored the relatively narrow interpretative approach of art history. Those that lay outside the theatrical model were routinely ignored. 'With few exceptions, there remains an overdetermined narrative of a dominant cinematic ideal that endured throughout the mid-century,' observes Haidee Wasson. 'Large and dark room, celluloid, projector, screen, seated audience – in short, the movie theater.'[28] Several studies of the past twenty years, however, have convincingly demonstrated the many ways film has been 'popular' both as a medium of wide appeal and consumption and as a technology and means of producing narrative employed by ordinary people under diverse, everyday circumstances. These include the work of Wasson on portable cinema, Charles Acland on film's pedagogical use in schools and other educational settings, Patricia Zimmermann and Karen Ishizuka on home movies, Amy Herzog on peep shows, Charles Tepperman on amateur cinema and Alison Griffiths on projected images in science museums and planetaria, in addition to Huhtamo's own work on the moving panorama and the screen's multiple incarnations.[29] Thomas Elsaesser sees media archaeology playing a significant part in this 'new film history'. By encouraging investigation beyond the teleological narrative of evolution and refinement told by the 'winners' (in this case, those concentrating on the rivalry between the commercial film industry and the avant-garde), these innovative forays have consequences for our understanding of cinema and the wider field of moving-image media. 'What an archaeological practice very quickly teaches us is not only that it is hard to tell winners from losers at this stage in the game,' Elsaesser explains, 'but that we are constantly rediscovering losers in the past who turn out to have become if not winners then the great-grandfathers of winners.'[30]

Whether we call projected moving-image artworks 'expanded cinema', 'gallery films', 'cinema of exhibition', 'other cinema', 'paracinema' or something else, tracing the progression and critical significance of the projected image's passage into art spaces solely in relation to standard movie-theatre practices or avant-garde movements implies a grossly simplified history of the moving image.[31] The medium of film and the experience of cinema existed in multiple formats that changed shape with the century's rapid shifts in media technologies and social conditions. The 1950s saw several widescreen processes emerge from Hollywood, for example, to radically alter the movie-theatre experience. The drive-in – first developed in the 1930s – provided new visual and social opportunities by situating cinema in the landscape. By the end of the 1950s, a quarter of all American movie theatres were drive-ins.[32] Throughout the century, home-movie making and viewing proved a common and significant form of cinema outside commercial and avant-garde networks. At mid-century, millions of home-movie cameras were sold annually.[33] From the 1960s to 1990s, pornographic peep shows represented a primary means for viewing recorded sexual acts on film and video. Popping up in cities around North America and Europe, the peep show – which was not always a solitary experience – represented hundreds of millions of dollars in annual revenue before home video, cable and satellite distribution absorbed the market.[34]

All of these practices of cinema have impacted the making of moving-image art. This book refracts contemporary art's relationship to the projected image through the prism of these unexpected – yet historically and culturally significant – examples. Warhol was not far from the mark when he said 'It's the movies that have really been running things in America ever since they were invented. They show you what to do, how to do it, when to do it, how to feel about it, and how to *look* how you feel about it.'[35] In closely examining his example alongside those of the other artists presented here, the episodic historical framework of the chapters that follow maps new ground in the deep-seeded relationship between art, cinema formats and vernacular culture. The structure is chronological, with each chapter focused on the circumstances around the creation and reception of key works by a single artist. The choice of Rauschenberg, Warhol, Hatoum and Gordon is meant to demonstrate a continuing dialogue between art and popular cinema forms across divergent contexts, aesthetics and agendas that has gone largely unnoticed despite the considerable commercial success and cultural visibility of these artists. It spans the historical and cultural frames of abstract art, conceptual art, pop art, feminist art, installation art, performance art and appropriation art, not to mention expanded cinema and what has been called 'post-cinema'.[36]

Each of these artists employs different strategies that collectively indicate a sustained engagement between art and popular cinema forms through variable (and sometimes incompatible) aesthetic stances and social agendas. Focusing on four artists allows detailed consideration of manifold interpretations of a specific work and practice that often encompasses multiple historical moments and exhibitions. Of course, works and practices never exist in isolation. Every chapter therefore places its principal examples in relation to the production of other artists, among them Allan Kaprow, Nam June Paik, Stan Brakhage, Jonas Mekas, Carolee Schneemann, VALIE EXPORT, Tacita Dean, Philippe Parreno and Phil Collins, to demonstrate a wider field of influence for such models, while also indicating paths for further study. More artists and cinema forms could – and should – be considered within such parameters. The ranks of artists working with film and video have been broad and deep, as museum exhibitions, gallery shows, biennials, art fairs and of course other books on this subject attest. Considerations of moving-image art created outside the Western context are also necessary. Film and cinema have flourished in cultures across the globe, often in ways rarely encountered in North America and Europe. This prosperity underpins recent works by non-Western artists – including Subodh Gupta, Nástio Mosquito and Cao Fei – that incorporate projected moving images. Hopefully, scholarly assessments of the influence of historical forms of popular moving-image culture on such work will not be long in coming.

The book's opening chapter revisits Robert Rauschenberg's 1953 exhibition of his *White Paintings* in relation to the rise of widescreen cinema. Rauschenberg's display of 'blank' white canvases in different aspect ratios a few blocks from the world premiere of CinemaScope in Manhattan is a decisive act in art's relationship to moving-image culture in the second half of the twentieth century. In his emphasis on the potential play of ambient light on these screen-like surfaces, Rauschenberg drew a correspondence between art and cinema as both avant-garde painting and commercial film faced post-war identity crises (one tied to the formal problems of abstraction, the other the economic competition of television). This historical and geographical convergence of new screen forms in the gallery and theatre indicated lingering uncertainty over the nature of artistic production and visual phenomena in relation to wider social and economic structures. Consideration of contemporary accounts of CinemaScope and Rauschenberg's paintings – drawn from newspapers, trade journals and art magazines – demonstrates their shared commitment to the primacy of the spectator's immersion within the spatial interplay of the lighted surface and immediate surroundings. Considering the widespread, optimistic press coverage of CinemaScope's arrival and effects, this chapter argues that the *White Paintings'* polarising effect on the New York art world was exacerbated by their physical and temporal proximity to an ambitious new model of cinema.

In the expansion of art into new media contexts, Andy Warhol's Factory would become the most famous and closely documented site of such activity. Chapter 2 moves from the gallery and theatre into the studio to demonstrate how Andy Warhol's mid-1960s film production often eschewed those settings, instead taking on characteristics of home-movie culture in its aesthetics and presentation methods. Making the spectacle of a vernacular cinema and its multiple screen forms a primary component of his work, Warhol filmed friends and acquaintances in activities common to home movies, including sleeping, eating and simply sitting in front of the lens. Outside occasional (and sometimes notorious) movie-theatre screenings, Warhol tended toward alternative social and receptive conditions of film by projecting his works in diverse viewing spaces through a variety of improvised exhibition models and screen surfaces. From his Factory studio to friends' apartments, he used retractable mass-produced home-movie screens, wrinkled bed sheets and living-room walls to vary the conditions of projection and transform film into an unpredictable, yet deeply communal event. These strategies anchor his film-making in the common mid-century domestic practices of family shooting and viewing as a means to promote, reify and maintain intimate social relationships. Such casual conditions – uncommon even for the performance-based art of the 1960s, yet the norm in amateur cinema – were readily described in contemporaneous reports on Warhol in mainstream publications such as *Life* and *Newsweek*. They were minimised in later critical accounts of his work, however, and have since been discarded in most gallery exhibitions of his films.

Chapter 3 examines moving-image art's engagement with issues of intimacy and embodiment through the relationship between the feminist, body-based performance art of Mona Hatoum and the pornographic peep show, which flourished in urban spaces in the 1970s and 1980s. After working through the political implications of body and screen in live performance pieces in the 1980s, Hatoum created the video installation *Corps étranger*. Housed in a columnar structure recalling peep shows as well as medical visualising equipment such as the MRI (magnetic resonance imager), the 1994 piece included floor-based projections of an endoscopic exploration of the artist's body.

Created after the home-video boom that virtually eliminated the commercial viability of the peep show, *Corps étranger* and associated installations by

Hatoum capitalise on the presence of the screen as physical object to explore fetishisation and abjection in representations of the body in public settings. Just as the peep show offered fantasies of intimacy and proximity, *Corps étranger*'s floor-based screen facilitates bodily contact among viewers as well as the interpenetration of physical and imaged bodies. Seen in relationship to the heavily regulated material conditions of porn screening booths – from lighting and surface area to doors and glory holes – as gleaned from first-hand accounts, proceedings of government commissions on pornography, and popular press reports, the work's affinity with the peep show via the displaced screen runs against the grain of its critical reception. Descriptions of the work often concentrate on the screen as a recess or void to be circumvented, rather than a material interface for bodily exchange. Such readings reveal the difficulties of integrating alternate mass-media exhibition models – especially marginal or controversial ones – into both the museum space and the viewer's consciousness.

The celebration of cinema's centenary in the mid-1990s – amid declarations of its imminent demise – is the setting of Chapter 4. Assessments of film's first century would not only reinforce perceptions of the theatre model as cinema's only noteworthy incarnation, but also spark a major reinvestment of the projected image (often based on that misperception) in art contexts that has continued to this day. This chapter concentrates on the work of Douglas Gordon during that period, recognising his installations of projected images as akin to an archaeology of cinema. Gordon consistently eschews the physical and ideological conditions of the movie theatre in the art gallery, even as he excavates popular cinema for his material. Working almost exclusively with found footage or classic Hollywood films, he often fossilises their narratives by projecting the image at an excessively slow rate. His screens are precariously placed, angled against walls, columns and each other like rescued artefacts. Discernible in multiple works by Gordon prior to 2000, this evocation of the 'ruins' of cinema reaches its apotheosis in *5 Year Drive-By*, a monumental, short-lived outdoor installation erected in the California desert near Twentynine Palms in 2001. Crossing the adventurous appeal of drive-ins with the exile of the projected image to the topographical and historical margins of modern mass culture, *5 Year Drive-By* harboured a projection of John Ford's *The Searchers* (1956) moving at a geological rate of one frame every fifteen minutes. Studied alongside descriptions of drive-ins culled from film-industry documents, magazine articles and exhibitors' advertisements, *5 Year Drive-By* emerges as an exploration of cinema's stake in myths of Western expansion and neo-liberal progress. Projected day and night, the Twentynine Palms installation tested the legibility of the screen as a screen rather than, say, a whitewashed billboard. Caught in limbo between performance and object, the screen resembled the abandoned remains of a misguided modernism awaiting rediscovery or disintegration at the moment networked, mobile-media culture would transform basic understandings of cinema.

Through these episodes in art's interaction with the multiple specialised, but popular, cinema models of the twentieth century, this book may establish continuation where others find rupture, and rupture where others might sense continuity. What it primarily aims to illustrate, however, is the way common and banal practices may be dismissed or misunderstood, but will have far-reaching consequences in unexpected contexts. As Daniel Birnbaum claims, 'When new cultural formations appear they tend to use fragments from already obsolete forms . . . The future of exhibition making will deploy devices we once knew but had forgotten about.'[37] *Screen Presence* recuperates what we once knew but may have forgotten, not toward predicting the future, but rather to make sense of a more recent past, a past common to art and the moving image.

Notes

1. Catherine Fowler, 'Room for Experiment: Gallery Films and Vertical Time from Maya Deren to Eija Liisa Ahtila', *Screen* 45:4 (Winter 2004): 324–43, p. 324.

2. Tamara Trodd identifies split histories of 'experimental artists' films and gallery-based, projected images', with the latter 'often develop[ing] from and referenc[ing] the wider history of visual arts in general'. Tamara Trodd, 'Introduction: Theorising the Projected Image', in Tamara Trodd (ed.), *Screen/Space: The Projected Image in Contemporary Art* (Manchester: Manchester University Press, 2011), pp. 6–7. See also the chapters on painting and sculpture in Catherine Elwes, *Installation and the Moving Image* (New York: Wallflower Press, 2015).

3. Haidee Wasson, 'IN FOCUS: Screen Technologies', *Cinema Journal* 51:2 (Winter 2012): 141–4, p. 143.

4. Raymond Bellour, '"Cinema, Alone"/Multiple "Cinemas"', *Alphaville* 5 (Summer 2013), see http://www.alphavillejournal.com/Issue5/HTML/ArticleBellour.html (accessed 1 September 2015).

5. 'Black box' extends back to the *camera obscura* as the material and conceptual basis of photography and cinema. It has been used to describe imaging devices and apparatuses including the television ('little black box') and desktop computer. See Noam M. Elcott, *Artificial Darkness: An Obscure History of Modern Art and Media* (Chicago: University of Chicago Press, 2016). The term 'white cube' as a description of the art gallery appears to have been coined by Brian O'Doherty in his 1976 critique of contemporary gallery design. See Brian O'Doherty, *Inside the White Cube: The Ideology of the Gallery Space* (Santa Monica: Lapis Press, 1986 [1976]). Black-box/white-cube binaries in relation to moving images in art

spaces figure in Sabine Breitwieser, *White Cube/Black Box: Skulpturensammlung, Video, Installation, Film* (Vienna: Generali Foundation, 1996) and Andrew V. Uroskie, *Between the Black Box and the White Cube: Expanded Cinema and Postwar Art* (Chicago: University of Chicago Press, 2014).

6. Helen Anne Molesworth, *Image Stream* (Columbus: Wexner Center for the Arts, 2003), p. 8. Other statements by proponents of the moving image's entrance into art spaces that nevertheless frame it as a threat or burden include Kate Mondloch's claim that 'high-definition digital projections and architectural-scale screens have *colonized* gallery spaces and exhibitions across the globe', and Matthias Michalka's declaration that 'Today visual artists *can hardly avoid*, in the frame of their reflections on society, dedicating their efforts (to no small degree) to the moving image that has become a central point of reference in general'. Kate Mondloch, *Screens: Viewing Media Installation Art* (Minneapolis: University of Minnesota Press, 2010), p. xii; Matthias Michalka, 'Asides on Art and Film', in Pawel Althamer (ed.), *Art & Film: Curated by Vienna* (Nürnberg: Verlag für moderne Kunst, 2010), p. 40; my emphasis.

7. Erika Balsom, 'A Cinema in the Gallery, a Cinema in Ruins', *Screen* 50:4 (Winter 2009): 411–27, p. 411; my emphasis.

8. A. L. Rees, 'Expanded Cinema and Narrative: A Troubled History', in A. L. Rees, Duncan White, Steven Ball and David Curtis (eds), *Expanded Cinema: Art, Performance, Film* (London: Tate Publishing, 2011), p. 20.

9. Molesworth, *Image Stream*, pp. 10–11.

10. Malcolm Turvey, Hal Foster, Chrissie Iles, George Baker, Matthew Buckingham and Anthony McCall, 'Round Table: The Projected Image in Contemporary Art', *October* 104 (Spring 2003): 71–96, p. 94.

11. Among examples in addition to those referenced elsewhere in the Introduction, see Alison Butler, 'A Deictic Turn: Space and Location in Contemporary Gallery Film and Video Installation', *Screen* 51:4 (Winter 2010): 305–23; Catherine Fowler, 'Remembering Cinema "Elsewhere": From Retrospection to Introspection in the Gallery Film', *Cinema Journal* 51:2 (Winter 2012): 26–45; Jonathan Walley, 'Materiality and Meaning in Recent Projection Performance', *Velvet Light Trap* 70 (Fall 2012): 18–34; Jonathan Walley, 'The Material of Film and the Idea of Cinema: Contrasting Practices in Sixties and Seventies Avant-Garde Film', *October* 103 (Winter 2003): 15–30; Philippe-Alain Michaud, 'Light Line: The Geometric Cinema of Anthony McCall', *October* 137 (Summer 2011): 3–22; Stephen Monteiro, 'Performing Color: Mechanized Painting, Multimedia Spectacle and Andy Warhol's *Chelsea Girls*', *Grey Room* 49 (Fall 2012): 32–55.

12. Sheldon Renan, *An Introduction to the American Underground Film* (New York: E. P. Dutton, 1967), pp. 227–8.

13. Bradley Eros, 'There Will Be Projections in All Dimensions', *Millennium Film Journal* 43–4 (Summer–Fall 2005): 63–100, p. 65.

14. Ian White, 'Life Itself! The "Problem" of Pre-Cinema', in Stuart Comer (ed.), *Film and Video Art* (London: Tate, 2009), p. 14.

15. Erika Balsom, *Exhibiting Cinema in Contemporary Art* (Amsterdam: Amsterdam University Press, 2013), p. 14.

16. Andrew V. Uroskie, 'Siting Cinema', in Tanya Leighton (ed.), *Art and the Moving Image: A Critical Reader* (London: Tate, 2008), pp. 397–8.

17. Yann Beauvais, 'Deconstructing Cinema', *Art Press* 262 (November 2000): 42–7, p. 47.

18. These omissions may be the result of film studies' initial concentration on narrative structures such as montage and genre. The 2011 edition of *Introduction to Film Studies* makes mention of the avant-garde, alternative and pornographic cinema on five of its 535 pages (down from nineteen pages on avant-garde and alternative cinema in the 1999 edition), while home movies, drive-ins and other such cultural practices are altogether absent. Even CinemaScope is mentioned once only. Jill Nelmes (ed.), *Introduction to Film Studies*, 5th edn (New York: Routledge, 2011); Jill Nelmes (ed.), *An Introduction to Film Studies*, 2nd edn (New York and London: Routledge, 1999). Similarly, *The Routledge Companion to Film History* makes brief mention of home movies (as a counter example to 'popular cinema' as commercial cinema) and excludes CinemaScope, pornography and drive-in theatres. William Guynn (ed.), *The Routledge Companion to Film History* (New York: Routledge, 2011).

19. Turvey *et al.*, 'Round Table', p. 86. Foster's own assessment affirmed that 'There are all kinds of projected images . . . and it's important to keep in mind the differences between them'. In searching for a genealogy and typology, unfortunately, his inquiry fell back on medium specificity rather than cultural usage, citing 'image installations, cinema, video, digital, etc.' as examples. Ibid. p. 71.

20. Maeve Connolly, *The Place of Artists' Cinema: Space, Site and Screen* (Bristol: Intellect, 2009), p. 10.

21. Giuliana Bruno, *Surfaces: Matters of Aesthetics, Materiality, and Media* (Chicago: University of Chicago, 2014), p. 151.

22. Jonathan Walley, 'Identity Crisis: Experimental Film and Artistic Expression', *October* 137 (Summer 2011): 23–50, p. 27.

23. Gene Youngblood, *Expanded Cinema* (New York: E. P. Dutton, 1970), pp. 41–2.

24. Balsom, 'A Cinema in the Gallery, a Cinema in Ruins', p. 412.

25. Erkki Huhtamo, 'From Kaleidoscomaniac to Cybernerd: Notes toward an Archaeology of the Media', *Leonardo* 30:3 (1997): 221–4, p. 222.

26. Erkki Huhtamo and Jussi Parikka, 'Introduction: An Archaeology of Media Archaeology', in Erkki Huhtamo and Jussi Parikka (eds), *Media Archaeology: Approaches, Applications, and Implications* (Berkeley: University of California Press, 2011), p. 4.

27. Jay David Bolter and Richard Grusin, *Remediation: Understanding New Media* (Cambridge, MA: MIT Press, 1999).

28. Haidee Wasson, 'Suitcase Cinema', *Cinema Journal* 51:2 (Winter 2012): 148–52, p. 149.

29. Ibid. p. 149; Haidee Wasson, 'Protocols of Portability', *Film History* 25:1–2 (2013):

236–47; Charles R. Acland, 'The Crack in the Electric Window', *Cinema Journal* 51:2 (Winter 2012): 167–71; Patricia R. Zimmermann, *Reel Families: A Social History of Amateur Film* (Bloomington: Indiana University Press, 1995); Karen L. Ishizuka and Patricia R. Zimmermann (eds), *Mining the Home Movie: Excavations in Histories and Memories* (Berkeley: University of California Press, 2008); Amy Herzog, 'In the Flesh: Space and Embodiment in the Pornographic Peep Show Arcade', *The Velvet Light Trap* 62 (Fall 2008): 29–43; Alison Griffiths, *Shivers Down Your Spine: Cinema, Museums, and the Immersive View* (New York: Columbia University Press, 2008); Charles Tepperman, *Amateur Cinema: The Rise of North American Moviemaking, 1923–1960* (Oakland: University of California Press, 2015); Erkki Huhtamo, *Illusions in Motion: Media Archaeology of the Moving Panorama and Related Spectacles* (Cambridge, MA: MIT Press, 2013); Erkki Huhtamo, 'Elements of Screenology: Toward an Archaeology of the Screen', *ICONICS: International Studies of the Modern Image* 7 (2004): 31–82; Erkki Huhtamo, 'Screen Tests: Why Do We Need an Archaeology of the Screen?', *Cinema Journal* 51:2 (Winter 2012): 144–8.

30. Thomas Elsaesser, 'Early Film History and Multi-Media: An Archaeology of Possible Futures?', in Wendy Hui Kyong Chun and Thomas Keenan (eds), *New Media, Old Media: A History and Theory Reader* (New York: Routledge, 2006), p. 22.

31. Stan Vanderbeek coined the term 'expanded cinema' in the mid-1960s. More recently, Catherine Fowler has proposed the term 'gallery films', Jean-Christophe Royoux has offered 'cinema of exposition' and Raymond Bellour has employed 'an other cinema'. See Stan Vanderbeek, '"Culture: Intercom" and Expanded Cinema: A Proposal and Manifesto', *Tulane Drama Review* 11:1 (Fall 1966): 38–48; Fowler, 'Room for Experiment'; Jean-Christophe Royoux, 'Remaking Cinema', in Jaap Guldemond (ed.), *Cinéma, Cinéma: Contemporary Art and the Cinematic Experience* (Eindhoven: Stedelijk van Abbemuseum, 1999), pp. 21–7; Raymond Bellour, 'Of an Other Cinema', in Leighton (ed.), *Art and the Moving Image*, pp. 406–22.

32. Kerry Segrave, *Drive-in Theaters, a History from Their Inception in 1933* (Jefferson: McFarland & Co., 1992), pp. 235–6; Phil Hannum, '$51,809,395 for 250 New Theatres in 1956', *Boxoffice* (4 August 1956): 18–20, p. 18.

33. 'Progress Report: Photographic Industry Shows Marked Gains', *New York Times* (17 May 1959), p. X19. Even in the early 1980s, with consumer-grade video threatening amateur film formats, about seven million US households still owned home-movie projectors. 'New Scene Stealer: The Video Camera', *New York Times* (25 September 1981), pp. D1, D15.

34. In 1981, a single Times Square peep-show booth purportedly could generate as much as $5,000 a day, or $1.8 million a year. William Serrin, 'Sex is a Growing Multibillion Business', *New York Times* (9 February 1981), pp. B1, B6.

35. Andy Warhol, *America* (New York: Harper & Row, 1985), p. 11; emphasis in text. While Warhol may be referring primarily to Hollywood films with this example, the study of his practices presented in Chapter 2 demonstrates how his conception of 'the movies' stretched well beyond commercial film.

36. Dudley Andrew, 'The "Three Ages" of Cinema Studies and the Age to Come', *PMLA* 115:3 (May 2000): 341–51.
37. Daniel Birnbaum, 'The Archeology of Things to Come', in Hans Ulrich Obrist, *A Brief History of Curating* (Zurich and Dijon: JRP|Ringier/Presses du reel, 2008), p. 298.

CHAPTER 1

A Wider Audience: Robert Rauschenberg, the White Paintings *and CinemaScope*

On a September evening in 1953, six thousand people gathered outside the Roxy Theater in New York City, matched by nearly as many invited guests, for the world premiere of 20th Century-Fox's *The Robe*.[1] The turnout likely pleased studio executives, who hoped the event would be remembered less as the premiere of a Technicolor biblical epic starring a young Richard Burton, than as the beginning of a new era in cinema exhibition. The studio had mounted a year-long media blitz promoting *The Robe* as the debut of CinemaScope, a widescreen projection process meant to transform the way the public saw films and understood cinema. 'You have read about it . . . you have heard about it . . . soon you will see it for the first time', proclaimed the studio's *New York Times* advertisement. 'Nothing you have ever seen in any theatre will match the scope . . . the spectacle . . . the power . . .'[2]

As the post-war success of television cut into film-industry profits, Hollywood gambled that CinemaScope and similar widescreen formats would redefine and rescue the cinema through unprecedented sensorial experiences.[3] Television manufacturers had advertised their products as comparable to cinema ('A TV picture so clear, so sharp . . . you'll think you're at the movies!'[4]). Fox sought a fundamental aesthetic shift with CinemaScope, one in which audiences accustomed to viewing images through the clearly demarcated frame of conventional cinema or television would lose their bearings before a large, slightly curved picture plane where the lateral edges of the image exceeded the field of vision. Bolstered by multi-track sound, the new format was meant to weaken the boundaries between picture and exhibition space, immersing the viewer in an environment television could not possibly match.

CREATING SPECTACLE

Although CinemaScope did not 'simulate third dimension to the extent that objects and actors seem to be part of the audience',[5] as Fox's marketing department had claimed, *The Robe*'s Roxy premiere generated favourable reactions overall, and widescreen projection became the most significant change to Hollywood production since the advent of sound in the 1920s.[6] *The Robe* would have a three-month run at the Roxy, becoming the second-highest grossing film in history.[7] 'Hollywood has finally found something louder, more colorful and breathtakingly bigger than anything likely to be seen on a home TV screen for years to come', *Time* magazine reported.[8] 'This huge motion picture … proved in itself to be essentially a smashing display of spectacle', wrote the *New York Times* reviewer, while the *Daily Mirror* informed readers, 'With CinemaScope, the audience enjoys the rare experience of becoming a vivid part of the spectacle, instead of a mere witness'.[9] *Newsweek* concurred, elaborating that 'The wide-screen techniques … make it possible for the spectator to feel, to a degree impossible with old-style movies, that things are going on "all around"'.[10] Even ambivalent reviews noted 'exciting employments of [CinemaScope] may be anticipated confidently' and that 'The most obvious comment upon the widescreen process is also the most important one: It is very well suited to spectacle'.[11] CinemaScope would succeed as a format for about a decade, rising to over seventy-five films a year in 1955 with production at all major studios except Paramount, which maintained the rival VistaVision process. CinemaScope encompassed nearly every genre, from children's animation with *Lady and the Tramp* to adult melodrama with *Rebel Without a Cause* (both 1955).

On the eve of CinemaScope's unveiling, a young artist from Texas hung two, multi-panel canvases covered in smooth, white house paint in a basement art gallery eight blocks away from the Roxy. These *White Paintings*, exhibited for only three weeks at Eleanor Ward's newly opened Stable Gallery, remain among Robert Rauschenberg's most important early works, representing a foundational moment in the history of post-war American art. In contrast to the media's frenzy for CinemaScope, the *White Paintings* received a small, but significant amount of attention in art periodicals and the mainstream press. The reaction to Rauschenberg's screen-like canvases, unlike the response to CinemaScope, was almost entirely negative. 'White canvas, conceived as a work of art, is beyond the artistic pale', wrote one critic in *Art Digest*.[12] Devoid of any apparent narrative content and appearing as blank supports 'untouched by any instrument',[13] the paintings were principally interpreted as a sophomoric stunt tapping the history of Dada and prior affronts to modernism to lampoon prevailing tastes for Abstract Expressionism and monochrome painting. A critic for *Arts and Architecture* called the *White Paintings* a 'gratuitously destructive act' and the *New York Herald Tribune* ranked the show one of the season's worst, while the exhibition of figurative paintings by Rauschenberg's friend, Cy Twombly, that ran concurrently at the gallery, had been more generously received.[14] 'Everyone was hostile, with the exception of a few artists', Ward remarked of the reaction to the *White Paintings*.

'One well known critic was so horrified he came out on the street literally clutching his forehead, and then fled down the block . . .'[15]

In their proportions, their uniformly white surfaces, and their situation in a windowless room, Rauschenberg's paintings more closely resembled projection screens – including the new CinemaScope variety – than modernist paintings. Indeed, Rauschenberg envisioned them functioning like screens. By reflecting changes in ambient light caused by action in the surrounding space, the paintings could make visitors feel that 'things are going on "all around"' with a screen performance that did not require the projected illusion of film. Rauschenberg would later claim, 'One could look at them and almost see how many people were in the room by the shadows cast, or what time of day it was'.[16] As objects intended primarily to exhibit such phenomena, he also believed that the paintings' surfaces were replaceable, and should be repainted as necessary to ensure proper reflectivity.[17] They need not be understood as works in themselves, then, but rather as foundations for the passing spectacle of everyday events. 'It is completely irrelevant that I am making them,' Rauschenberg claimed in 1951, '*Today* is their creator'.[18]

Although it seems no one directly invoked CinemaScope or movie screens during the exhibition's run, a *New York Herald Tribune* critic claimed that confused visitors to Rauschenberg's show had reported 'they were able to detect a slight suggestion of a shadow' on the 'untouched pieces of canvas'.[19] Composer John Cage's defence and promotion of the series in the same issue of the *New York Herald* – 'they . . . are not destroyed by the action of shadows', he would insist – positioned the paintings as steeped in a Zen renunciation of self by serving as the ground for the free play of light.[20] In his 2003 study of the *White Paintings*, Branden Joseph claimed that 'Rauschenberg aimed not at a productive intervention into culture but at an affirmation of difference attributed (indeed, at that point still too literally attributed) to the natural realm'.[21]

This chapter considers the competing interpretations of the *White Paintings* as empty paintings and screen-like objects as emblematic of larger mid-century tensions between art and popular visual spectacle, most notably in art's relationship to cinema. The *White Paintings* quite literally reflected these tensions in the gallery at the moment movie studios and journalists vigorously promoted widescreen cinema as an artistically inclined endeavour with origins in historical painting and live theatre. Of course, CinemaScope was a multi-million-dollar technological apparatus contrived in Hollywood as a reproducible, commodified means of entertainment. It included multi-track sound and sophisticated anamorphic optics to present moving, colour images to large, seated audiences housed in enormous darkened spaces. The *White Paintings*, conversely, were handcrafted objects obstinately created outside systems of commodification as quiet, experimental gestures at Black Mountain College in rural North Carolina in 1951 and seen by relatively few viewers in brightly lit gallery spaces. Despite these obvious differences, CinemaScope and Rauschenberg's series shared several formal and experiential traits. Both included oversized, highly reflective surface areas intervening in the visual field. Both relied on visible light fluctuations on those surfaces to produce their effects. Both were deployed to change the viewer's sense of space, participation and event within an established medium, in part by testing the limits of the image frame within the field of vision. If Fox hoped CinemaScope would revolutionise cinema by immersing viewers in ways reminiscent of large-scale historical painting and live theatrical performance, Rauschenberg hoped the *White Paintings* would revolutionise painting by bringing the gallery experience closer to the mechanisms of cinema and other forms of temporally and spatially based performance. As Mark Cheetham says, 'These paintings facilitated and celebrated a theatrical absorption that linked painting, location, and spectator'.[22] In exposing such theatricality in the gallery experience, Rauschenberg undermined the mechanisms of painting for traditionalists and modernists alike.[23] While not overtly introducing what one would commonly call 'cinema' into the gallery space – there was neither film nor projector, after all – a painting from the series had already been exhibited with projected images in multimedia performances involving Rauschenberg and Cage at Black Mountain College. Hanging in the Stable Gallery, these paintings referenced cinema's basic qualities of visible and constant light changes on a reflective surface of pre-determined dimensions, thus conveying aspects of the *cinematic* while anticipating key aesthetic concerns found in later moving-image based artworks.

It is reasonable to think that the *White Paintings*' polarising effect on the 1953 New York art world may have been exacerbated by their historical, formal and geographical proximity to CinemaScope's premiere. 'The justified excitement over the opening of CinemaScope and "the Robe" has simmered down to the point where a fellow can speak of it in a normal voice and be heard' a *New York Times* reporter kidded two weeks after the *Robe* premiere, just as Rauschenberg's show was about to close.[24] Rauschenberg's placement of his two-panel and seven-panel *White Paintings* in the Stable's basement created a provocative echo of the screen technologies of the culture industry, potentially inducing dynamic feedback loops not only between the two paintings but also between the series and the history of the moving image. His 6 x 8-foot, two-panel *White Painting*, hanging in one corner of the basement, perfectly matched the 1.33:1 aspect ratio of television and silent-era cinema (Figure 1.1). It also closely resembled the 1.375:1 ratio of the sound era that was deemed the 'Academy' ratio and continued to be referred to within the

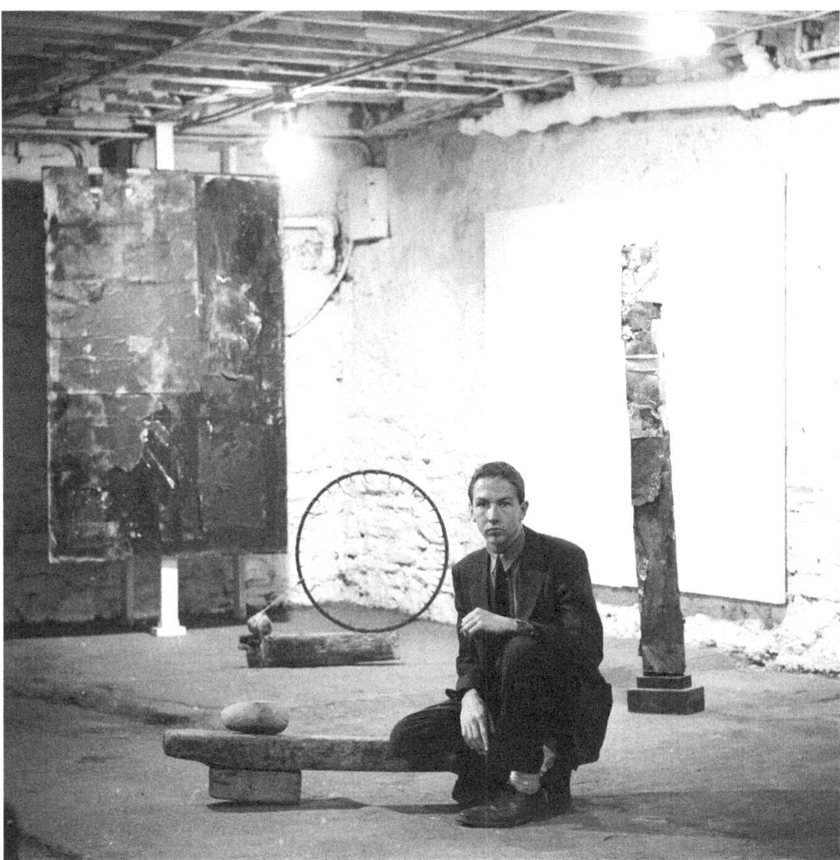

Figure 1.1   *Allan Grant, Robert Rauschenberg at an exhibition of his works at the Stable Gallery in New York, 1953. The LIFE Picture Collection / Getty Images © Estate of Robert Rauschenberg / SODRAC, Montreal / VAGA, New-York (2015)*

film industry as 1.33:1 (or 4:3). His monumental seven-panel example, placed at the other end of the basement, took the form and proportions of new widescreen formats, with a 1.75:1 aspect ratio that neared the eventual widescreen standard of 1.85:1 (Figure 1.2).[25] This 6 x 10½-foot painting could just as easily have alluded to the giant canvases that had become the coin of Jackson Pollock and other New York Abstract Expressionists, however. As art historian Irving Sandler later remarked, 'In 1953, Robert Rauschenberg exhibited canvases painted flat white, the first of a succession of works that scandalized the New York School'.[26] The apparent lack of colour and brushwork on these surfaces contributed to the immediate affront. In the long run, however, what proved most scandalous was their deflection of the material away from an emphasis on static, abstract images meant to reflect

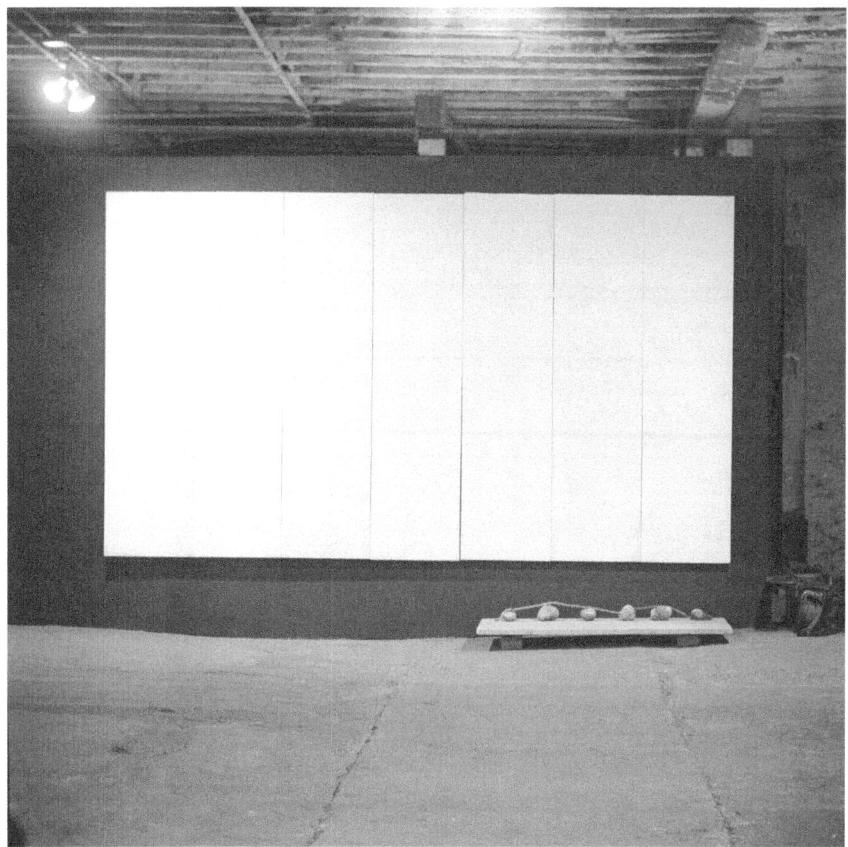

Figure 1.2   *Allan Grant,* White Painting *(seven panels), at an exhibition by Robert Rauschenberg at the Stable Gallery in New York, 1953. The LIFE Picture Collection / Getty Images © Estate of Robert Rauschenberg / SODRAC, Montreal / VAGA, New-York (2015)*

the artist's personality, toward the ambient events of the exhibition space that emerge as an image within the frame of the stretched canvas. 'I did them as an experiment to see how much you could pull away from an image and still have an image', Rauschenberg remarked.[27] This turn from artist to environment spectacularised the exhibition space in a way that opened the door for Minimalism, expanded cinema, Happenings and other types of art that privileged the 'audience's' phenomenological experience of time and space as integral to the work. By the 1960s, as the neo-avant-garde turned aesthetic concerns away from the discrete, finished object to collective performance, contingency, and mass culture, the 1953 exhibition of the *White Paintings* would be cited as a pivotal moment in art's conceptual shift. 'On the edge of such an abyss all that is left to do is *act*', claimed Allan Kaprow in 1964.[28]

Painting and Theatre

In the years following World War II, American commercial cinema was heading toward clear disaster after almost a half-century of growth. Between 1947 and 1952, weekly movie attendance plummeted from nearly eighty million to about forty million spectators.[29] In 1948, the US Supreme Court upheld anti-trust legislation that forced Hollywood studios to divest of their theatres. Increasing migration to the suburbs and rising television ownership had cast serious doubt on the future of primarily city-based movie going. By 1952, more than a third of all American households had television sets.[30] 'There's only one way to beat television', one studio head conceded in 1953, 'That's to get in it'.[31]

Hollywood considered partnerships that included projecting television broadcasts in movie theatres, but opted first to overhaul the theatre environment.[32] At the base of this change was the transformation of image sizes and screen proportions to starkly differentiate movies from the flickering frame of the living-room television set. 'Each and every studio has its shoulder to the wheel to find ways and means to improve the present screen, with possibly one or two exceptions', explained *Los Angeles Times* Hollywood beat reporter Edwin Schallert in April 1953. 'What may come of it all in the long run isn't known, but this has certainly given movieland a basic liveliness previously absent.'[33]

Most viable options relied on existing technologies and techniques, such as the stereopticon and the anamorphic lens.[34] The first wave of change involved three-dimensional cinema produced by shooting with a double-lens camera and exhibiting the results in a double projection of nearly superimposed green- and red-toned images. After initial excitement over this process in late 1952, the awkwardness of its cardboard eyewear and its limitations for colour film-making – a key to elevating movies above the televisual image – sent studios searching for other solutions. Larger and wider screens became the favoured alternative, since they could create an illusion of depth without eyewear through their increased size and curvature (meant to compensate for peripheral lens distortion). Widescreen cinema also could be coupled with multi-channel sound systems that scattered individual audio cues across the exhibition space to integrate the audience into screen space aurally as well as visually.

The first major stride in this direction was Cinerama, introduced in New York in September 1952. Requiring three cameras during filming and as many projectors in exhibition, Cinerama was a triptych of contiguous images aligned horizontally across a 145-degree, curving sweep of enormous screens to produce a single overall view. Although its first release, *This Is Cinerama*, began with a brief summary of the history of cinema and included images of the Milan Opera and the Vienna Boys' Choir, it primarily concentrated on locations and camera movements that would induce awe through monumental forms and powerful action. These included a 'sudden wild [railway] ride', a helicopter view over Niagara Falls, and a 'flight through the tortuous giant canyon of Zion National Park'.[35] Cinerama emphasised visual effect over narrative progression. As Pop artist Richard Hamilton recalled of his first Cinerama experience, 'The theatre publicity and lobby displays made no attempt to inform about subject-matter of the film – audience participation is what they were selling'.[36]

Envelopment in the overwhelming image was critical to Cinerama's effect, but this hinged on creating an even and seamless visual field from three adjacent images. 'There is some distortion more noticeable in some parts of the house than in others', observed a *New York Times* reporter after Cinerama's premiere. 'The three projections were admirably blended, yet there were visible bands of demarcation on the screen.'[37] Differences across the three images would continue to diminish the effect of immersion, despite a five-person technical crew constantly adjusting image alignment, projection brightness and sound levels during screenings. The problem would not be solved until a single-projector model was introduced in 1963, by which time other widescreen processes were firmly established in most theatres.[38]

As much as Cinerama produced a movie-going experience of a new magnitude, its material and technical requirements prohibited it from becoming a common process for commercial film-making and exhibition. Nevertheless, the excitement it generated encouraged the industry to explore similar entertainment formats, prompting a surge in widescreen experimentation throughout 1953. From WarnerSuperScope (Warner Bros.), to Vistascope (Columbia) and VistaVision (Paramount), the surge would peak in September with 20th Century-Fox's successful CinemaScope release.

Achieved by shooting and projecting standard 35-mm film through an anamorphic lens that can compress the image in production and subsequently expand it on screen, CinemaScope was more than just a larger screen or wide-lens effect. French scientist Henri Chrétien had developed the process in the 1920s and Fox president Spyros Skouras bought it in 1952 as the key technical component to producing wider images without costly changes to cameras and projectors. 'Subsequently one after another of the major studios announced some version of "wide screen", and now most of the industry has formed a disorderly caravan behind [Fox], headed helter-skelter toward the land of happily-ever-after', *Life* magazine reported in July 1953. 'The audience, of course, will decide whether it is a sunrise or a sunset they are heading into.'[39]

Understanding the pressing need for technological standardisation, Fox licensed CinemaScope to other studios while mandating the process for all its productions. Since movie theatres would have to be re-equipped with large, curved screens and multi-channel sound systems, the use of CinemaScope by multiple studios would likely accelerate these changes. In anticipation of CinemaScope's possible radical transformation of the terms of production and viewing, many studios had slowed production during 1953 to await the results of *The Robe*'s release. By that summer Fox was already processing equipment orders from four thousand theatres, with the expectation of filling a thousand of them by the New Year.[40] Fuelled in part by *The Robe*'s success, annual US box-office receipts rose for the first time in seven years.[41]

Sceptics criticised CinemaScope and other widescreen initiatives as desperate measures by studio executives already stung by the failure of 3-D. A writer for the *Quarterly of Film, Radio and Television* predicted that 'The technical means will have been provided to give us a more complete external-theatrical experience', yet 'shallow effect' would prevail over story as 'the present rush for size and sensation seems to indicate that there is little belief that mature and thoughtful stories are any answer to the box-office problem'.[42] Fox's CinemaScope marketing plan concentrated on the transformation of movie viewing into an 'external-theatrical experience', not only by emphasising the physical magnitude of the image area, but also by relating CinemaScope to other, more culturally elevated art forms known for 'thoughtful stories'. Although initial press screenings of the process included a car crash and a flight over the Rocky Mountains, these were shown alongside scenes from *The Robe*, based on a best-selling historical novel, and *How to Marry a Millionaire*, Fox's follow-up CinemaScope feature based on a Broadway play.[43] Studio production head Darryl Zanuck claimed that the new process combined 'the intimacy of a play, the movement and variety of films, plus an unprecedented potential for the effective presentation of both'.[44]

One reporter at *The Robe*'s premiere remarked that 'with CinemaScope the audience enjoys the rare experience of becoming a vivid part of the spectacle, instead of a mere witness'. Another claimed the CinemaScope experience 'made all beholders feel as if they were participants'.[45] Ariel Rogers has noted that early proponents and critics of widescreen agreed that increased audience 'participation' was the desired effect of this new form of cinema exhibition, but what exactly participation meant and how it could be measured was far less certain.[46] As the remarks from the *Robe* premiere suggest, many accounts 'presented the experience of widescreen as one that blurred the boundaries between viewer and image', explains Rogers.[47] In his history of widescreen processes, John Belton argues that 3-D films and Cinerama produced this effect not by attempting to recreate the presence of theatre but rather through a carnival-ride appeal that Hollywood studios would seek to mitigate with CinemaScope and similar screen systems. 'The model chosen … was less that of the amusement park, which retained certain vulgar associations as a cheap form of mass entertainment, than that of the legitimate theater,' Belton explains, recalling film critic André Bazin's assertion that the theatre's live actors moving in physical space elicited greater audience involvement than projections of filmed action.[48] A viewer's awe or wonder at the visual events transpiring on the screen would be combined with a sense of active participation in those events, triggered by the tendency to scrutinise parts of the image, as the entire field of the immense screen would be too large to allow a continuous view of the whole. Fox's initial announcement of CinemaScope emphasised these circumstances, explaining that 'Due to the immensity of the screen, few entire scenes can be taken in at a glance, enabling the spectator to view them as in life, or as one would watch a play when actors are working from opposite ends of the stage.'[49] In seeing the possibilities of intimacy, movement and variety in CinemaScope, Zanuck implied an equivalent range of sensorial and emotional experience for the viewer. Yet invoking theatre also meant elevating CinemaScope – and commercial films in general – from mass entertainment to high culture, further differentiating film from a television industry already drawing scrutiny for its potentially negative impact on informed public discourse and social formation.[50]

Concurrent to the rhetoric of theatrical intimacy and presence were comparisons between CinemaScope and the fine arts, a provocative strategy worth exploring in relation to Rauschenberg's *White Paintings*. 'In the history of painting', Belton explains, 'the canvas painting bordered by a wooden frame replaced the fresco or wall painting during the Renaissance; 1950s cinema reversed this change as the frame gave way to the wall'.[51] By selecting a biblical epic as its inaugural film for the process, Fox positioned CinemaScope and the cinema as the modern context for the serious, monumental subjects found in the most grandiose paintings.[52] Written by Lutheran minister Lloyd C. Douglas, the novel that served as the source of the film had sold over two million copies. Its didactic tale of spiritual discovery follows the Roman tribune Marcellus, who participates in Christ's crucifixion only to find salvation through exposure to early Christians and the inexplicable powers of Christ's discarded robe. Fox insisted on links to historical painting – the most prestigious in the hierarchy of Western painting genres – even if the media preferred promotional images of Marilyn Monroe and Betty Grable stretched across patio recliners in *How to Marry a Millionaire* to the sweeping Roman pageantry of *The Robe*.[53]

The souvenir programme for *The Robe* included a double-page centre spread of a scene from the film to give readers a sense of CinemaScope's

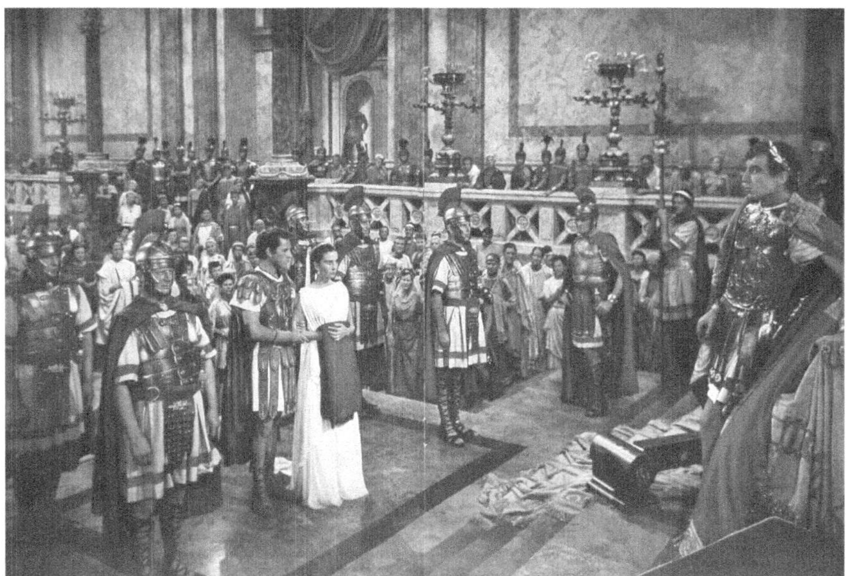

Figure 1.3   *The final scene of* The Robe, *the first film shot in CinemaScope, as illustrated in the* Robe *souvenir programme, 1953.*

visual sweep. Rather than choosing a scenic exterior or moment of complex movement, of which the film had many, the studio published the film's closing confrontation between Caligula and Marcellus (Figure 1.3). Depicting a crowd of forty or fifty in a Roman palace, the composition tellingly exudes the proscenium-restricted theatricality of a play, rather than the possibilities for dynamic perspectives made possible by the movie camera. Here CinemaScope is high theatre. It is also akin to history painting, as the scene resembles the large paintings typically produced by European academies to commemorate events of the court. Jacques-Louis David's 20 x 32-foot *Consecration of the Emperor Napoleon I* (1806–7) would be one well-known example (Figure 1.4). At an aspect ratio of 1.5:1, the 12 x 18-inch programme image is not nearly as wide as CinemaScope, but nearly matches in miniature the 1.6:1 ratio of David's masterpiece.

Accompanying instructions in the programme urge readers to hold the palace image up close to the face, to simulate the visual experience of CinemaScope (Figure 1.5). These instructions reinforce the film's relationship to painting and the museum by depicting a spectator who appears to be standing, as though in a museum gallery, rather than seated, as one would be at the theatre or cinema. Mimicking the well-known cliché of the art aficionado, this male spectator appears to scrutinise the surface. Much like

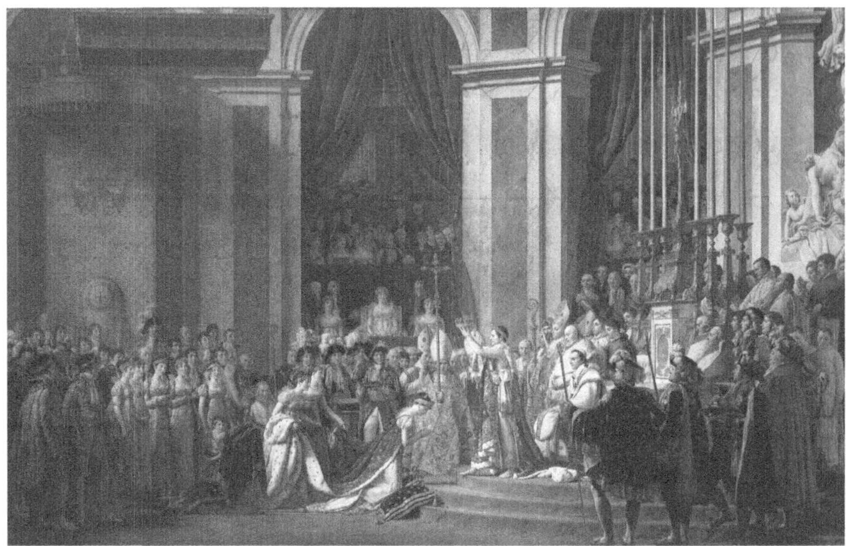

Figure 1.4	*Jacques-Louis David,* The Consecration of the Emperor Napoleon and the
Coronation of Empress Joséphine on December 2, 1804, *1806–7, oil on canvas. Louvre, Paris*

Rauschenberg's *White Paintings*, however, the rectangular surface seems to offer nothing, save for the vertical seam where its panels abut. Through the pairing of *The Robe*'s palace scene and the anonymous male spectator before an empty frame, the programme intersects the visuality of theatre, history painting and the modern gallery.

When describing CinemaScope's potential visual impact, *Robe* director Henry Koster referenced history painting by invoking a work much larger, and more obscure, than David's. *The Crucifixion* (1895), by Polish artist Jan Styka, was a 45 x 195-foot painting that stretched across the front wall of a purpose-built, two-thousand seat auditorium at Forest Lawn cemetery outside Los Angeles (Figure 1.6). At an astounding 4.33:1 ratio, the painting was the basis of a sound and light show that recalled the panoramas and dioramas of the previous century, while suggesting the horizontal sweep of wider movie screens.[54] Koster believed that CinemaScope could 'duplicate this imposing panorama in all its essentials'.[55]

The Robe's establishing shot of the crucifixion – three small, silhouetted crosses on Mount Calvary, pressing at the top of the screen against a darkened sky as the road to Jerusalem winds below – amounts to a reverse-angle of Styka's painting, which looks down through the crosses toward the city. One of the first shots to be filmed, it was included in press screenings of CinemaScope at the Roxy and elsewhere in spring 1953, implying an affinity between the process' enormous picture (25 x 65 feet on the Roxy's new

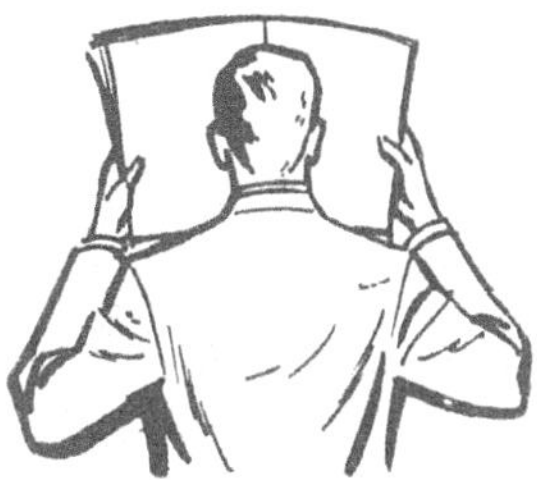

Figure 1.5 *Instructions in the* Robe *souvenir programme for viewing the double-page illustration of* The Robe's *final scene.*

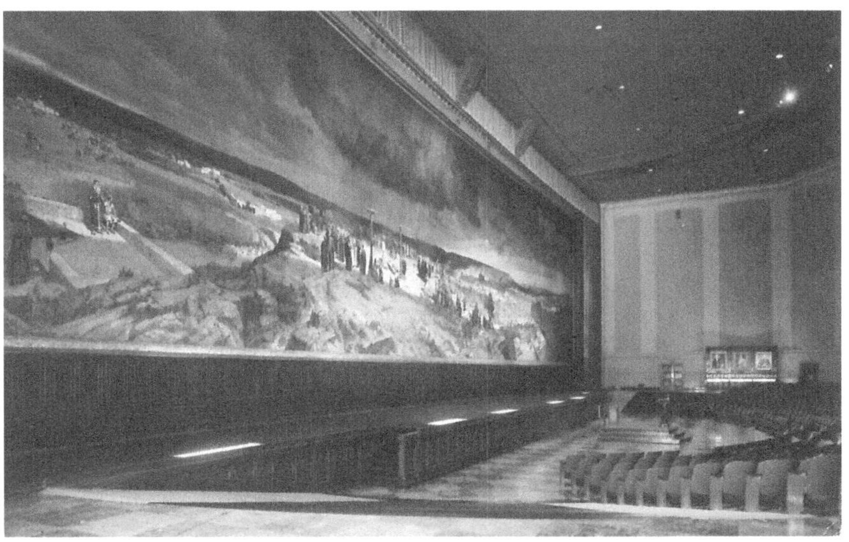

Figure 1.6 *Jan Styka,* The Crucifixion, *1895, in the Hall of the Crucifixion, Forest Lawn Memorial Park, Glendale, California, circa 1960. Image provided courtesy of Forest Lawn Memorial-Park Association.*

screen) and history and mural painting.[56] 'The Crucifixion scene is particularly impressive with its wide arc of sky and outline of surrounding country', the *Wall Street Journal* stated in its review of the finished film. 'There is more of everything than in conventional films, which is all to the good where masses of people and scenery are necessary.'[57]

A more immediate link between *The Robe* and painting, however, was the work of Dean Cornwell. A successful muralist, Cornwell won commissions for murals in Radio City in New York and the rotunda of the Los Angeles Public Library. He also painted biblical episodes and contemporary scenes of the Holy Land. In 1947, the original owners of *The Robe*'s film rights, RKO Pictures, hired him to create several double-page illustrations for Douglas' novel.[58] Fox organised a touring exhibition of these paintings in department stores in major cities nationwide throughout the summer of 1953 to promote the film. They were accompanied by a tableau of the crucifixion site and 'story panels' providing insight into the Fox release.[59] In a telling confusion of art and cinema, a *New York Amsterdam News* report noted that 'Totalling [sic] eight large canvases, the series is one of the most distinguished contemporary filmings of Biblical history'.[60]

Building on these invocations of painting, when *The Robe* finally began its run, press reviews relied on art metaphors to describe its visual effects. The *New York Herald Tribune* called the film a 'Technicolor mural' and the *New York Times* observed that 'plainly, the size of this new canvas invites panoramic artistry'. A journalist at the Chicago premiere stated that 'many of the scenes are like beautiful murals', while *Time* described the production as 'overpower[ing] the eye with movie murals of slave markets, imperial cities, grandiose palaces and panoramic landscapes . . .'[61] The emphasis on murals as the closest visual equivalents to CinemaScope is not insignificant. Perhaps the most ancient method of creating a large image, the mural requires precisely the sort of intense, selective viewing that CinemaScope promoters had attributed to both the stage and their new film process. Not prone to be 'taken in at a glance', as modern art critic Clement Greenberg wrote of murals, they instead 'deliver themselves from point to point, in instants . . . [and] the connecting of those instants – their flow into one another – is instantaneous too'.[62]

Depth, Edge and Centre

By successfully bringing the theatre, the panorama, history painting and the mural into the conversation around CinemaScope, Fox had positioned this new cinema experience as middlebrow cultural fare that might appeal to a swelling middle class otherwise prone to rely on the television set for its visual entertainment. By referencing cultural signifiers considered moribund by highbrow urban modernists, however, CinemaScope just as readily represented to them yet another form of low-brow, derivative mass-cultural appropriation. A vital part of the Western painting tradition, the illustrative, representational images invoked in discussions of CinemaScope had been shed by the avant-garde in the cul-de-sac of endless repetition of accepted subjects of history, religion and classical myth. Equally accessible to middle- and low-brow sensibilities, this 'kitsch', as Greenberg had famously described such popular visual forms to *Partisan Review* readers in 1939, was considered the cultural fodder that fed capitalism, totalitarianism and other oppressive political ideologies. Formulaic and dishonest, according to Greenberg, kitsch is 'ersatz culture . . . using for raw material the debased and academicized simulacra of genuine culture', a description that would encompass the work of Styka, Cornwell and any other modern artist following aesthetic rules shaped by the European Academies. 'For what is called the academic as such no longer has an independent existence, but has become the stuffed-shirt "front" for kitsch.'[63]

Greenberg attended Rauschenberg's Stable Gallery exhibition in 1953, but did not publish his views on what he saw. In the weeks immediately preceding his visit, however, he published something of a follow-up to his earlier essay. Entitled 'The Plight of Our Culture', it attempted to combat post-war expansion of mass-market consumerism by reasserting low-, middle- and high-brow cultural distinctions. The critic assured readers that 'lowbrow, "machine", commercial culture' was 'easy' and available everywhere 'to offer its relief to all those who find any sort of higher culture too much effort'.[64] Cinema, by nature, was nothing if not machine culture. Even the interwar multimedia efforts of Constructivists and Surrealists to integrate cinema into the avant-garde had been lost on Greenberg and much of the post-war New York art scene that encountered the *White Paintings*. László Moholy-Nagy's 1920s work on cinema and painting is particularly noteworthy in the context of Rauschenberg's gesture. As early as 1928, Moholy-Nagy called Kazimir Malevich's 1918 monochrome painting, *Suprematist Composition: White on White*, 'a miniature cinema screen'. He explained

> Here is to be found the interpretation of Malevich's last picture – the plain white surface, which constituted an ideal plane for kinetic light and shadow effects which, originating in the surroundings, would fall upon it.[65]

This history was disregarded in interpretations of Rauschenberg's work at the time of his exhibition, except perhaps by Cage, who had studied Moholy-Nagy's writings.[66] Hollywood's interest in paintings by conservative – even reactionary – artists such as Styka and Cornwell in linking film to the fine arts could only have deepened any belief that commercial cinema represented ersatz culture.[67] Under these conditions, the slightest formal evocation of commercial cinema – even in a new format – would be intolerable in the gallery space, not only to proponents of abstract painting's detached originality, but also to anyone defending more traditional modes of painting.

As the appropriation of historical painting by Hollywood and movie critics reached its apotheosis at the Roxy, Rauschenberg's *White Paintings* exposed the other side of the avant-garde's 'revolutionary' break. While some gallery visitors may have detected Rauschenberg's effort to radically revise the terms of viewer participation in art, others construed the two paintings as a joke at the expense of art insiders. The possibility of a put-on seemed greater when these paintings were considered alongside other works by Rauschenberg included in the show, such as several abstract *Elemental Sculptures* in wood, metal and string, and at least four large-scale, textured collages in paper and gloss black paint (sometimes referred to as Rauschenberg's 'black paintings'). The incidental, handmade aesthetic of the sculptures and black paintings aligned them with fashionable currents of formal abstraction and *art brut*. The minimal, industrial appearance of the *White Paintings* made them alien intruders, even when compared to the simple, polychromatic forms of the more rigid Colour Field paintings being produced at the time. Yet, in 1953, cinema's widescreen systems had emphasised a major perceptual shift for two-dimensional visual media. This shift informed the potential meanings of the *White Painting*'s representation of 1.33:1 and 1.85:1 aspect ratios, since widescreen ratios promoted a diminished awareness of lateral frame edges that correspondingly increased the sense of image space as an uninterrupted continuation of audience space.[68] This change in visual spectacle was conducive to increased viewer interaction with Rauschenberg's *White Paintings*, as it encouraged gallery visitors to move back and forth between the two ratios and perhaps become increasingly aware of subtle perceptual distinctions between the light events taking place on these uniform, but differently shaped surfaces.

Although the collision of the two-panel and seven-panel *White Paintings* in the Stable Gallery basement effectively 'brought to life' the material conditions behind the movie industry's aesthetic experiments of 1953, their origins were elsewhere. As mentioned previously, they were painted in the summer of 1951 in Black Mountain, North Carolina, as part of a series of six *White Paintings* (five multi-panel and one single-panel). For all six the artist applied oil-based, white house paint with a roller to stretched canvas, creating smooth, evenly coated and uninflected surfaces. The dimensions varied across the series, but were measured by the half-foot. The single-panel version was 4 x 4 feet. The 6 x 10½-foot seven-panel work was composed of 6 x 1½-foot units.

In writing to New York dealer Betty Parsons from Black Mountain in October 1951, Rauschenberg described the *White Paintings* as 'dealing with the suspense, excitement and body of an organic silence, the restriction and freedom of absence, the plastic fullness of nothing, the point a circle begins and ends'.[69] In this description the paintings might represent an end game, archly satisfying conditions of modernism famously laid out by Greenberg. As a champion of the Abstract Expressionists, Greenberg had adumbrated a seductive teleology of modern art that began with Edouard Manet and the Impressionists and moved toward an increasing awareness and recognition of medium specificity to culminate in the works of Pollock and other New York School painters.[70] In Greenberg's description, each of the plastic arts inexorably drifted from representational mimicry in order to confront its essential material and ontological conditions. This required rejecting perspectivalism in painting to create works that affirmed the defining flatness of the picture plane. In a later assessment of the history of the medium, Greenberg would go so far as to say, 'It was the stressing of the ineluctable flatness of surface that remained . . . more fundamental than anything else to the processes by which pictorial art criticized and defined itself under Modernism'.[71]

In 1956, Greenberg would summarise the contribution of a decade of Abstract Expressionism to his concept of modernism by yoking the reduction of any illusion of depth to achromatic palettes and increased canvas size as advanced painting's 'conspicuous features'. Black-and-white evoked value contrasts, yet the Abstract Expressionists used this most basic pairing of contrast 'precisely in an effort to repudiate value contrast as the basis of pictorial design'. While Kazimir Malevich may already have pushed beyond any Abstract Expressionist with his 1918 painting *Suprematist Composition: White on White*, Greenberg considered this 'a mere symptom of experimental exuberance [that] implied nothing further' (Figure 1.7). The mid-century increase in size was triggered by the renunciation of depth, according to Greenberg, within which abstract painters 'could develop pictorial incident without crowding'. 'The flattening surfaces of their canvases', he explained, 'compelled them to move along the picture plane laterally and seek in its sheer physical size the space necessary for the telling of their kind of pictorial story'.[72] Lateral expansion in cinema, on the other hand, was a means of *enhancing* the illusion of depth at the risk of diluting the potential visual narrative. Rudolf Arnheim had argued in the 1930s that a sense of the screen's outer limits was necessary to a film's visual impact. 'It is just such restrictions which give film its right to be called art', he concluded.[73] Reacting to CinemaScope, Charles Barr would later explain

> It is not only the horizontal line which is emphasized in CinemaScope (this is implied by critics who concentrated on the *shape* of the frame qua shape – as though it were the frame of a painting – and concluded that the format was

Figure 1.7   *Kazimir Malevich*, Suprematist Composition: White on White, *1918, oil on canvas. Museum of Modern Art, New York*

suitable only for showing/framing crocodiles and procession). The more open the frame, the greater the impression of depth: the image is more vivid, and involves us more directly.[74]

Envisioning the *White Paintings* as 'pure surface', Rauschenberg sought an image plane that negated both edge and centre – particularly in his seven-panel version – therefore resolutely rejecting the modernist flatness Greenberg espoused. 'I was frustrated because there was a restriction that something had to have an edge', Rauschenberg said. 'I couldn't deal with that. Architecture is just another edge. I couldn't keep it going. How far can you push something that doesn't have a center?'[75] The loss of the edge meant the loss of the threshold between viewer space and picture space. Rauschenberg accomplished this in the *White Paintings* by creating multi-panel surfaces on a scale that would challenge visual perception of the painting's outer limits as the viewer neared the work, much like *The Robe*'s printed programme instructed readers to hold its illustrations close to their faces to approximate the effect of CinemaScope. Whether on a movie screen or a primed canvas, the centre can only be eliminated by diminishing the edge. The absence of brushstrokes, patterns and colour simultaneously minimised reference to the edge in the *White Paintings*, while opening up their centre as an amorphous space.

Lawrence Campbell's review of the Stable Gallery show concluded that 'while most paintings are painted to be seen from a distance, Rauschenberg's are made to be seen from close-up'.[76] The *White Paintings'* unblemished surfaces invited scrutiny, potentially drawing viewers in to search for subtle irregularity or nuance, at which point they would lose their sense of edge and centre. This allowed viewers to become more aware of the light and shadow reflected on the surface, and the fact that these originated in *their* space. Any further attempt to focus on the surface would be frustrated by these variations in light much as a film's projection will make it nearly impossible to concentrate on a screen surface as surface. This loss of the object's edge and centre in examining the *White Paintings*, to be replaced by a world of superficial light play from sources above and behind the viewer, reproduced the basic conditions – if not the magnitude or intensity – of widescreen cinema.

One could argue that Rauschenberg's decision to construct his works out of multiple, separate panels would undermine his effort to eliminate edges by creating new ones across the image field. This segmentation reinforces the object's modularity and utility, however, while further undermining centrality. Pieces can be mounted and dismounted individually. Paintings can be expanded, reduced or rearranged. Since there is no particular order or sequence to the panels, there can never be a designated centre panel as such, and any identifiable edge to the work is arbitrary and contingent. 'The physical edges of the module allowed the painting an extension limited only externally by its place of display', explains Mark Cheetham, 'rather than by the dimensions of the support'.[77] In the context of 1953 these noticeable, evenly spaced divisions of the field echoed the seams occasionally detected by audiences at widescreen cinemas. As CinemaScope required theatre owners to add additional panels to their existing screens or purchase Miracle Mirror screens (recommended by 20th Century-Fox) to be assembled from multiple units, screen surfaces sometimes manifesting creases or segmental breaks. Even for carefully installed screens at larger, urban theatres, the extended width required segmentation of the screen material. Mentioning seams 'that have been so apparent in the wide screens thus far shown', a review of a Washington, DC, CinemaScope press screening explained that 'the plastic process knitting the strips of screen together takes some time to ease into proper hanging shape'.[78]

The multi-unit nature of the *White Paintings* also produces a remarkable affinity with early theories of the aesthetic import of widescreen. Director Jacques Rivette, writing in *Cahiers du cinéma* in 1954, praised the 'beauty of the void' in widescreen, explaining that

> extreme use of the breadth of the screen, the physical separation of the characters, empty spaces distended by fear or desire, like lateral units, all seems to be – much more than depth – the language of true filmmakers, and the sign of maturity and mastery.[79]

In a detailed examination of the CinemaScope aesthetic, David Bordwell detects a tendency toward 'clothesline staging' in the lateral vastness of widescreen, which places actors and objects at regular intervals along the same plane in horizontal settings. 'Scope's width invited – demanded, some directors felt – a partitioning of the visual field. This creates a strip of modules, and these can be juxtaposed in breadth or depth', Bordwell explains. 'The partitioning strategy tends to treat the screen not as a wraparound window on a large chunk of reality, but rather as a surface to be broken down in rhythmic units.' In shot-reverse-shot sequences, for example, the screen might be divided into fifths. Citing examples that stress CinemaScope's abstract possibilities, such as the overlapping lines of grain elevators in *Picnic* (Joshua Logan, 1955), Bordwell concludes that 'in a sense, Scope didn't expand the visual field; it cropped it'.[80]

Certainly Rauschenberg was not referencing such a widescreen aesthetic, since it developed only after the Stable Gallery exhibition. Nevertheless, the demarcation of abutting panels in a work like the seven-panel *White Painting* could produce a part-whole visual experience similar to the effects described by Rivette and Bordwell. As Rivette asked in his treatise on widescreen, 'Wouldn't great *mise-en-scène*, like great painting, be flat, hinting at depth through slits rather than gaps'.[81] Rauschenberg's work delivers those slits as a material certainty on a surface far more flat, both physically and perceptually, than CinemaScope's often slightly curved screens.

SCREEN PERFORMANCE

In exploring the cinematic implications of the Stable Gallery presentation, it is worth considering the evolution of Rauschenberg's thinking around these works from 1951 to 1953, since the cinema unexpectedly intersects their existence at multiple points. Branden Joseph claims that Rauschenberg's understanding of the paintings' significance shifted from an object-based concern with modernism's reductive drive to an interest in the works' potential for participatory action. John Cage would play a determining role in this transformation. 'By 1953, [Rauschenberg] had come through his association with Cage to regard them as something more: as exemplifications of a positive force of difference made visible through their "transparency" to temporal and environmental factors', Joseph posits.[82]

Rauschenberg embarked on the series under the tutelage of Josef Albers, having absorbed the emphasis on simple forms and pure fields of colour that had culminated in the ex-Bauhaus instructor's celebrated *Homage to the Square* series. 'He said many times a day, "Art's a *Schwindel*"', Rauschenberg would say many years later. 'Actually, the "white paintings" came directly out of his schooling. He taught me such respect for all colors that it took me years before I could use more than two colors at once. I didn't know which one I was "schwindling".'[83]

Rauschenberg first attempted to exhibit the *White Paintings* in autumn 1951 at the Betty Parsons Gallery. Parsons had given him his first New York show earlier that year, but she rejected the *White Paintings*, perhaps wary of upsetting her impressive group of Abstract Expressionists that included Jackson Pollock, Mark Rothko, Barnett Newman and Clyfford Still.[84] However different in genealogy or intent, his monochromes came dangerously close to the large, segmented white-on-white paintings by Newman that Parsons had exhibited – to disastrous reviews – immediately before Rauschenberg's first show.[85] Stable Gallery owner Eleanor Ward first exhibited Rauschenberg's work in January 1953 with a black-paint collage in the *First Stable Gallery Annual.* Having founded the gallery that year, she visited Rauschenberg's Fulton Street studio in late spring and approved the *White Paintings* for an autumn show to run concurrently with Twombly's. In preparation for the event, Rauschenberg and Twombly spent the summer refurbishing the basement of the new gallery, which had previously sheltered police horses. They hauled out years of accumulated debris and whitewashed the walls.[86]

Rauschenberg spread his paintings and sculptures throughout the gallery's two floors. The decision to show only the two- and seven-panel *White Paintings* is remarkable in the context of the screen revolution that was unfolding in the neighbourhood around them. Not only did the paintings demonstrate the difference between cinema's new widescreen forms of 1.85:1 or more (CinemaScope reached 2.66:1 for the *Robe* release, before settling in at 2.55:1) and the Academy ratio of TV and cinema's past: the seven-panel painting's 1.75:1 ratio also represented the maximum allowable width for a movie screen before camera techniques are required to compensate for peripheral distortion.[87]

In a fortuitous turn that demonstrates the curiosity surrounding

Rauschenberg's exhibition, *Life* magazine photographer Allan Grant documented the installation for an anticipated spread that never ran.[88] Grant's photographs depict the two *White Paintings* in the Stable basement, accompanied by at least one collage and four *Elemental Sculptures* (see Figures 1.1 and 1.2). The 6 x 4-foot, two-panel work was placed on the gallery's freshly painted white stone walls, situated diagonally from a large, but narrower, black paint and paper collage. The seven-panel *White Painting* hung directly opposite the collage, on a smooth surface that appears to have been the only dark wall in the show.[89] Since Rauschenberg and Twombly had renovated and painted the space immediately before the exhibition, it is likely Rauschenberg had prepared the surface especially for the *White Painting*. Suspended on this dark ground, the larger *White Painting* suggested a window or screen frame in a way that the neighbouring *White Painting* on a white wall did not. In Grant's photographs at least one overhead gallery light is directed toward the larger painting, demonstrating the modulation of light described by Rauschenberg and others. In this enclosed environment, light waves bouncing off the rough stone foundation, the sculptural forms and the buckled surface of the glossy collage potentially created a complex network of light events on the *White Paintings'* spotless surfaces. Ambient light emanating from the street above added to the spectacle, according to the gallery owner. 'There was a sort of grating at one end of the room, high up', Ward describes, 'through which a little daylight filtered in, and it gave the whole room a sort of underwater feeling'.[90]

Rauschenberg's attempt to convert the gallery space into a type of cinematic apparatus for creating and capturing screen phenomena, with his wide white painting as the vortex of viewer interface, drew on the artist's unusually close relationship to the cinema during the post-war period of movie spectatorship decline. After serving in the US Navy during the war, he worked as a movie stand-in in California and built sets for a film production company while studying at the Kansas City Art Institute. His one-man show at the Betty Parsons Gallery in May 1951 included paintings (now lost) that *Art News* described as 'large-scale, usually white-grounded canvases' and Rauschenberg would later call 'paintings mostly silver & wh[ite] with cinematic composition'.[91] While painting the *White Paintings* at Black Mountain that summer, he made a camera-less 16-mm film by painting frames of a standard, three-minute reel of scenes in New York's Central Park shot earlier by his wife, Susan Weil.[92] Film, projection and painting decisively converged for Rauschenberg the following summer, when a *White Painting* was used in a multimedia event organised by Cage in Black Mountain's dining hall. Subsequently entitled *Theater Piece No. 1*, the one-off event eliminated barriers between audience and performance, becoming an important forerunner of

Happenings and the New Theatre that emerged in New York by the close of the decade.

Accounts of *Theater Piece No. 1* vary, but it included Cage, Merce Cunningham, M. C. Richards, David Tudor, Charles Olson and Rauschenberg engaged in individual activities structured within time references pre-established by Cage. Richards, Olson and Cage read texts, Tudor played the piano, Cunningham danced and Rauschenberg played old records on a gramophone. This was accompanied by slide and film projections. A multi-panel *White Painting* (likely Rauschenberg's four-panel version) was hung in cruciform from the single-story building's low-pitched ceiling, suggesting an ecclesiastical object but also repeating the pattern of intersecting aisles that demarcated both audience and performance space. By several accounts the painting acted as the projection screen, though it is likely that the film and slides were also projected onto other surfaces.[93]

As an interface for audience, action and image, the *White Painting* was not merely a screen-like presence in *Theater Piece No. 1*, but a multimedia object hanging at the threshold of theatre, cinema and the visual arts.[94] The *White Painting*'s role as a base for visualising action in Cage's piece would make it a provocative counter example to the theory of 'action painting' that art critic Harold Rosenberg published in the pages of *Art News* in the six-month gap between the presentation of *Theater Piece No. 1* and the announcement of CinemaScope. Rosenberg claimed in 'The American Action Painters' that post-war painting's power derived from the capacity to present the creative process as a temporally grounded physical act unfolding within a specific emotional or psychological state. 'At a certain moment the canvas began to appear to one American painter after another as an arena in which to act', Rosenberg claimed. 'What was to go on the canvas was not a picture but an event.'[95] This would place the artist and the viewer in new positions, where image and object might seem secondary. 'What gives the canvas its meaning is not psychological data but *role*, the way the artist organizes his emotional and intellectual energy as if he were in a living situation . . . Since the painter has become an actor, the spectator has to think in a vocabulary of action.'[96] Rosenberg's theory extends beyond action, however, by introducing the language of theatre into the painting. The painting must represent the *performance* of being an artist above any other subject or theme. Reflecting the gap between object and action thus opened, Barnett Newman would describe the quandary facing painters. 'What is painting? It's filling up a canvas. You have a canvas that's so wide and so high, and you fill it up with paint', Newman explained. 'But it can't look as though you've just filled it up with paint. That's the paradox.'[97]

Throughout 1953, *Art News* ran a series of articles on the creative methods of individual artists that would confirm Rosenberg's reasoning. With due attention to Abstract Expressionism, the series included Franz Kline and Jack Tworkov, both of whom knew Rauschenberg from Black Mountain, and Willem de Kooning. While the popular press reported on Hollywood's scramble to widescreen and the coming of CinemaScope, the *Art News* series emphasised the artist's reliance on inner conflict and the unconscious to execute a work. Kline 'may find a theme that has been unconsciously working its way into the open', Tworkov may become 'deeply . . . involved in the process and unaware of what he is doing', and de Kooning's torturous paint-ing process may indicate a 'vacillating, Hamlet-like history'.[98] Across these stories, immersion in a work begins with the artist's descent into creation, and the value of the viewer's experience hinges on the surface materials' ability to transmit this struggle.

The *White Paintings* represent a reinterpretation and extension of these underlying precepts, from painting as the arena of performance of an artist's subjective engagement with universal questions of human existence to the object as a replaceable, supporting element in an environmental, time-based performance of spectator and spectacle. Their passage from Albers-inspired paintings in 1951 to projection screen in *Theater Piece No. 1* in 1952 set this trajectory in motion, resulting in a hard landing in the basement of the Stable Gallery in 1953, where two *White Paintings* became liminal objects vacillating uncomfortably between painting and screen. 'Initially, this American-made *vide* represented a supernatural purity of a symbolic order', suggests Edward Strickland, working from Rauschenberg's own description of the series (in his October 1951 letter to Parsons) as being 'one white as God' that embodies 'the plastic fullness of nothing'. However, Strickland explains,

> Presented publicly . . . it was very problematically transformed from a meta-physical to a functional entity: a reflective tool as an environmental presence and a projective tool as a component in a multimedia extravaganza. In either case it was precisely the unsullied purity of its whiteness that permitted the contamination by images, be they silhouettes or film.[99]

In essence, Strickland describes the *White Paintings'* transformation from a container for abstract ideas into an instrument of light-based spectacle, or from primarily painting to primarily screen. The contemporary record dem-onstrates the conversion was problematic only for those unwilling to accept these objects as a means for creating ephemeral images out of the fluctuat-ing intensity and direction of light waves passing through their environ-ment. This is clear in Hubert Crehan's *Art Digest* editorial rebuking the *White Paintings* at the Stable Gallery. 'Can we even look at the stark [canvas] duck with pleasure?' Crehan asks. 'I think that we cannot – it allows no leeway for intensification or variation of experience.'[100] Cage, however, would point out that '[Rauschenberg] changes what goes on, on a canvas, but he does not change how a canvas is used for paintings – that is, stretched flat to make rectangular surfaces which may be hung on a wall'.[101] Rauschenberg changed 'what went on' by moving the point of signifying action from the painter and the moment of paint falling on canvas (as was familiar to mid-century art audiences through Pollock's drip technique) to the action of the viewer and the exhibition environment. This cleverly reinterpreted and undermined ideas of painting-as-event.

'Before such emptiness, you just wait to see what you will see', explained Cage, asking the question that may have been on the minds of other Stable visitors: 'Is Rauschenberg's mind then empty, the way the white canvases are?'[102] With no trace of an artist's physical performance on the surface, some viewers literally drew a blank. 'A blank canvas provokes a blank look', Crehan declared.[103] Dore Ashton's review of the exhibition in the same issue of *Art Digest* elaborated that 'Rauschenberg has decided that paintings have lives of their own. They come dressed as they are. One comes as seven pure white panels of sized canvas, symmetrical and identical, blank-faced, untouched by any instrument.' Ashton concluded by raising precisely the issue Rauschenberg would claim was primary to the work.

> But isn't Rauschenberg's experience, his unique experience, like a small thorn in the hide of an elephant? Doesn't art require a hint of the banal, a hint of the social role of man to locate it in time and history[?][104]

Indeed, in the context of their exhibition amid the excitement and apprehension surrounding widescreen cinema, the *White Paintings* were a small thorn in the hide of the art gallery experience. Crehan likened them to 'dada shenanigans', while de Kooning thought Rauschenberg had to be 'fooling around, not really serious'.[105] Newman – perhaps eager to distance these canvases from his own highly contested near-monochrome works – reportedly exclaimed 'Humph! Thinks it's easy. The point is to do it with paint.'[106] Greenberg couched his own reaction in terms of his defence of high culture's 'effort' in the face of popular culture's facility. He claimed years after visiting the exhibition that upon seeing the 'blank canvases' in the Stable Gallery he was 'surprised by how *easy* they were to "get", how familiar-looking and even slick they were'.[107] James Fitzsimmons in *Arts and Architecture* pronounced the *White Paintings* the 'low point of Rauschenberg's exhibition'. As Fitzsimmons saw it,

> There is less than meets the eye. Of course, a blank white canvas might be an aid to contemplation, but the four white walls the landlord provides will do as well . . . The function of a canvas . . . is aborted when it is misused in this way.[108]

By comparing the canvas to the white wall, Fitzsimmons raises a possibility in line with Rauschenberg's reasoning: the canvas, like a wall, can be a backdrop for events. Pointing to the *White Paintings'* screen-like qualities as neutral grounds for changing physical events, Fitzsimmons surmises that 'Rauschenberg has backed himself into a corner, where there is nothing for him to do but make wall coverings'.[109]

CONCEPTUALISM AND CAMP

CinemaScope aspired to endow film with cultural sophistication while the *White Paintings* insinuated popular spectacle in the culturally elite context of the art gallery. In the decade following the *Robe* premiere and the *White Paintings'* exhibition, their reputations would change drastically. By the 1960s the *White Paintings* were celebrated as a critical neo-avant-garde step toward the participatory culture imbuing art, from Minimalism to Conceptualism and Happenings to Fluxus.

Amid the handful of reactions to the *White Paintings* published in 1953, John Cage's letter published in their defence in the *New York Herald Tribune* two months after the show had closed would receive as much attention as the paintings themselves. An *ekphrasis* of negation, excerpts from the letter would be reprinted in mass-market books on art as early as 1955, guiding subsequent interpretations of the paintings.[110] After its long list of renunciations ('No subject, no image . . . No white . . .') that recalls Buddhist sacred texts, Cage's letter declared

> I have come to the conclusion that there is nothing in these paintings that could not be changed, that they can be seen in every light and are not destroyed by the action of shadows.[111]

The emphasis on contingency and ephemerality tied to an underlying permanence reinforces the *White Paintings'* identity as screens, with light and shadow as the determining factors. In 1961 Cage famously called the paintings 'airports for lights, shadows and particles'.[112] Dominique Païni claims that such activity remains a critical component of moving-image installations in art spaces in the twenty-first century. 'What the visitor-spectator discovers when approaching [projection screens] is the agitated, febrile dust, an infinite number of vibrating atoms. The incarnation of the moving image is dust.'[113]

Cage first met Rauschenberg at the artist's Betty Parsons Gallery exhibition in 1951 but only befriended him at Black Mountain College the following year. The *White Paintings* mirrored Cage's ideas on silence and chance as constitutive elements of creative production. He would cite the series as the inspiration behind his influential 1952 composition *4'33"*, composed and performed the same summer as *Theater Piece No. 1*. The composition presented concertgoers four minutes and thirty-three seconds of 'silence', punctuated by David Tudor's raising and closing the piano's keyboard cover to signal the movements, and the inevitable ambient sounds of the setting.[114] The paintings and *4'33"* would influence later film-based art performances, such as Nam June Paik's *Zen for Film* (1962–4), which projected clear film leader and its accumulation of scratches and dust, and William Raban's *2'45"* (1972), a piece that entailed filming a blank screen and then re-filming and projecting further generations of the film at subsequent screenings.[115] In 2001, Philippe Parreno would make explicit the link between Rauschenberg's paintings, Cage's composition, chance and the cinema with *El Sueño de una Cosa* (2001–2). In this installation viewers were confronted by a replica of Rauschenberg's seven-panel *White Painting* (though it bears repeating that the idea of an 'original' *White Painting* flies in the face of Rauschenberg's conception of the series as replaceable objects). Hung on a museum's standard white-cube walls, every four minutes, thirty-three seconds the gallery's window shades lowered and the lights dimmed for a one-minute digitally programmed film of shots of Arctic landscapes projected onto the canvas. The sequence of images, accompanied by Edgar Varèse's 1954 composition *Déserts*, changed with every viewing so that the spectator's experience was never the same.

After the Stable Gallery exhibition, the *White Paintings* did not appear in public for a decade, by which time Pop and Minimalism had landed firmly on the head of Abstract Expressionism. Rauschenberg would include the seven-panel painting in his first museum show, at the Jewish Museum in New York in 1963.[116] Following Cage's lead, curator Alan Solomon called it 'the definitively stated fact of the impossibility of creating a void', pointing out that 'the interplay of the environment with the painting, into which accident and circumstance enter freely, enlarge without limit the seemingly narrow range of possibilities in the white surface'.[117] In a review for *The New York Times*, Brian O'Doherty declared, 'If you can't lick the environment, join it.' O'Doherty recognised in Rauschenberg's work 'a conquest of common, everyday reality from a bridgehead of abstract expressionism. He is trying to materialize an ambiguous limbo between high art and low life.'[118]

Assessing Rauschenberg's impact on American art of the 1960s, Andrew Forge surmises that the *White Paintings* were the first simple action in the reconfiguration of art around contingency and spectacle. 'The ambiguity of that enterprise – paintings as nonpainting, nonpaintings as painting', Forge explains, 'prefigures the restlessness which leads him later toward the theater, dance, spectacle, and to experiments with sound and light and the multiplicity of materials and mediums in the studio'.[119] Indeed, Rauschenberg became heavily involved in performance. He collaborated regularly with the Merce Cunningham and Trisha Brown Dance Companies, for whom he designed projection-based sets. As part of Experiments in Art and Technology, which he co-founded with Billy Klüver, Fred Waldhauer and Robert Whitman in 1966, he created *Open Score*, a performance that included a tennis match and the projection of infra-red, closed-circuit images of the audience responding in the dark to various instructions from Rauschenberg.[120]

Allan Kaprow championed the *White Paintings* as part of the emergence of such multimedia art practices. Remarking that when they were exhibited in 1953 no one could definitively claim whether or not they were art, Kaprow determined that a decade later the verdict was clear. 'For [Rauschenberg] and for us who saw them', Kaprow recalled, 'the black and white paintings were an end to art and a beginning'. He located the importance of the *White Paintings* in the spectator's realisation of his presence in the 'blanked screen' via his shadow. 'He may have caught a glimmer of the point', remarked Kaprow, perhaps in reference to his own experience, 'that now much, if not everything having to do with art, life and insight, was thrown back at him as his responsibility, not the picture's'.[121]

Describing the spectator's engagement in terms of responsibility pointed to a radically different idea of participation from that promoted by CinemaScope, which by the mid-1960s had slipped out of favour for the less elongated 1.85:1 aspect ratio that is still common today. Although it introduced widescreen as a viable theatrical model, 20th Century-Fox's attempt to convert everyday movie going into extravagant spectacle proved too ambitious. 'CinemaScope, initially hailed as "a poor man's Cinerama", ultimately devolved into a poor man's CinemaScope', relates Belton, 'playing on small screens in small theaters, stripped of its stereo sound'.[122] Seventy-millimetre film processes such as Todd-AO gained favour for prestige productions from *Oklahoma* (1955) to *Star Wars* (1977), providing projected images that were sharp and distortion-free even on the largest screens. According to Bordwell, after CinemaScope's 1950s success it remained in use for a 'low-end output' of fifteen to twenty films a year.[123] These later films sometimes sought to convey the amusement-park thrills previously attributed to Cinerama, as in *Fantastic Voyage* (1966), a Cold War thriller that portrayed shrunken scientists coursing through the bloodstream of a Soviet defector in a microscopic submarine. Whereas the *White Paintings'* importance rose sharply in the story of new art's multimedia, performative attributes, CinemaScope had become pedestrian entertainment at the edge of relevancy, such that even 20th Century-Fox abandoned it by 1967.

Notes

1. Richard P. Cooke, 'The Theatre: The Big Try', *Wall Street Journal* (18 September 1953), p. 4.

2. *The Robe* advertisement in *The New York Times* (16 September 1953), p. 39.

3. For a detailed consideration of this episode in commercial film's history, consult John Belton, *Widescreen Cinema* (Cambridge, MA: Harvard University Press, 1992), pp. 69–157.

4. Emerson television advertisement, *Life* (9 November 1953), p. 14.

5. '20th Century Has New Movie Device', *Los Angeles Times* (2 February 1953), p. A1.

6. While widescreen became the dominant mode of American commercial film exhibition from the 1950s, it has a much longer history, including the 1920s examples of three-camera Polyvision employed in Abel Gance's *Napoleon* (1927) and Fox's development of Grandeur, which used 70-mm film. See Belton, *Widescreen Cinema*, pp. 34–51 and Robert E. Carr and R. M. Hayes, *Wide Screen Movies: A History and Filmography of Wide Gauge Filmmaking* (Jefferson: McFarland and Company, 1988), pp. 3–9.

7. The film earned $17.5 million in North American box-office receipts against $4.6 million in costs. See '"The Robe" Concludes Record Run Dec. 15th', *New York Amsterdam News* (12 December 1953), p. 35; David Pratt, 'Widescreen Box Office Performance to 1959', *The Velvet Light Trap* 21 (1985): 65–6, p. 65; 'Filming of "The Robe" Completed in 10 Years', *Los Angeles Times* (1 May 1953), p. B8.

8. 'The New Pictures', *Time* (28 September 1953), p. 84.

9. Bosley Crowther, 'The Screen: "The Robe" Shown in CinemaScope', *New York Times* (17 September 1953), p. 32; *New York Daily Mirror* reviewer Frank Quinn, as quoted in 'New York Critics Are Enthusiastic', *Boxoffice* (19 September 1953), p. 8. Recognising in CinemaScope 'a new art evolution in film' at its Hollywood premiere a week later, the *Los Angeles Times* exulted, 'One can summon a whole array of adjectives to describe what takes place. "Magnificent" is by all odds the first.' Edwin Schallert, '"The Robe" Hailed as Epochal Film', *Los Angeles Times* (25 September 1953), p. A1.

10. 'New Films', *Newsweek* (28 September 1953), p. 96.

11. Crowther, 'The Screen: "The Robe" Shown in CinemaScope', p. 32; Cooke, 'The Theatre: The Big Try', p. 4. For a rare negative review, see The Associated Press, '"The Robe" Unveils CinemaScope Film Process in New York', *Chicago Daily Tribune* (17 September 1953), p. C5.

12. Hubert Crehan, 'The See Change: Raw Duck', *Art Digest* 27:20 (15 September 1953), p. 25.

13. D[ore]. A[shton]., '57th Street', *Art Digest* 27:20 (15 September 1953): 20–1, 25, p. 21.

14. James Fitzsimmons, 'Art', *Arts and Architecture* LXX (October 1953), p. 34; Emily Genauer, 'Art and Artists: The Bests and Worsts of the Year', *New York*

Herald Tribune (20 June 1954), sec. 6, p. 13. For an assessment of Twombly's participation and its reception, see Kirk Varnedoe, *Cy Twombly: A Retrospective* (New York: The Museum of Modern Art, 1994), pp. 17–9.

15. Eleanor Ward, as quoted in Varnedoe, *Cy Twombly*, p. 59, note 72. Ward eventually removed the guest book for the show 'because so many awful things were being written in it'. Ward, as quoted in Calvin Tomkins, *Off the Wall: A Portrait of Robert Rauschenberg* (New York: Picador, 2005), p. 77.

16. Robert Rauschenberg, as quoted in Tomkins, *Off the Wall*, pp. 64–5. In Rauschenberg's short 1968 text entitled 'Autobiography' he elaborates 'The wh[i]t[e] paintings were open composition by responding to the activity within their reach'. Ibid. p. 292.

17. Rauschenberg recycled some of the *White Painting* panels in his assemblage-based *Combines* between 1953 and 1962. The panels of the seven-panel *White Painting*, for example, were converted into *Trophy II (for Teeny and Marcel Duchamp)* in 1961, which appears to have areas of the original white coating breaking through subsequent layers of paint, fabric and sheet metal. Other instances of re-use include *Yoicks* (1953), which appears to incorporate the two-panel *White Painting*, *Collection* (1954), *K249765* (1956) and *Stripper* (1962). When it came time to exhibit works from the series in later years Rauschenberg had panels repainted or rebuilt as necessary. In 1962 he sent specifications and materials to Ponthus Hulten to have new versions made for exhibition there and the two-panel *White Painting* was reproduced for an exhibition at the Moderna Museet in 1965. The seven-panel *White Painting* exhibited at the Jewish Museum in New York in 1963 would have been a new version, given the original was recycled for *Trophy II*. For the *White Paintings 1951* exhibition at the Leo Castelli Gallery in 1968, he instructed his assistant, Brice Marden, to remake the entire series. These were updated yet again, either in 1971 or 1973, by assistant Hisachika Takahashi and exhibited at the Ace Gallery (1973) and the Smithsonian Institution (1976). All versions retain the original 1951 date, however. See Robert S. Mattison, *Robert Rauschenberg: Breaking Boundaries* (New Haven: Yale University Press, 2003), pp. 52–3; Mark A. Cheetham, *Abstract Art against Autonomy: Infection, Resistance, and Cure Since the 60s* (Cambridge: Cambridge University Press, 2006), p. 49; Tomkins, *Off the Wall*, pp. 245–6; Walter Hopps, *Robert Rauschenberg: The Early 1950s* (Houston: Houston Fine Art Press, 1991), p. 80; Roberta Bernstein, 'Introduction', in Larry Gagosian Gallery, *Rauschenberg: The White and Black Paintings 1949–1952* (New York: Larry Gagosian Gallery, 1986), p.[3]; National Collection of Fine Arts, *Robert Rauschenberg* (Washington, DC: Smithsonian Institution, 1976), p. 66. The black paintings were also considered objects that could be modified or remade, but that has never been done. See Bernstein, 'Introduction', p. [4].

18. Rauschenberg, as quoted in Branden W. Joseph, *Random Order: Robert Rauschenberg and the Neo-Avant-Garde* (Cambridge, MA: MIT Press, 2003), p. 29; emphasis in text.

19. Emily Genauer, 'Musings on Miscellany', *New York Herald Tribune* (27 December 1953), sec. 4, p. 6.

20. Ibid. p. 6.

21. Indeed, Joseph later acknowledges that these paintings 'tend to act as neutral projection screens'. Joseph, *Random Order*, p. 81. In addition to the first chapter of Joseph's book, for more on Cage and the series' Cageian aesthetic, see Roni Feinstein, 'The Early Work of Robert Rauschenberg: The White Paintings, the Black Paintings, and the Elemental Sculptures', *Arts* 61 (September 1986): 28–37 and Mattison, *Robert Rauschenberg*, p. 52. Among Cage's pronouncements on the paintings, see John Cage, 'On Robert Rauschenberg, Artist, and his Work', *Metro* 2 (May 1961), reprinted in John Cage, *Silence: Lectures and Writings* (Middletown: Wesleyan University Press, 1961). For speculation on the range of interpretations of the series, see Calvin Tomkins, *The Bride and the Bachelors: Five Masters of the Avant Garde* (New York: Penguin Books, 1965), p. 203.

22. Cheetham, *Abstract Art Against Autonomy*, p. 49.

23. The threat of theatricality to modern art would later be expressed most extensively by Michael Fried, working from theories developed by Clement Greenberg that are explored in this chapter. See Michael Fried, 'Art and Objecthood', in Michael Fried, *Art and Objecthood* (Chicago: University of Chicago, 1998).

24. Bosley Crowther, 'Now CinemaScope! A Look at "The Robe" and the New System in Which it is Put On', *New York Times* (27 September 1953), p. X1. Rauschenberg's Stable Gallery show ran from 15 September to 3 October 1951.

25. On the success of 1.33:1 and 1.85:1 ratios, see Belton, *Widescreen Cinema*, pp. 15–33, 218.

26. Irving Sandler, *The New York School: The Painters and Sculptors of the Fifties* (New York: Harper & Row, 1978), p. 174.

27. Robert Rauschenberg and Barbara Rose, *Rauschenberg* (New York: Vintage Books, 1987), p. 45.

28. Allan Kaprow, 'Should the Artist Become a Man of the World', *Art News* 63:6 (October 1964): 34; emphasis in text.

29. Joel W. Finler, *The Hollywood Story* (London: Octopus Books, 1988), p. 289.

30. Gary R. Edgerton, *The Columbia History of American Television* (New York: Columbia University Press, 2007), p. 137. See also Christopher H. Sterling and John Michael Kittross, *Stay Tuned: A History of American Broadcasting*, 3rd edn (Mahwah: Lawrence Erlbaum Associates, 2002), pp. 337–8.

31. Republic Pictures president Herbert Yates, as quoted in 'Critical Times', *Time* (21 September 1953), p. 106.

32. Ed Ainsworth, '3 R's of 3D: Agents See Theater with Everything', *Los Angeles Times* (25 May 1953), p. A1.

33. Edwin Schallert, 'New Screen Introduced at U-I; Merle Travis and Larsen Get Breaks', *Los Angeles Times* (2 April 1953), p. B9.

34. For this history, see Belton, *Widescreen Cinema*; Carr and Hayes, *Wide Screen Movies*; Kenneth MacGowan, 'The Screen's "New Look": Wider and Deeper', *Quarterly of Film Radio and Television* 11:2 (Winter 1956): 109–30; John Belton (ed.), *American Widescreen* issue, *Velvet Light Trap* 21 (1985). A contemporaneous

list of competing processes can be found in Leonard Spinrad, 'Mapping the Growing Wide-Screen, 3-D Maze: Or, a Guide to Some of the Entries in the Movies' Multi-Dimensional Field', *New York Times* (12 April 1953), p. X5.

35. Edwin Schallert, 'Cinerama Gives Films New Thrills', *Los Angeles Times* (30 April 1953), p. A1.

36. Richard Hamilton, 'Glorious Technicolor, Breathtaking Cinemascope and Stereophonic Sound', in Richard Hamilton, *Collected Works, 1953–1982* (London: Thames and Hudson, 1982), p. 122.

37. Waldemar Kaempffert, 'Solid Motion Pictures Produced by Curved Screen and Peripheral Vision', *New York Times* (5 October 1952), p. E9. A year later, these problems persisted: '[Cinerama's] subtle divisions are still noticeable and sometimes bothersome.' 'New Films', *Newsweek* (28 September 1953), p. 96.

38. Belton, *Widescreen Cinema*, p. 109; Bob Thomas, 'Bothersome Seams Eliminated', *Daytona Beach Morning Journal* (11 June 1963), p. 12. For additional explanation of the problems involved, consult Dennis Sharp, *The Picture Palace and Other Buildings for the Movies* (London: Hugh Evelyn, 1969), pp. 202, 204.

39. Robert Coughlan, 'Spyros Skouras and his Wonderful CinemaScope', *Life* (20 July 1953): 81–4, 86, 89–90, 92, 94, p. 82.

40. Ibid. p. 94.

41. Robert Sklar, *Movie-Made America* (New York: Random House, 1975), p. 285.

42. Richard C. Hawkins, 'Perspective on "3-D"', *Quarterly of Film Radio and Television* 7:4 (Summer 1953): 325–34, p. 333.

43. Edwin Schallert, 'CinemaScope Seen by First Audience', *Los Angeles Times* (19 March 1953), p. 6.

44. Darryl F. Zanuck, 'CinemaScope in Production', in Mark Quigley Jr (ed.), *New Screen Techniques* (New York: Quigley Publishing Company, 1953), p. 156. The studio furthered that 'The CinemaScope filming technique gives the actor the satisfaction of "living" his part, not fragmentarily, but completely, this yielding a greater performance'. 'The Story of CinemaScope', *The Dynamo* 1:1 (December, 1953), unpaged.

45. Frank Quinn of *The Mirror*, as quoted in 'New York Critics Are Enthusiastic', and J. M. Jerauld, 'Tremendous First Night Impression is Created by 20th-Fox Process', *Boxoffice* (19 September 1953), p. 8.

46. Ariel Rogers, *Cinematic Appeals: The Experience of New Movie Technologies* (New York: Columbia University Press, 2013), pp. 19–60.

47. Ibid. p. 57. Rogers claims that the sense of touch and a sensation of motion were also potential attributes of participation.

48. Belton, *Widescreen Cinema*, p. 191. For Bazin's views on widescreen cinema, see André Bazin, 'Three Essays on Widescreen', *Velvet Light Trap* 21 (1985): 8–16.

49. Thomas M. Pryor, 'Fox Films Embark on 3-Dimension Era', *New York Times* (2 February 1953), p. 17.

50. See, for example, Theodor Adorno's 1950s writings on television in Theodor W. Adorno, *The Culture Industry: Selected Essays on Mass Culture*, ed. J. M. Bernstein (New York: Routledge, 2001).

51. Belton, *Widescreen Cinema*, p. 196.

52. Painting had been invoked as early as 1930 in industry discussions of widescreen formats. When the Academy of Motion Picture Arts and Sciences studied the possibility of changing the standard aspect ratios of the frame at the time, supporters of widescreen pointed to the history of painting and the predominance of rectangular proportions. Lloyd Jones, 'Rectangle Proportions in Pictorial Composition', *Journal of the Society of Motion Picture Engineers* 14:1 (January 1930): 32–7. For discussion of the aesthetic debate surrounding the history of widescreen before the 1950s, see Belton, *Widescreen Cinema*; Kenneth MacGowan, 'The Wide Screen of Yesterday and Tomorrow', *Quarterly of Film Radio and Television* 11:3 (Spring 1957): 217–41.

53. Such an image from *How to Marry a Millionaire* appears in Coughlan, 'Spyros Skouras and His Wonderful CinemaScope', pp. 82–3. Another image of Monroe used to illustrate CinemaScope's film compression appears in Allen Long, '3-D: A Two-Eyed Wonder', *Science News Letter* 64:5 (1 August 1953): 74–5, p. 74. As one review of the April press screening of CinemaScope proclaimed, 'A musical sequence from *How to Marry a Millionaire* was one of the most impressive pieces shown . . . The shim-sham shimmies of a dancing Marilyn Monroe had unusual vigor.' Thomas A. Wise, 'CinemaScope's Debut: 3-D Process Leaves Cinerama Slight Edge', *Wall Street Journal* (25 April 1953), p. 1. For more on CinemaScope's relationship to Monroe, see Rogers, *Cinematic Appeals*, pp. 40–55.

54. 'Religion: The Biggest Yet', *Time* 57:14 (2 April 1951), p. 85. While the panorama offered nineteenth-century viewers elevated views of landscapes and city skylines that seemed laterally endless in their cylindrical configuration, the diorama was based on changes in light on painted, diaphanous surfaces.

55. Philip K. Scheuer, 'Directors See Greater Art, Reality Evolving from 3D', *Los Angeles Times* (22 February 1953): D1, D3, p. D3. Directors who criticised widescreen would also revert to painting to support their claims. For example, John Ford, who grudgingly submitted to CinemaScope for *The Long Gray Line* in 1955, similarly explained that 'you never see a painter use that kind of composition – even in the great murals, it still wasn't this huge tennis court', noting that CinemaScope makes 'your eyes pop back and forth, and it's very difficult to get a close-up'. Vincente Minnelli, required to use CinemaScope for several films including his Van Gogh biography, *Lust for Life* (1955), argued that 'the four to three ratio of the standard movie screen approximates the shape of conventional paintings. Such a configuration has stood the test of ages.' John Ford, as quoted in Peter Bogdanovich, *John Ford* (Berkeley: University of California Press, 1968), p. 92; Vincente Minnelli and Hector Arche, *I Remember It Well* (Garden City: Doubleday, 1974), pp. 279–80.

56. Wise, 'CinemaScope's Debut', p. 1; Bosley Crowther, 'CinemaScope Seen at Roxy Preview', *New York Times* (25 April 1953), p. 10. An even larger screen, 32 x 72 feet, was installed at the Fox Theatre in Detroit, Michigan. See 'Behind the Year Ahead', *The Dynamo* 1:1, unpaged.

57. Cooke, 'The Theatre: The Big Try', p. 4.

58. Irene Powers, 'Many Will See Dean Cornwell on his Return', *Chicago Daily Tribune* (23 February 1953), p. B6; '*The Robe*: Novel of Early Christianity Has Become a Popular Classic', *Life* (8 December 1947): 90–4, p. 90. For Cornwell's illustrations, see Lloyd C. Douglas, *The Robe,* (Chicago: Peoples Book Club, 1942). Background on RKO's original involvement is in Edwin Schallery, 'New Era Dawns for The Robe', *Los Angeles Times* (16 August 1953), p. D1.

59. See '*Robe* Campaign Plan Outlined by Einfeld', *Boxoffice* 63:13 (25 July 1953), p. 9; 'Bullock's to Display Religious Paintings', *Los Angeles Times* (24 August 1953), p. A3. For studies of Cornwell, see Patricia Janis Broder, *Dean Cornwell: Dean of Illustrators* (New York: Balance House, 1978); University of Missouri, Museum of Art and Archaeology, *Dean Cornwell: Painter as Illustrator* (Columbia: University of Missouri, Museum of Art and Archaeology, 1978); Carol Lowrey, *A Legacy of Art: Paintings and Sculptures by Artist Life Members of the National Arts Club* (New York: National Arts Club/Hudson Hills Press, 2007), pp. 76–7.

60. 'CinemaScope Will Be Launched with "Robe"', *New York Amsterdam News* (21 February 1953), p. 26. The article reports that the paintings were insured for $50,000. Exhibiting artwork around the US to promote a film had a precedent in 1940, when United Artists producer Walter Wanger hired Grant Wood, Thomas Hart Benton and seven other artists to create a dozen paintings inspired by John Ford's *The Long Voyage Home* (1940). The works, accompanied by photographs from the production of this screen adaptation of several plays by Eugene O'Neill, formed a travelling art exhibition. In praising the idea as an effort to bring American artists 'closer to the interest of the great mass of our people', the exhibition catalogue also voiced the hope that 'the artists' interpretations will encourage the public to search the film from an entirely new angle, from the artist's angle, seeking that which is especially significant in action and in characterizations'. Scott Eyman, *Print the Legend: The Life and Times of John Ford* (Baltimore: The Johns Hopkins University Press, 1999), p. 231; Edward Alden Jewell, 'Art Used in Films to be Shown Here', *New York Times* (14 August 1940), p. 21.

61. Otis L. Guernsey Jr, '*The Robe*', *New York Herald Tribune* (17 September 1953), p. 19; Crowther, 'Now CinemaScope!', p. X1; Mae Tinée, 'Crowd Sees *The Robe* Unfurl CinemaScope', *Chicago Daily Tribune* (24 September 1953), p. C1; 'The New Pictures', *Time* (28 September 1953), p. 84.

62. Clement Greenberg, 'Intermedia' (1981), in Robert C. Morgan (ed.), *Clement Greenberg: Late Writings* (Minneapolis: University of Minnesota, 2003), p. 95.

63. Clement Greenberg, 'Avant-Garde and Kitsch' (1939), in John O'Brian (ed.), *Clement Greenberg, The Collected Essays and Criticism: Volume 1, Perceptions and Judgments, 1939–1944* (Chicago: University of Chicago, 1986), pp. 12–13.

64. Clement Greenberg, 'The Plight of Our Culture' (1953), in O'Brian (ed.), *Clement Greenberg, The Collected Essays and Criticism: Volume 3, Affirmations and Refusals, 1950–1956*, p. 135.

65. László Moholy-Nagy, *The New Vision and Abstract of an Artist*, trans. Daphne M. Hoffmann, 4th edn (New York: George Wittenborn, 1947 [1928]), p. 39.

66. As the present study concerns primarily the significance of Rauschenberg's *White Paintings* within the artistic and cultural climate of 1950s American art and media culture, this facet of the story, which also includes the theories and works (*The Large Glass, Tu m'*) of Marcel Duchamp, must be set aside. For greater consideration of this aesthetic legacy in regard to the *White Paintings*, see Joseph, *Random Order*, pp. 33–42.

67. Beyond Cornwell's iconographic focus on Christianity and colonisation, as part of the National Commission to Advance American Art he led efforts to block non-American – particularly Mexican – artists from working in the US in the 1930s. Such nationalistic gestures certainly made him acceptable to a Hollywood caught in the throes of McCarthyism. See 'Dartmouth Scored in Alien Art Row', *New York Times* (10 June 1933), p. 15.

68. Betty Granger, 'Three-Dimensional Films Set to Revolutionize the Industry', *New York Amsterdam News* (7 February 1953), p. 25.

69. Rauschenberg and Rose, *Rauschenberg*, pp. 26, 29.

70. This teleology was set in motion in the pages of *Partisan Review* in 1940 with 'Towards a Newer Laocoon'. Clement Greenberg, 'Towards a Newer Laocoon' (1940), in O'Brian (ed.), *Clement Greenberg, The Collected Essays and Criticism: Volume 1*, pp. 23–38.

71. Clement Greenberg, 'Modernist Painting' (1960), in O'Brian (ed.), *Clement Greenberg, The Collected Essays and Criticism: Volume 4, Modernism with a Vengeance, 1957–1969* (Chicago: University of Chicago Press, 1993), p. 87.

72. Clement Greenberg, '"American-Type" Painting' (1955), in O'Brian (ed.), *Clement Greenberg, The Collected Essays and Criticism: Volume 3*, p. 226. For a study of the problems that monochrome paintings – including Rauschenberg's – posed for Greenberg, see Thierry de Duve, 'The Monochrome and the Blank Canvas', in Serge Guilbaut (ed.), *Reconstructing Modernism: Art in New York, Paris, and Montreal, 1945–1964* (Cambridge, MA: MIT Press, 1990).

73. Rudolf Arnheim, *Film as Art* (Berkeley: University of California Press, 2003 [1931]), p. 17.

74. Charles Barr, 'CinemaScope: Before and After', *Film Quarterly* 16:4 (Summer 1963): 4–24, p. 9; emphasis in text.

75. Rauschenberg and Rose, *Rauschenberg*, pp. 45–6, 65.

76. While Campbell directly mentioned only the black-paint collages, his assertion applies just as well to the *White Paintings*. L[awrence]. C[ampbell]., 'Rauschenberg and Twombly', *Art News* 52:5 (September 1953), p. 50.

77. Cheetham, *Abstract Art Against Autonomy*, p. 48.

78. Richard L. Coe, 'CinemaScope Gives a Preview', *The Washington Post* (27 June 1953), p. 7.

79. Jacques Rivette, 'The Age of *metteurs en scène*', *Cahiers du cinéma* 31 (January 1954): 45–8, reprinted in Jim Hillier (ed.), *Cahiers du cinéma: The 1950s: Neo-Realism, Hollywood, New Wave* (Cambridge, MA: Harvard University Press, 1985), pp. 279 and 278.

80. David Bordwell, *Poetics of Cinema* (New York and London: Routledge, 2008), pp. 310–11; David Bordwell, 'Schema and Revision: Staging and Composition in CinemaScope', in Jean-Jacques Meusy (ed.), *CinemaScope Between Art and Industry* (Paris: Association française de recherche sur l'histoire du cinéma, 2003), p. 219. See also Francesca Liguoro and Giustina D'Oriano, 'The Frontiers of Vision', in ibid. p. 300; David Bordwell, 'Widescreen Aesthetics and Mise en Scene Criticism', *Velvet Light Trap* 21 (1985): 18–25; Harper Cossar, *Letterboxed: The Evolution of Widescreen Cinema* (Lexington: University of Kentucky, 2011), chapter 3.

81. Rivette, 'The Age of *metteurs en scène*', p. 278.

82. Joseph, *Random Order*, p. 80. Regarding the relationship between Rauschenberg's surfaces and their surroundings, see also Craig Owens, *Beyond Recognition* (Berkeley: University of California Press, 1992), pp. 75–9.

83. Rauschenberg and Rose, *Rauschenberg*, p. 23.

84. These painters had already asked Parsons earlier that year to drop other artists from her roster. With her refusal, they soon left for other galleries, particularly the Sidney Janis Gallery. See Lee Hall, *Betty Parsons: Artist, Dealer, Collector* (Harry N. Abrams: New York, 1991), pp. 101–3.

85. The critical reception of Newman's 1951 exhibition was so awful that he gave up one-man shows for several years. Rauschenberg's 6 x 9-foot, three-panel *White Painting* could almost be called a re-creation of one painting from that show, Newman's *The Name II* (1950), a 9 x 8-foot white oil and magna canvas segmented into three vertical panels by Newman's tell-tale 'zips' – here, thin bands of a variant shade of white. *The Name II* was described by one critic as 'elephantine panels' marked by 'sterility, preciousness, and above all pretentiousness'. Belle Krasne, 'The Bar Vertical on Fields Horizontal', *The Arts Digest* (1 May 1951), p. 16. See also Richard Shiff, Carol Mancusi-Ungaro and Heidi Colsman-Freyberger, *Barnett Newman: A Catalogue Raisonné* (New Haven: Yale University Press, 2004), pp. 216–9; Ann Temkin, 'Barnett Newman on Exhibition', in Ann Temkin (ed.), *Barnett Newman* (New Haven: Yale University Press, 2002), pp. 44–5.

86. Rauschenberg and Rose, *Rauschenberg*, p. 47; Tomkins, *Off the Wall*, p. 77.

87. Quigley Jr (ed.), *New Screen Techniques*, p. 110; MacGowan, 'The Screen's "New Look"', pp. 120–1. The measurements of the two-panel *White Painting* are based on the example from Rauschenberg's collection dated 1951 and exhibited in the Sons & Lumières exhibition at the Centre Pompidou in 2004. See Centre Pompidou, *Sons & Lumières: Une histoire du son dans l'art du XXe siècle* (Paris: Éditions du Centre Pompidou, 2004), pp. 266–7.

88. Rauschenberg and his wife, Susan Weil, had already appeared in the magazine in 1951 to demonstrate their large-scale prints made by placing diverse objects, bodies and forms on blueprint paper then exposing it to light. These works are cameraless photos, much like the *White Paintings* are projectorless cinema. One of these photos would appear in the Museum of Modern Art's 'Abstraction in Photography' show in the summer of 1951, at the time the *White Paintings* were

created. 'Speaking of Pictures . . . Blueprint Paper, Sun Lamp, a Nude Produce Some Vaporous Fantasies', *Life* (9 April 1951): 22–4.

89. See additional photos from the exhibition in Walter Hopps, *Robert Rauschenberg: The Early 1950s* (Houston: Houston Fine Art Press, 1991), pp. 157, 189–90, 192–3. Incidentally, Rauschenberg would hang one of his large *Black Paintings* (c.72 x 108 inches) on this very wall in a later exhibition. See ibid. pp. 155, 181–2.

90. Ward, as quoted in ibid. p. 77.

91. Dorothy Seckler, 'Reviews and Previews: Robert Rauschenberg', *Art News* 50:3 (May 1951): 59; Tomkins, *Off the Wall*, p. 291.

92. Mary Emma Harris, *The Arts at Black Mountain College* (Cambridge, MA: MIT Press, 1987), p. 188.

93. Accounts suggest these projections may have included slides and an eight-millimeter film by Nicola Cernovich. The most extensive account of the event is found in Martin Duberman, *Black Mountain: An Exploration in Community* (New York: E. P. Dutton, 1972), pp. 350–8. For a description written shortly after the performance and confirming film projections, see Francine du Plessix Gray, 'Black Mountain: The Breaking (Making) of a Writer', in Mervin Lane (ed.), *Black Mountain College: Sprouted Seeds* (Knoxville: University of Tennessee Press, 1990), p. 300. Regarding Cage's recollection of the *White Paintings* as screens, see Tomkins, *Off the Wall*, p. 68 and John Cage, Michael Kirby and Richard Schechner, 'An Interview with John Cage', *The Tulane Drama Review* 10:2 (Winter 1965): 50–72, pp. 52–3. As for Rauschenberg's memory, Walter Hopps wrote in 1991 that 'Rauschenberg states that projections on his *White Paintings* were never intended and did not happen'. Hopps, *Robert Rauschenberg: The Early 1950s*, p. 66.

94. Rauschenberg would return to the hanging screen in 1966 for his own multi-media performance piece, *Open Score*. Incorporating a tennis match on a darkened court and a live video feed from infrared cameras projected onto screens hanging overhead, *Open Score* was performed in the 9 Evenings: Theatre and Engineering series he organised in New York with EAT (Experiments in Art and Technology).

95. Harold Rosenberg, 'The American Action Painters', *Art News* 51:8 (December 1952): 22–3, 48–50, p. 22; reprinted in David Shapiro and Cecile Shapiro (eds), *Abstract Expressionism: A Critical Record* (Cambridge: Cambridge University Press, 1990), p. 76.

96. Ibid. pp. 78–9; emphasis in text. The idea of the abstract artist as actor was taken up even by those disinclined to such art, as when Ben Shahn states '[It] is the *act* of painting which is emphasized . . . The artist becomes actor, sometimes in a drama of his own psyche'. Ben Shahn, *The Shape of Content* (New York: Vintage Books, 1957), p. 68.

97. Barnett Newman, 'Picture of a Painter', *Newsweek* (16 March 1959), p. 58.

98. Robert Goodnough, 'Kline Paints a Picture', *Art News* 51:8 (December 1952): 36–9, 63–4, p. 37; Fairfield Porter, 'Tworkov Paints a Picture', *Art News* 52:3

(May 1953): 30–3, 72–3, p. 31; Thomas B. Hess, 'de Kooning Paints a Picture', *Art News* 52:1 (March 1953): 30–3, 64–7, p. 30.

99. Edward Strickland, *Minimalism: Origins* (Bloomington: Indiana University Press, 1993), p. 37.

100. Crehan, 'The See Change: Raw Duck', p. 25.

101. Cage, 'On Robert Rauschenberg, Artist, and his Work', p. 100.

102. Ibid. p. 107.

103. Crehan, 'The See Change: Raw Duck', p. 25.

104. A[shton]., '57th Street', pp. 21, 25. For more on the shift from 1951 and 1953, see Joseph, *Random Order*, p. 57.

105. Crehan, 'The See Change: Raw Duck', p. 25; Willem de Kooning, as quoted in Mary Lynn Kotz, *Rauschenberg: Art and Life* (New York: Harry N. Abrams, 1990) p. 79.

106. Newman, as quoted in Harold Rosenberg, *The De-definition of Art* (New York: Horizon, 1972), p. 91.

107. Clement Greenberg, 'Recentness in Sculpture' (1967), in O'Brien (ed.), *Clement Greenberg, The Collected Essays and Criticism: Volume 4*, pp. 251, 254; my emphasis. An equally important, but far less 'easy' affront to Abstract Expressionism is Rauschenberg's *Erased de Kooning Drawing* (1953), wherein he spent several weeks carefully erasing a drawing donated to him by the painter.

108. James Fitzsimmons, as quoted in Kotz, *Rauschenberg/Art and Life*, pp. 79, 82.

109. Ibid. p. 82. As Andrew Forge would note in 1969, the *White* and *Black Paintings* 'are on the brink of being not painting at all since a white wall or a tarred fence would have served some of their functions – except for the task given the onlooker'. Andrew Forge, *Rauschenberg* (New York: Abrams, 1969), p. 37.

110. Sarah Newmeyer, *Enjoying Modern Art* (New York: Mentor Books, 1955), pp. 226–7.

111. As quoted in Genauer, 'Musings on Miscellany', section 4, p. 6. For the letter's parallels with Buddhist literature, see David W. Patterson, 'Words and Writings', in David Nicholls (ed.), *The Cambridge Companion to John Cage* (Cambridge: Cambridge University Press, 2002), pp. 97–8.

112. John Cage, 'On Robert Rauschenberg, Artist, and his Work', p. 102.

113. Dominique Païni, 'Movies in the Gallery: Flow on Show', *Art Press* 287 (February 2003): 24–9, p. 27.

114. Kyle Gann, *No Such Thing as Silence, John Cage's* 4'33" (New Haven: Yale University Press, 2010). For more on the relationship between Cage and Rauschenberg, see Joseph, *Random Order,* pp. 33–68; Caroline A. Jones, 'Finishing School: John Cage and the Abstract Expressionist Ego', *Critical Inquiry* 19:4 (Summer 1993): 628–65, pp. 647–54.

115. Malcolm LeGrice's *White Field Duration* (1973) is another example. Cage's observations on the relationship between *Zen for Film* and the *White Paintings* are worth repeating here: 'In the case of the Nam June Paik film, which has no images on it, the room is darkened, the film is projected, and what you see is the dust that has collected on the film. I think that's somewhat similar to the case

of the Rauschenberg painting, though the focus is more intense. The nature of the environment is more on the film, different from the dust and shadows that are the environment falling on the painting, and thus less free.' John Cage, 'On Nam June Paik's *Zen for Film* (1962–64)', in Richard Kostelanetz (ed.), *John Cage, Writer* (New York: Limelight Editions, 1993), p. 109. See also William Raban, 'Reflexivity and Expanded Cinema: A Cinema of Transgression?', in A. L. Rees, Duncan White, Steven Ball and David Curtis (eds), *Expanded Cinema: Art, Performance, Film* (London: Tate Publishing, 2011), pp. 98–107.

116. Brian O'Doherty, who attended the Jewish Museum show, would later remark that Rauschenberg had brought to the art experience 'not just the vernacular object but something much more important, the *vernacular glance*'. As the *White Paintings* were only 'palimpsests of the fluctuating environment [that] have a kind of short term function', according to O'Doherty their mere presence 'vulgarizes the idea of formal aesthetic inquiry'. Brian O'Doherty, *American Masters: The Voice and the Myth* (New York: Random House, 1973), p. 199; emphasis in text.

117. Alan R. Solomon, *Robert Rauschenberg* (New York: The Jewish Museum, 1963), unpaged.

118. Brian O'Doherty, 'Robert Rauschenberg', *New York Times* (28 April 1963), p. 137.

119. Forge, *Rauschenberg*, p. 124.

120. See Nancy Spector, 'Rauschenberg and Performance, 1963–67: A "Poetry of Possibilities"', in Walter Hopps and Nancy Spector (eds), *Robert Rauschenberg, a Retrospective* (New York: Solomon R. Guggenheim Museum, 1997), pp. 226–45. It was Rauschenberg's large-scale paintings of transferred found images, however, that more directly brought the cinema to bear in his work. O'Doherty claims that Rauschenberg's work included the 'conflict between the filmic and the pictorial'. In *Barge*, for example, the thirty-two-foot canvas' 'super-CinemaScope format' encourages a linear reading of the images like 'a filmic series, which the images themselves, grainy, gray and black and white, obviously invite', according to O'Doherty. O'Doherty, *American Masters*, p. 205.

121. Allan Kaprow, 'Experimental Art', *Art News* (March 1966): 60–3, 77–82, pp. 78, 63. On the matter of environmental circumstances and the mobile spectator as part of the operation and impact of the work, see also Fried, 'Art and Objecthood', and Robert Morris, 'Notes on Sculpture, Part 1' and 'Notes on Sculpture, Part 2', in Robert Morris, *Continuous Project Altered Daily: The Writings of Robert Morris* (Cambridge, MA: MIT Press, 1993), pp. 1–22.

122. Belton, *Widescreen Cinema*, p. 162.

123. Bordwell, *Poetics of Cinema*, p. 282

CHAPTER 2

The Screen Scene: Andy Warhol, the Factory and Home Movies

Film- and performance-based art was still a rarity in most museum and gallery spaces in the mid-1960s, yet it had decisively entered the studio, the co-op and related contemporary art settings. In North America, Europe and elsewhere, screenings, concerts, recitals, readings, environments and other forms of performative, interactive production had become an integral part of what would be called the neo-avant-garde. Gaining purchase in the trans-media historical avant-garde that included Constructivism, Dada and Surrealism – instead of the seeming entropic path laid out by Abstract Expressionism and 'advanced' painting – Happenings and Pop, Fluxus, Minimal and Conceptual art dissolved barriers of media specificity by emphasising performance, spectacle and duration as components (or the totality) of the piece. A decade after the Stable Gallery exhibition, Robert Rauschenberg's *White Paintings* had become almost quaint by comparison.

Within this context, Andy Warhol would establish an art career of continuous collaboration, shaped by the synthesis of media and social interaction. A major aspect of this *Gesamtkunstwerk* was Warhol's film-based social practices throughout the 1960s, which are increasingly recognised as one of his greatest artistic legacies. Warhol's production and exhibition methods of the period relied heavily on vernacular film culture, particularly home-movie practices, to transform film into a binding thread of the large, motley group of personalities that formed his Factory studio community (Figure 2.1). 'It was people who were fascinating,' Warhol explains in *POPism*, his 1960s memoir co-written with Pat Hackett, 'and I wanted to spend all my time being around them, listening to them, and making movies of them.'[1] While the frequent appearance of his films in museums and galleries today may represent validation for works that received little public affection when they were made, the conditions of their exhibition – often looped digital-video transfers presented like slow-moving paintings – regularly dissociate them from their initial use as mechanisms in the construction of collective identity. Just as home movies tend to privilege practice – the making and sharing – over the object in their contribution to social cohesion, Warhol's films before 1966 constituted a social practice primarily centred on and in the Factory as a

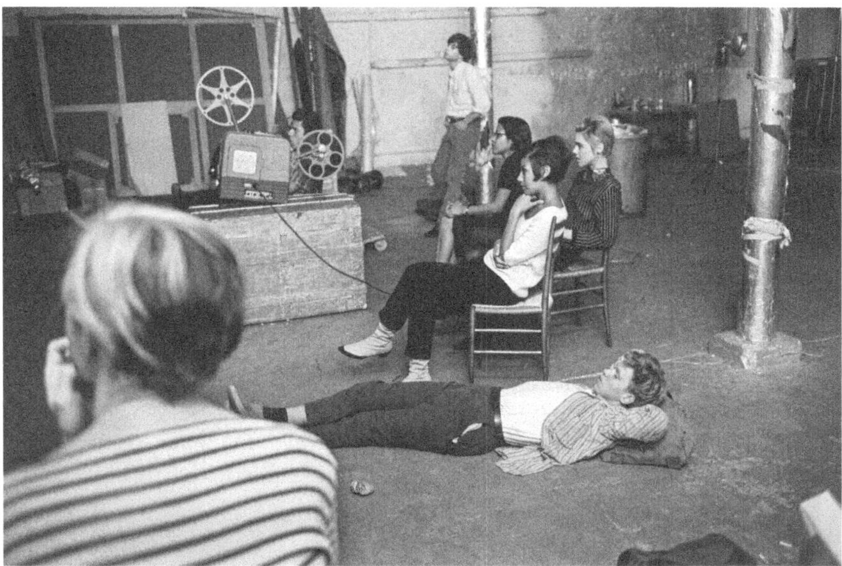

Figure 2.1   *Bob Adelman, Screening at Andy Warhol's Silver Factory, 1965. © Bob Adelman*

discrete community. As Warhol later claimed, 'We didn't think of our movies as underground or commercial or art or porn; they were a little of all those, but ultimately they were "our kind of movie"'.[2] This description is perhaps the best summation of Warhol's sizable film project, framing it as a collective effort that catered first and foremost to those who participated in it.

A few years after the Factory closed, *Art in America* would note film-making as one of Warhol's major contributions to contemporary art, another being 'the achievement of a relatively interesting group-life-style, with a distinct coloration'.[3] In fact, each of these contributions had been pivotal in helping produce and sustain the other. While Warhol certainly had commercial aspirations for his work, these do not negate the films' inward focus on a relatively close-knit group of people. What made these films 'our kind of movie' for the Factory crowd was their clarification and perhaps definition of who this 'we' was, to the extent that it is hard to imagine this group without taking the films into account.[4] Home movies are inevitably their makers' 'kind' of movies. What Gillian Rose has said of family photos holds just as true for movies: 'Family photos are particular sorts of images embedded in specific practices, and it is the specificity of those *practices* that define a photograph as a family photo as much as, if not more than, what it pictures'.[5] Recognising and articulating methods of Factory film-making and viewing, with their roots in the poorly esteemed but widely practiced twentieth-century popular film form of home movies, is therefore a critical step to a better understanding of the value of Warhol's filmography, including some of its most inscrutable and alienating works, such as *Sleep* (1963).[6]

HOLLYWOOD AND HOME MOVIES

Andy Warhol described his activity at the Factory as 'Movies, movies, and more movies. We were shooting so many', he boasted, 'we never even bothered to give titles to a lot of them. Friends would stop by and they'd wind up in front of the camera, the star of that afternoon's reel'.[7] Warhol's film-making from 1963 to 1966 – before he turned to producing features for commercial release – was a loose, largely improvised and communal endeavour that brought him and his entourage into a cinema-suffused lifestyle. Whether shooting films in the silver-lined luminescence of the Factory, his post-industrial loft studio on 47th Street, or gathering there with others to watch the results projected on makeshift screens, Warhol's film activity matched elements of professional production with methods and conditions more commonly associated with home-movie making.

Warhol's films from that period – whether considered minimalist experiments, camp escapade or both – have commonly been interpreted as perspicuous, amusing and sometimes stinging responses to the commercial cinema of the movie theatre. '[I]f you consider the context in which he is making the films . . . I would consider his films specifically were designed as a provocation – or an alternative in a sense – to commercial Hollywood', noted art critic and Factory regular Gregory Battcock. 'All of his films were references to commercial cinema in one way or another.'[8] Film historian Matthew Tinkcom claims that 'Warhol's films of the underground period sought to emulate the feel of Hollywood, not by emulating conventional narrative patterns, but by creating their own versions of glamour'.[9] Actor and film critic Amy Taubin, who, like Battcock, had been filmed by Warhol at the Factory, interprets the films as 'a response to [the] Hollywood films Warhol grew up on'.[10] Probably thinking of underground film-makers like Jack Smith, with whom Warhol worked at the start of his film career, Taubin explains that 'Warhol learned from the avant-garde how to produce a (per)version of Hollywood in his own studio for little more than the cost of a roll of 16mm film and developing'.[11]

Warhol assembled a crew of assistants in this endeavour, including Gerard Malanga, Chuck Wein and Billy Name, and hired playwright Ronald Tavel to write screenplays or, more accurately, create 'situations'.[12] Warhol adapted characters and stories from standard studio genres, making use of Batman, Dracula and Tarzan. He adapted Anthony Burgess' *A Clockwork Orange* six years before Stanley Kubrick's Warner Brothers production. He filmed hundreds of 'screen tests' of assistants, acquaintances and Factory visitors, culling from these a few more-or-less regular players he called his 'Superstars'. At the peak of production in the mid-1960s Warhol maintained a brisk output of reels at the Factory, transforming the mid-town Manhattan loft from a painting studio into something approaching a sound stage. He made some of these films available for exhibition rental nationwide.[13]

Alongside these attributes, however, there are significant traits of home-movie culture in Warhol's Factory film activity, from the choice of subjects to techniques of filming and modes of exhibition. As defined by Patricia Zimmermann in *Mining the Home Movie*, home movies are 'a subset of the amateur film movement located within individual and/or familial practices of visual recording of intimate events and rituals and intended for private usage and exhibition'.[14] Warhol's early work regularly foregrounded such intimate, everyday activity in capturing the 'family drama' that was the Factory, as Caroline Jones has described it.[15] Whether silent or direct-sound, the films were in 16-mm format, they lacked titles and credits (including even the copyright notice), they were composed of single-take reels, and they depicted people sleeping, eating, getting haircuts, staring at the camera, putting on make-up, singing, talking on the phone, fighting, flirting, kissing and having sex.[16] Warhol even filmed his mother, Julia Warhola, doing housework while improvising the unlikely role of an aging Hollywood star bickering with her young husband, played by the artist's boyfriend at the time, Richard Rheem (Figure 2.2). While Warhol publicly promoted some of these films by advertising them in the media and screening them in theatres for short periods, more often than not they were seen only at the Factory, primarily by the people who participated in their making.

Participants were rarely paid for their involvement. '[Pay] would have spoiled the fun of making these movies', explains Gerard Malanga, one of the few Warhol collaborators on payroll at that time.[17] The story – if there was a story – was sometimes chosen at the last moment, and who participated might depend on who happened to turn up at the studio that day. No matter what combination of personalities ended up in-frame and what was happening, the camera usually kept rolling. 'Warhol conceived of narrative as a series of situations', film-maker J. J. Murphy points out, 'in which his non-professional performers would engage in improvised role playing as opposed to following a carefully constructed plot'. The strategy 'implicitly contained a significant risk of failure'.[18] Risk became its guiding aesthetic trait, to be exulted or derided. 'Mistakes make the genre of home movies powerful and real', explains film-maker Péter Forgács, calling this its 'perfection of imperfection'.[19] Warhol certainly perfected his imperfection. 'Whatever happens, planned or not, is the film', explained John Wilcock, a co-founder of Warhol's

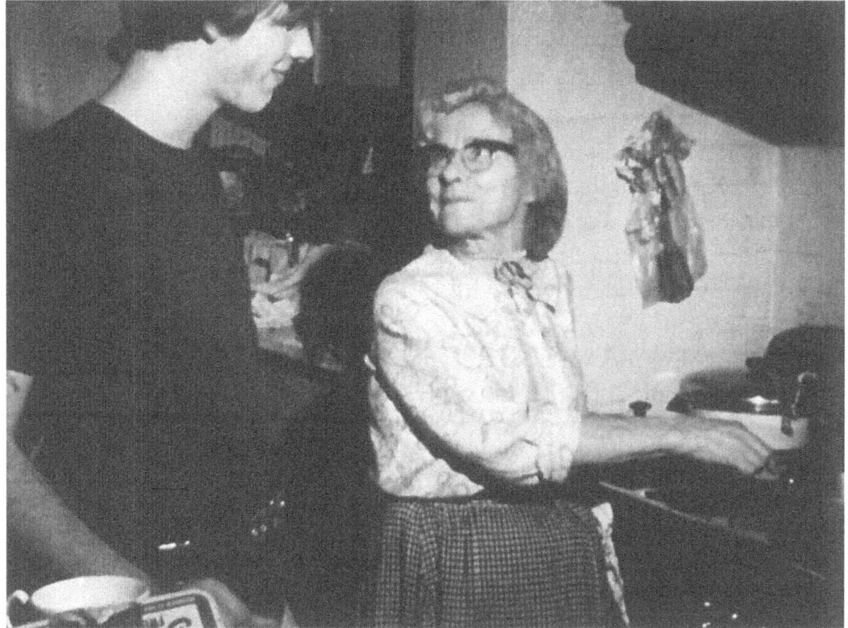

Figure 2.2 *Andy Warhol,* Mrs. Warhol, *1966, film frame.* © *The Andy Warhol Museum, Pittsburgh, PA, a museum of the Carnegie Institute, all rights reserved*

Interview magazine, in a 1965 profile piece for *The Village Voice*. 'Sometimes in the studio . . . there will be interruptions: telephone calls, people going up or down in the elevator, somebody dropping something or walking inadvertently in front of the camera. All is recorded. No trace of surprise or annoyance registers on Warhol's face.'[20]

These descriptions are confirmed by dozens of films shot at the Factory. 'Participation' becomes an ambiguous term in these works as people come and go. Sometimes they appear unaware a film is being shot or uncertain what to do. In the sound films those filming may interact with the participants in direct ways that recall home-movie making. In *Afternoon* (1965) Warhol shot several people on and around a sofa, asking them throughout to perform in simple ways, such as talking to each other, drinking and dancing. At points he sounds like the impatient father, pleading with them to 'Look into the camera', 'Do something', 'Talk one at a time' and 'Make faces'. A sense of inaction marks *Afternoon* and other films when the camera remains stagnant for banal activities; a sense of opportunities lost arises when the camera moves in the 'wrong' direction as an action takes place. Such properties – those that make a Warhol film 'Warholesque' – owe more to the culture of home movies (and, in the more sexually oriented films, the home movie's pornographic equivalent – the stag film) than they do to commercial cinema and prior avant-garde and experimental film-making.[21] In his book on twentieth-century amateur film-making, Charles Tepperman explains that even those amateur productions that had as many resources as Warhol's 'retain traces of their amateur status in moments of accidental beauty or in deliberate choices of playful or intimate subject matter'.[22] Warhol's debt to such film-making traditions was frequently acknowledged – whether as an asset or liability – in the press of the period. 'If [Andy Warhol] wants such a collection for "home movies" fine', wrote a critic of the Factory films in *Adam Film Quarterly*, 'but please, Mr. Warhol, don't foist them upon the movie-houses'.[23] Until recently, however, this genealogy has been overlooked in studies of Warhol's art and films.[24] Stephen Koch's *Stargazer: Andy Warhol's World and His Films*, published in 1973 and appearing in a new edition in 1985, long set the tone for understanding Warhol's Factory films. 'The "art" films Warhol began his career making as part of the impecunious but vital Independent movement presided over by Jonas Mekas have given way to a series of commercial sex farces', Koch explained, signalling the end of Warhol's 'commitment to high modernism'.[25] Peter Wollen has cast the films as reflecting 'a minimalist factory that simply recorded rather than transformed' while nevertheless indulging in camp. Explaining minimalism and camp as the Factory's bifurcated reaction to dominant commercial cinema, Giuliana Bruno states that 'the outlines of Warhol's cinematic opus can be read as a movement from "primitive cinema" to Hollywood modes of representation, for his film work retraces the very course of cinema's history'. She explains, 'Warhol began by shooting silent black-and-white films that remake silent cinema, and then moved toward stargazing'. Although Bruno recognises that Warhol's earliest works are 'recordings of people exhibiting daily behavior, enjoying leisure inactivity or pleasure time', content and form are read exclusively in terms of commercial cinema models, whether circa 1905 or 1965.[26]

This bias extends to the exhibition of these films. Warhol's few public screenings before the release of *The Chelsea Girls* in 1966 have received inordinate attention; one need only think of the numerous descriptions of bored audiences walking out of theatre presentations of *Sleep* (1963) and *Empire* (1964), alienated by static, silent films shot at 24 frames per second (fps) but projected at a slower 16 fps.[27] This emphasis has impacted interpretations of the function of these films and the intent of their director. Critic and film-maker Parker Tyler's influential 1967 analysis of Warhol's early films, 'Dragtime or Drugtime: or Film à la Warhol', is a good example. It frames Warhol's films as intended for 'the passive attention of a fixed (that is, seated) spectator in a film theater'. Tyler explained that this situation 'makes the viewing time required for [Warhol's] films into a drag exquisitely nuanced or excruciatingly redundant'.[28]

Although such conditions may have existed in Warhol's public screenings, he more frequently presented his films to friends and acquaintances at the Factory or elsewhere, often casually and spontaneously, in circumstances resembling home-movie watching. He insinuated the films into impromptu and informal gatherings, showing whatever reels happened to be on hand or opening canisters that had just returned from the lab. 'Even though we never knew ourselves till the very last minute which films we were going to screen', Warhol claimed, 'somehow, as if by magic, the people who were in the movie, or friends of theirs, would always know to turn up'.[29] He presented films at the high-society cocktail parties of wealthy collaborators, as when he projected the *Screen Tests* of Jane Holzer at her Park Avenue apartment after the opening of his *Flowers* show in November 1964.[30] He also included them in a memorial gathering at the Factory that autumn, showing films starring Freddy Herko shortly after the dancer's suicide.[31] Even when shown in public, his films were not limited to movie-theatre screenings, but also appeared under conditions related to home-movie viewing. The September 1964 presentation of excerpts from his silent films at the New York Film Festival, held at the Lincoln Center for the Performing Arts, did not happen on the theatre's screen but as projected loops using consumer-grade equipment in the lobby. 'To screen the films, Lincoln Center has acquired . . . small box-type projectors resembling television sets, designed to make it easy to show 8mm. movies in the home,' the *New York Times* reported.[32]

David E. James, in his chapter on Warhol in *Allegories of Cinema: American Film in the Sixties*, reflects commonly held beliefs – perpetuated by writers such as Koch and even Warhol himself – surrounding the artist's film exhibition practices. James claims that

> Many of the films were never shown, shown only during parties at the Factory when other things were going on, or shown as part of multiple sensoria like the Exploding Plastic Inevitable [in 1966]; or they were screened publicly and the audience walked out.[33]

Although James' account may hold true for particular films, many statements by Warhol and Factory participants suggest otherwise, emphasising the importance of informal shooting and viewing – far removed from parties and other events – as integral to the Factory's everyday, participatory culture. Wilcock, for example, ventured in 1965

> If Warhol has any specific point of view about his films, it is probably that whatever happens, he's having a ball learning how to make home movies, and it's merely gravy to him if the movies become valuable art

> works because he happens to have made them . . . Meanwhile, the movies, screened once, pile up in silver cans in his silvered studio. The filming is fun. Like most amateur movie making, it casts that extraordinary spell that makes the onlookers believe that they can go in and out of the action at will. Up front, in the light, are the 'actors,' often a bunch of people improvising on a basic script.[34]

Although Wilcock underestimated Warhol's commitment to film-making, his description of Factory practices meshes with other accounts. Dance and performance historian Sally Banes, one of the few scholars to recognise the impact of home-movie strategies on Warhol's methods, notes not only that Warhol filmed 'leisure-time activities of the type favored by amateur home-movie aficionados, but the festive holiday ambience of the film screenings resembled home-movie showings at family gatherings . . . People came and went at their pleasure, napped, chatted, and brought food to share'.[35]

Warhol's film work prior to 1966 appears to have been made as much for viewing on collapsible home-movie screens and bedsheets affixed to a wall as for screening in movie theatres. This begs the question: Why would such aspects of his film practices be overshadowed for years by considerations of the films' structuralist or minimalist tendencies, on the one hand, and their relationship to Hollywood as parody and camp, on the other? One answer is *Visionary Film*, P. Adams Sitney's influential 1974 work on American avant-garde cinema. In that book, Sitney named Warhol 'The major precursor of the structural film . . . although spiritually at the opposite pole from the structural film-makers'. Sitney conveniently ignored films such as *Tarzan and Jane Regained . . . Sort of* (1963), a camp travelogue shot while Warhol was visiting California, to instead celebrate the relatively static, silent 'monuments' of *Sleep*, *Eat* and *Empire*.[36] Zimmermann may offer another response, related to Sitney's selective assessment of Warhol's filmography, in noting the historically low stature accorded home movies in film and media studies. Home movies 'have been perceived as simply an irrelevant pastime or nostalgic mementoes of the past, dismissed as insignificant byproducts of consumer technology', she states. 'In the popular imaginary, home movies are often defined by negation: noncommercial, nonprofessional, unnecessary.'[37] It may be, then, that describing Warhol's cinema in terms of home-movie practices, even as only a part of its character and significance, risks diminishing it in the eyes of many. Indeed, while recent writings on his films have begun to explore their wider cultural sources and references, the exhibition of his films in museums and galleries continues to strip away any vestige of their messy amateur origins by presenting the filmic image as an ethereal, almost metaphysical apparition cut off from the materiality of everyday life.

HOME SCREENS

Warhol's film exhibition practices developed from three competing influences: screen techniques he adopted in his childhood and early painting career, the relationship between home-movie making and American consumer culture, and the coupling of art and environment implied by Rauschenberg's *White Paintings* and established in the 1960s neo-avant-garde. By the time he began making films in the Factory, Warhol was already familiar with amateur film-making and viewing. 'Although I didn't buy a movie camera till some time in '63', Warhol would later claim, 'it had certainly occurred to me to be a do-it-yourself filmmaker long before then'.[38] This matches Zimmerman's assertion that post-war amateur cinema as a leisure-time activity insinuated into the home 'simply another do-it-yourself ideology'.[39] Henry Geldzahler, the Metropolitan Museum curator who befriended Warhol at the start of his painting career, recalls Warhol borrowing a camera at that time and shooting Geldzahler in his apartment as he went about his daily activities. '[Warhol] came in and did a three-minute movie where I was smoking a cigar, and then I threw the cigar in the toilet, and I brushed my teeth, and then I flushed the toilet', Geldzahler recounts. 'For all I know, it was never printed. He was just trying to see what it looks like through a camera.'[40]

Warhol began making films at a time when cameras, projectors and other movie accessories had become common objects in American middle-class homes, promoted by manufacturers as among the essentials of modern family life. 'You just won't be able to remember it all in "still" pictures, alone', warned a 1953 advertisement for Kodak movie cameras. 'So movies are wonderful! But aren't they hard to make?' the ad asked readers. 'Not on your life! Movies are as simple as snapshots.'[41] A 1944 Bell and Howell ad offered 'The thrill of re-living your own personal history', explaining that 'Our research . . . promises you new and finer ways to *film* and *project* those precious bits of personal history on your own home screen'.[42] Warhol explored the social applications of the moving image by fostering the interdependence of daily routine, social interaction and the film event already implied through such marketing efforts. He would explain that, for his circle of friends and the hangers-on of that period, 'the movies became part of their lives; they'd get so into them that pretty soon you couldn't really separate the two, you couldn't tell the difference – and sometimes neither could they'.[43] This merging of life and movies, where the one not only informs the other but also ultimately depends on the other for coherence and meaning, fulfils the guiding myth of home-movie making and viewing as the technological means of representing, reifying and coalescing personal relationships.

Links between cinema and art run the length of Warhol's professional life. There are his gold-leaf shoe and boot collages named for actors including Mae West, Judy Garland and James Dean (the last appearing in *Life* magazine in 1956). There are the sketches copied from covers of magazines such as *Movie Play*.[44] There are the celebrated silkscreen portraits of Marilyn Monroe and Elizabeth Taylor in the early 1960s and those of Sylvester Stallone, Meryl Streep and Clint Eastwood in the 1980s. Similarly, the frenetic production of films with minimal action in the mid-1960s is paralleled by genre pastiche – from adventure to Western – and followed after 1967 by a string of commercial sexploitation films directed by Paul Morrissey and produced by Warhol that stretched well into the 1970s. Even Warhol's secondary activities, such as publishing *Interview* magazine (originally titled *inter/VIEW, A Monthly Film Journal*), bear close connections to cinema. Amid all of these is Warhol's frequent cinema going and unflagging desire to meet, photograph, interview – and gossip about – movie stars, which ended only with his death in 1987.[45]

As most accounts of Warhol's life document, his compulsion toward cinema as an organising biographical and creative trope runs even deeper, reaching into his Depression-era childhood in Pittsburgh. Like many kids growing up in urban America at that time, young Warhol (then Warhola) regularly went to the movies. He bought Hollywood screen magazines, collected promotional photos of stars and wrote to his favourite actors and actresses to request autographs.[46] Perhaps his most-prized possession of those years was the inscribed photo he had received from Shirley Temple. Amid the challenges of growing up the youngest son of poor Carpatho-Rusyn immigrants, the movies offered irresistible escape into a sparkling, care-free universe. 'Vacant, vacuous Hollywood was everything I ever wanted to mold my life into,' Warhol would claim as an adult.[47]

In addition to the photos, magazines and matinees, when he was seven years old Warhol's participatory cinema practices entered another dimension with his mother's gift of a toy projector to watch cartoons at home. 'We didn't have money to buy a screen', Warhol's brother John remembers, '[so] he'd show the pictures on the wall'.[48] Home-movie viewing thereafter supplemented both the public space of the movie theatre and Warhol's collection of memorabilia. Barely old enough to attend school, he was merging cinema and life in powerful ways by intersecting domestic architecture and family structure through projected spectacle. Requiring his intervention for the choice of the reel, the threading of the gate, the selection of an adequate projection surface and the cranking of the handle, the toy projector gave Warhol – for however brief a period – control over the terms of home viewing, and through this the social relationships within his family.

After studying painting and design at the Carnegie Institute of Technology and embarking on an advertising career in New York, Warhol's 1956 trip around the world with his friend, Charles Lisanby, provided another formative encounter with home movies, this time encompassing film making as well as viewing. Lisanby brought along an 8-mm movie camera and Warhol was able to watch himself on screen but, according to Lisanby, the artist was more fascinated by the aesthetics of home-movie shooting and projection. '[H]e was fascinated by the things that I had that were unedited', Lisanby recalled. 'In fact, he thought that the "Kodak" and all the dots and everything at the beginning or end of the leader . . . was as important as anything else.'[49]

The projected image would remain close to Warhol's creative process. When he left his lucrative commercial illustration career to begin 'serious' painting in the early 1960s, home projection provided the means for developing his distinctly impersonal painting style. He painted works including his iconic 1962 series of thirty-two Campbell soup cans from images cast by a Beseler Vu-Lyte opaque projector. In those pre-Factory days, working in the cramped quarters of his narrow Lexington Avenue townhouse, his white primed canvases became screens tacked to the living room or bedroom wall during the tracing and painting process.[50] 'If it was a drawing, he would draw, or if it was a painting, he would trace it off on canvas and then fill it in', recalled early assistant Nathan Gluck.[51] Projection space overlapped with living, social and creative space at the surface of the paper or canvas screen. By 1963 he had given up the Vu-Lyte to silkscreen his paintings and had acquired a Bolex 16-mm silent camera to add film-making to his repertoire. He switched to an Auricon sound camera one year later.

FROM HOLLYWOOD TO THE AVANT-GARDE

How would the sometimes spare and singular films Warhol made, including *Sleep*, *Empire*, *Kiss* (1963–4), *Eat* (1964), *Haircut (No.1)* (1963), *Poor Little Rich Girl* (1965), *Couch* (1964) and the *Screen Tests* (1964–6), relate to the conventions of home movies? Beyond their hard, minimalist surfaces, what these works depict are simple, quotidian events more likely to have been found on 8-mm reels arranged on a living room shelf than 35-mm reels stored in a Hollywood back lot or a museum collection (Figure 2.3). *Sleep*, with its repeated shots, slowed projection speed and nearly five-and-a-half-hour running time, has been described as 'a serial meditation on stillness, run through its variations and protracted within the irreal, yet tempered and concrete medium of film'.[52] It is all that, of course, but in its most basic socio-historical terms this extended event (that includes the repetition of certain shots) is the visual document of a couple's relationship. Warhol did not shoot

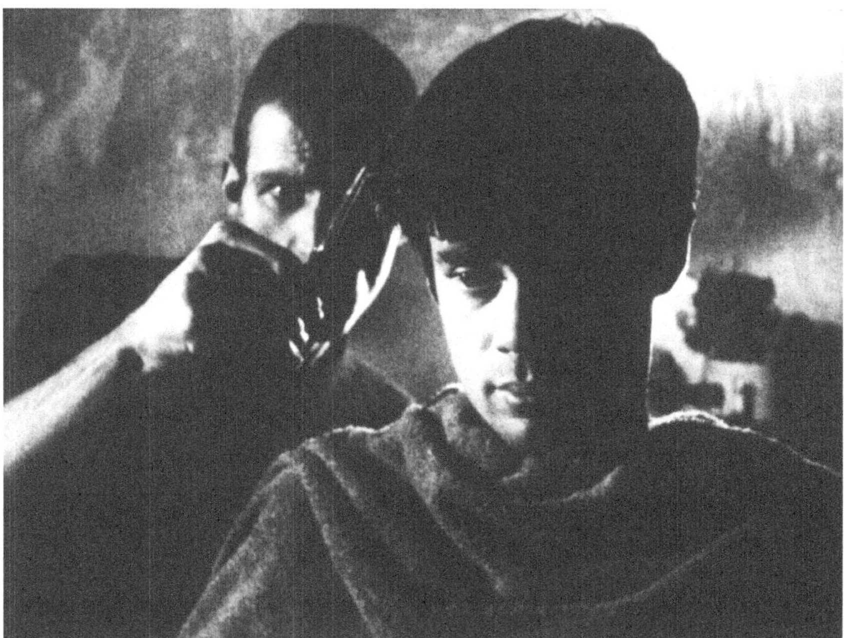

Figure 2.3 *Andy Warhol,* Haircut (No. 1), *1963, film frame.* © *The Andy Warhol Museum, Pittsburgh, PA, a museum of the Carnegie Institute, all rights reserved*

just any man sleeping, but his lover of the time, poet John Giorno. The relationship may be inferred from the intimate composition and duration of the work.[53] (A decade later he would shoot *Julia Warhola in Bed*, an astonishingly tender video portrait of his mother falling asleep.) Shots of family and friends asleep are common to home movies (think of all those post-dinner sofa shots at the holidays) and would return in later Warhol films. *Empire*'s static shot of one of New York City's top tourist attractions, the Empire State Building, similarly extends a requisite shot from any tourist's New York holiday. At eight hours of screening time the film produces a numbing caricature of such images, one that may bring to mind the tedium of watching a friend's 'endless' vacation reels. *Kiss, Eat, Couch* and other silent productions offer the viewer Warhol's circle engaged in various simple activities, many of which might surface in home movies (or in the case of *Couch*, an amateur stag film). These films hardly limit themselves to exploring the codes and grammar of cinema. In the selection and composition of content they could be said to describe a community. 'These movies are like games, not "serious" at all', Mekas would shrewdly explain of *Eat* and similar films as early as 1964, 'They are happy to call themselves "home movies"'.[54]

The hundreds of *Screen Tests*, where a lone subject usually is seated before a stark background and stares into the lens in close-up for four minutes, insert themselves into the droll aesthetic of home movies by confronting one of the most basic 'flaws' of the family film genre – the participant's recognition of the camera. A 1960s edition of Kodak's *How to Make Good Home Movies* explains that most people in front of the camera 'react stiffly, self-consciously, and inhibitedly'. To correct this, the book encourages readers to get their subjects 'engrossed in some sort of activity'.[55] Turning to the camera is a common action in Warhol films, both for the performers and the Factory visitors who stumble into the scene, but in the *Screen Tests* Warhol cleverly obeys and dismisses such advice by asking participants to concentrate on the very act of staring into the eye of the lens. As the series title indicates, the *Screen Tests* not only engage the home-movie genre but also relate to commercial cinema production. In doing so, however, they demonstrate the complex and rarely explored aesthetic, social and economic ties between Hollywood and the family film.

Marking the moment when an unknown actor or hopeful might emerge as a potential star, a screen test bridges amateur and commercial cinema, documentary and fiction. A 1961 contest advertised in *Life* magazine by Fairchild Camera and Warner Brothers capitalises on this ambiguity by encouraging consumers to make their own screen tests (Figure 2.4). It is hard to imagine Warhol, a *Life* subscriber and reader, overlooking Troy Donahue – the heart-throb chosen for his first silkscreen portrait a year later – in this full-page announcement promoting the contest and Fairchild's 8-mm Cinephonic sound camera. 'Entering this fabulous talent contest is as easy as acting in front of a home-movie camera. In fact that's all you do!' the ad assures readers, with a smiling Donahue pointing his lens at a trio of budding starlets. Encompassing production and exhibition, the ad suggests to readers 'Get your friends or family to help you make your Cinephonic "screen test". They'll have as much fun filming it as you have acting in it.' It urges them to rent a Fairchild projector to watch the results. 'You can enjoy showing your screen test to friends and family *before* you send the film to Warner Bros. in Hollywood.'[56] Intentionally or not, Warhol's later production and exhibition of his *Screen Tests* as an activity among friends uncannily resembles the formula laid out by Fairchild and the studio.

The popular dream – reflected in this contest – of crossing Hollywood and home-movie making emerges in *Tarzan and Jane Regained . . . Sort of*, one of Warhol's earliest films. Partly shot in Los Angeles, the eighty-minute film references Hollywood narratively and geographically, while bearing a remarkable resemblance to family vacation movies. Indeed, Warhol had bought his Bolex for this trip across country with painter Wynn Chamberlain, poet-

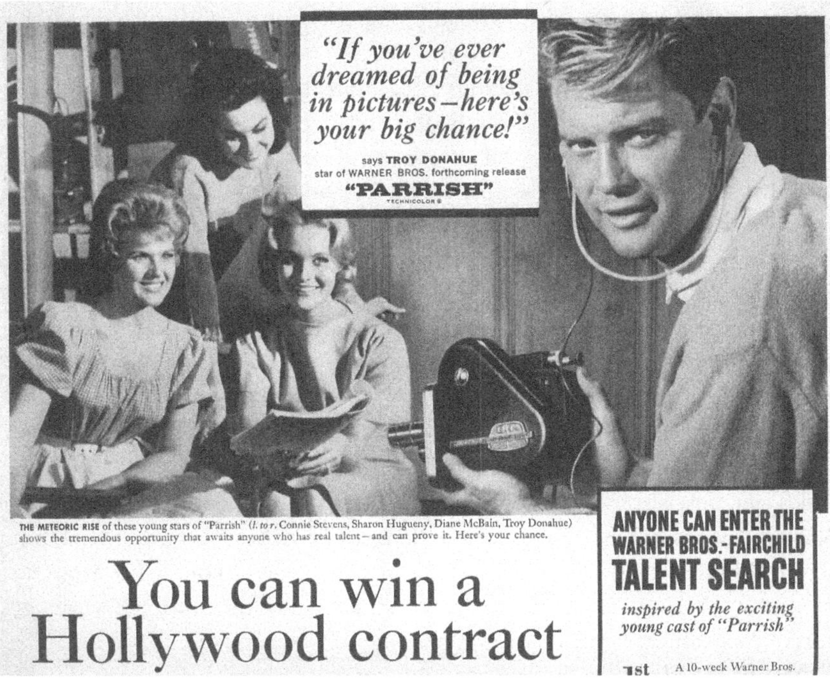

Figure 2.4   *Warner Bros.-Fairchild Talent Search advertisement (detail), 1961.*

actor Taylor Mead and studio assistant Gerard Malanga. 'Taylor Mead was such a great screen star, we thought it would be a great idea to do Taylor going across country', Warhol explains. 'So I bought this 16mm camera, and we just shot Taylor in California.'[57] The film opens with a typical vacation-movie sequence of highway scenes from a car window as the travellers approach their destination. The rest of the film concentrates on Mead as a comical Tarzan, with Naomi Levine occasionally accompanying him as Jane. Frolicking in a zebra-print child's bathing suit around a Beverly Hills hotel pool, Venice Beach body-building equipment and Santa Monica's famous pier, Mead indulges in a tourist film that doubles as Hollywood parody.[58] 'Warhol employs a home-movie or amateur aesthetic', J. J. Murphy claims, not only through 'quirky' camera movements and jump cuts, but also by creating a jungle adventure where 'dogs and cats can substitute for wild animals, a hotel swimming pool can be a river, [and] a doll can substitute for a person in a heroic rescue'.[59] Twentieth-century articles on amateur movie making often suggest mimicking the look and action of Hollywood films – particularly adventure films – through simplified costumes, stunts and special effects. *Tarzan and Jane Regained . . . Sort of* functions in this vein, shifting the context of the effort to the avant-garde merely by means of its participants.

The heavy emphasis on informality, improvisation and accident found in *Tarzan and Jane Regained . . . Sort of* and Warhol's subsequent films duplicates conditions of home-movie making while reflecting trends in contemporary avant-garde film-making by friends of Warhol, including Jonas Mekas, Jack Smith and Marie Menken – all of whom appear in Warhol's films – and other artists, such as Stan Brakhage. It is important to affirm Warhol's debt to – and divergence from – these peers to accurately gauge his relationship to home-movie production and exhibition. Smith, best-known for his 1963 film, *Flaming Creatures*, created camp works of elaborately staged and costumed visual and sexual excess. 'The preparations for every shooting were like a party', Warhol claimed.[60] Warhol acted in Smith's unfinished 1963 film, *Normal Love*, dancing with others atop a fake layer cake, and he shot his own footage of the production (*Jack Smith Shooting* Normal Love, 1963). What Susan Sontag terms the 'wilfully technical crudity'[61] of Smith's work, and Tyler describes as its 'rough stuff in the home movie style', impacted Warhol's work, and he readily acknowledged the debt.[62] 'I picked something up from him for my own movies – the way he used anyone who happened to be around that day, and also how he just kept shooting until the actors got bored', Warhol explained.[63]

Mekas, a Lithuanian émigré, was the nexus of alternative film-making in New York throughout the period, founding *Film Culture* magazine in 1955, the New American Cinema Group in 1960, and the Film-Makers' Cooperative in 1962. He also wrote the 'Movie Journal' column for *The Village Voice*, in which he chronicled and promoted Warhol's rise as a film-maker.[64] Mekas obsessively carried and used a Bolex camera to record daily events for a film diary of his life and the lives of those around him. He relied on a single-frame technique, however, that compressed and fragmented filmed events as though caught in the selective, imperfect net of memory.[65] Menken also relied on single-frame shooting and animation techniques to create impressionistic films of post-war New York. Brakhage, known to Warhol through Mekas, shot films of his family and friends in the Colorado countryside. With a similar emphasis on compression and fragmentation, Brakhage often explored the relationship between humanity and nature.[66] As much as all three film-makers relied on friends and family as participants in their productions – a tendency extending back to the height of avant-garde cinema in Europe in the 1920s – their works often bear vestiges of what Mekas had described in the 1950s as the 'film poem' by containing elements of 'personal lyricism'.[67] Indeed, even Smith's irreverently amateurish images deliver 'an extraordinary charge and beauty', according to Sontag.[68]

Warhol distinguished his work by unequivocally rejecting the film diary and lyrical poem while also downplaying the subjective camera.[69] He regularly trained an immobile lens on banal events – sleeping, eating, kissing, and the like – shooting them in single takes to avoid editing. In 1964, Mekas awarded Warhol *Film Culture*'s Independent Film Award, citing this simplicity of technique that rendered 'Eating as eating, sleeping as sleeping, haircut as haircut'.[70] 'Raw and crude was the way I liked our movies to look', Warhol would say, and other appraisals of his work during that period recognised a home-movie aesthetic, for better or worse.[71] *Art News* critic David Antin, representing a fine art rather than film perspective, described films like *Eat*, *Vinyl* (the 1965 adaptation of *A Clockwork Orange*) and *Banana* (1964) as 'all homemade and showing it, hav[ing] a consistently attractive, ratty look'.[72]

Such films play out the hazards and contradictions of home-movie culture as they were described in guides and manuals of the 1950s and 1960s. '*All good compositions . . . depend on their impact by standing out against a plain background*', asserted *How to Take Better Home Movies*. 'Subjects filmed against such solid areas can't help but stand out to advantage.'[73] Warhol reflects that advice in his early films – especially the *Screen Tests* – with bright or dark interior backgrounds, although he sets aside exhortations that the amateur 'make his movie more interesting by offering a variety of compositions'.[74] Similarly, *How to Make Good Home Movies* stressed the home-moviemaker's power to 'preserve the entire event, unfrozen and continuous, exactly as it happens'.[75] With a simple example of filming a boy getting his first snow shovel, however, the manual explained that movie makers should record only bits of the action. 'If you've merely followed along with your movie camera, shooting a little of each chapter . . . you'll find, much to your pleasure, that you've captured a wonderful slice of childhood, complete and continuous.'[76] Of course, many of Warhol's films underscore the paradox in such expectations by providing a version of the 'complete and continuous' produced with a motionless camera and reel-long shots that circumvent the episodic aesthetics associated with selective filming.

Tally Brown's participation in a Warhol production on her first visit to the Factory in the summer of 1964 recalls the comic antics of family films. Extremely tired, Brown fell asleep on one of the couches that contributed to the studio's strangely domestic atmosphere. Warhol then filmed attempts by various visitors and colleagues to tease her awake. 'When I saw the footage, I thought that I looked like a very petulant baby whale', she explained later, with 'all of these gadflies poking me and demanding things of me'. According to Brown, 'What makes this funny is that at least half a dozen of them became – well, they *all* became – colleagues of mine, when I became conscious. And at least half a dozen are still close friends'.[77] Warhol would claim 'I only wanted to find great people and let them be themselves and talk about what they usually talked about and I'd film them for a certain length of time and that would be the movie'.[78] His assertion follows Kodak's observation to amateurs that '[In] home movie-making . . . you generally take activity the way it comes'.[79] The practice of using Factory regulars and visitors like Brown as actors and crew troubled typical hierarchies and produced overlapping, interchangeable responsibilities that reinforced community through the shared burdens and pleasures of film-making. Battcock, who participated in several films, explained that 'You knew what you were doing was amusing and interesting, and certainly different, and not too serious'.[80] The camera became a way to bring people together, initiating a process that would frequently conclude in the film's exhibition on a Factory projector.

'The actors are simply his friends, who, at Mr. Warhol's direction, improvise for nothing', film critic Vincent Canby concluded in 1967.[81] As Warhol would say when describing his work with Edie Sedgwick, 'the whole idea behind making those movies in the first place was to be ridiculous'.[82] This intention, present to varying degrees across his work of the mid-1960s, estranges his films from commercial cinema in obvious ways while emulating the liberating potential of 'inept' leisure-time amateur movie making. '"Actors" often seem to be going through their own daily routines, whether campy or not', Tyler commented on Warhol's films, claiming that this 'just naturally takes the shape of a Happening rather extensively planned'.[83] Tyler's recourse to Happenings addresses the hybrid Warhol created in his film-making and projecting by tying them to wider events in art in the 1960s. Happenings and multimedia performances had become common elements of the New York neo-avant-garde art scene by the mid-1960s. Before he produced the Exploding Plastic Inevitable performances of 1966, Warhol preferred to attend such events rather than stage them, the exception being perhaps his film screenings.[84] 'Almost every group event in the sixties eventually got called a "happening"',[85] Warhol would joke, and he contributed to the phenomenon by creating loosely defined group events spanning mundane social affairs, business and lived artwork.

Two venues – the Judson Memorial Church and the Film-Makers' Cinematheque – encouraged Warhol in this endeavour and its relationship to his film activities. Warhol appreciated the versatility of the Happening by attending concerts, dance performances and other events involving artists including Robert Rauschenberg, Yvonne Rainer and Robert Morris at Judson Church. The Judson Dance Theater – started there in 1962 – became a valuable resource for Warhol, who called it one of the 'major feeders of personalities and ideas into the early Factory'.[86] It also provided him with the opportunity to experience the fluid and interdependent relationship between performance and audience as this might relate to his film-making. Ronald Tavel, for example, described the Judson Church event organised by Rainer where he and Warhol developed the idea for *Screen Test #1* (1965), a filmed interview with Warhol's lover, Philip Fagan. Performers and audience comprised a single group throughout the duration of Rainer's piece, confusing the distinction between spectacle and spectator. 'Everybody was waiting for it to begin, and it was over, finally, after two hours . . . That was it', Tavel explained. During the piece, however, 'Warhol [was] walking around doing business', which included recruiting Tavel to collaborate on the film. '[He] not only negotiated with me to make this film during the Happening', Tavel remarked, 'but to develop the esthetic. I'd love to know whether it had incubated in his mind . . . or whether it just occurred to him in talking to me then.'[87]

Warhol's interaction with Tavel at the performance suggests a clear sense of the role of audience action, rather than attention, in the architecture of an event. Mekas' Film-Makers' Cooperative, which became the Film-Makers' Cinematheque in 1964, would contribute to Warhol's understanding of film exhibition as a similarly informal, communal activity. Although less of a source for Factory participants, the Cooperative was a fusion of art production and community experience around unorthodox film exhibition practices. It was housed in Mekas' loft on Park Avenue South from 1962 to 1963 and provided nearly nightly screenings to which members brought whatever they were making, finished or not, for all to see. Packed with equipment, furniture and film canisters, the loft was so cluttered that Mekas slept under an editing table. 'The screen would be opened with the office as a dark backdrop', recalls participant Joan Adler, 'and the audience would drag up chairs, sit on the floor, or lie on the sofa'.[88] The versatility of Mekas' loft – as apartment, archive, editing suite and theatre – blurred the status of screenings, situating them as events between cinema, meeting, workshop and party. Although Warhol regularly attended these screenings, the audience was large enough that he could remain peripheral. 'Andy Warhol sat on the floor of my loft for months, watching movies, before I knew who he was', Mekas would later state.[89]

In spite of Mekas' penchant for chaos and conviviality, the Cooperative remained a relatively formal organisation with its nightly screenings mimicking movie-theatre schedules, and its economic and political mission framing it as a clubhouse, editorial office, depository and distribution centre for members' works. Indeed, the Film-Makers' Cinematheque would one day handle the nationwide distribution of Warhol's *Chelsea Girls* (1966). When Warhol started screening films at the Factory, he borrowed from Mekas' methods for social gatherings while setting aside their institutional, cine-club characteristics. From 1963, Warhol would show his films on occasion in theatres through programmes presented by the Film-Makers' Cooperative, but many of them never made it to that venue. The only sure place to find them was at the Factory, where they not only became a routine part of its collective activities, but proved a valuable resource for defining the space and its inhabitants as a socially integrated community loosely akin to the home and family.

MOVIES MAKE THE HOME

In describing a hypothetical ocean crossing, an advertisement for Ciné-Kodak cameras from Warhol's youth linked home movies to the survival of social relationships and collective memory. 'Interesting people. Gathered together for one brief interval of adventure. Brief, except to you', the ad stated.[90] Suggesting to readers the home movie's capacity to preserve family events and the serendipitous relationships that shape them was a common theme in advertising consumer-grade film equipment throughout the twentieth century. In marketing home movies to American households after World War II, film suppliers, equipment manufacturers and other consumer goods companies endorsed the concept of amateur film as a social conduit and family activity. Television's post-war threat to the movie theatre, as described in Chapter 1, also put home-movie sales at risk. The physical requirements of home projection could hardly compete with the stream of broadcast images ready to flood the living room at the turn of a dial. While television diminished the market for the movie cartoons and serials that Warhol had projected on the walls of his boyhood home, personal movie making became increasingly important to selling film technology as an essential component of the visual culture of family.

Unlike television, home-movie equipment would permit consumers to translate their own lives into visual narratives. 'Home movies capture the familiar expressions . . . the smiles and gestures that *are* your dear ones', stated a 1952 Kodak Brownie camera advertisement. 'The parties . . . the celebrations . . . the days that mean most spring to life whenever you wish . . . on your movie screen.'[91] These homemade narratives could be presented at any time, as often as necessary, before differing audiences on varied occasions. In production and reception, the home movie shaped and fortified family and social ties through creative integration and self-representation.

Advertisements for home-movie equipment typically depicted this sense of social reinforcement through visual cues depicting movie making and viewing as foundations for greater family harmony and unity. A 1959 ad for Kodak Cine 8-mm cameras, for example, presents a young woman filming three children on a pony ride in the park (Figure 2.5). In a lower corner of the ad, the same children are shown watching the scene projected in a panelled room typical of 1950s American domestic architecture. One child in the

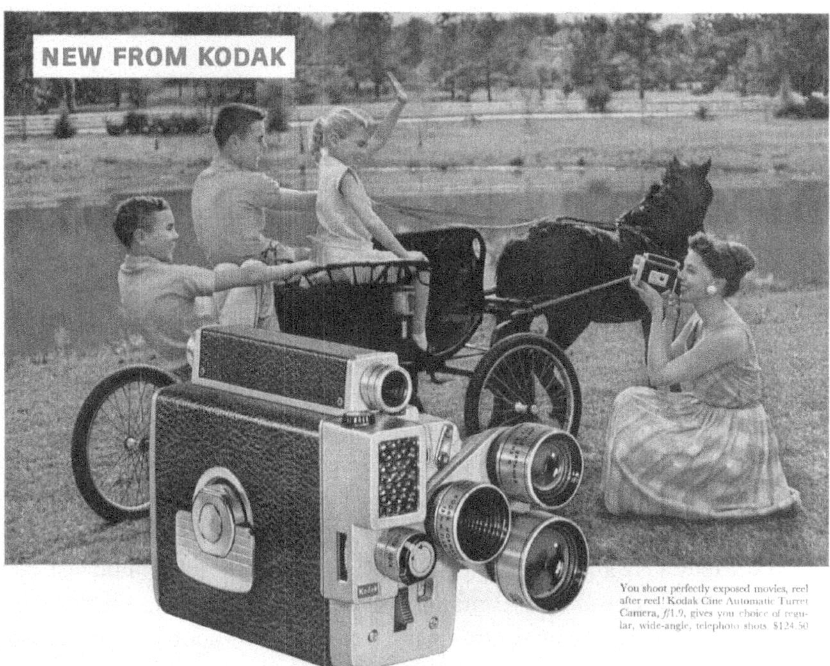

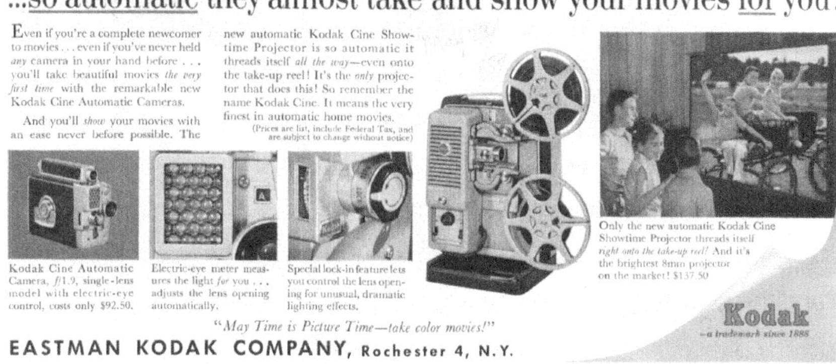

Figure 2.5 *Eastman Kodak Company advertisement for Kodak Cine 8-mm cameras and projectors, 1959.*

audience turns to another, smiling and resting her hand on his shoulder, as though commenting on the event or simply expressing her delight. That these children – presumably siblings – are wearing the same smiles and clothing throughout the ad conveys a timeless stability that appears to be created, or at least facilitated, by home cinema culture.

Referencing the value of audience action, Warhol famously claimed that his early, 'static' films

> were also made to help the audiences get more acquainted with themselves . . . You could do more things watching my movies than with other kinds of movies: you could eat and drink and smoke and cough and look away and then look back and they'd still be there. It's not the ideal movie, it's just my kind of movie.[92]

Expressing an interest in 'testing' audience reactions, Warhol's explanations nevertheless rebuke criticism that he actively sought to alienate viewers, suggesting instead the power of film exhibition as a conduit to social interaction beyond the viewer-image interface. From the perspective of Warhol's relationship to home movies, his early production of slowed events in single takes with a static camera must be considered not solely an effort to wear down narrative mechanisms of film language and make viewers conscious of the act of viewing, but also an effort to engender new ways of participating. It is the catalyst of a larger event that does not stop at the minimalist film on the screen but embraces contingent events of the viewing space as the fluidity and conviviality of production extends to conditions of exhibition. 'The aesthetics that went into the making of these films spilled out into the presentations of the films', Mekas has remarked, a situation that undoubtedly perplexed many film reviewers.[93]

However well-known and documented, the instances before 1966 when Warhol presented his works in movie theatres before the general public were greatly outnumbered by his projections elsewhere on more casual and even familial terms.[94] Warhol film assistant Chuck Wein told a reporter in 1965 that 'We call what we are doing *Synscintima*. "Syn", for synthetic, "scin" for scintillating, and "intima" for the personal or intimate nature of the films. We have dubbed the whole thing "reel-real", or the idea of the reel of film creating the reality.'[95] While Warhol never indulged in such solemn theorising, Wein's pronouncement nevertheless described a strategy that overlaps with the aims of home movies. By shooting familiar subjects and situations, the 'reel world' structures and transforms the real world. As Parker Tyler explained, in Warhol's films 'The line between life and theater, reality and fiction, is not so much blurred as deliberately, cursorily informalized'.[96]

Roger Odin's research on the structure and significance of family films emphasises this unique functioning of home-movie making and viewing. Odin classifies home movies as a special genre hinging exclusively on self-identification and the reification of social networks, thereby provoking an almost necessary alienation of viewers outside those networks. This was often the case with Warhol's films. Defining the home movie as a document 'made by one member for other members of the same family, filming events, things, people, and places linked to the family', Odin believes that making the film is not the only goal, but becomes a reason to 'take part in a *collective* game in the family domain'. Accordingly, this can entail family members 'finding themselves together in front of a camera' simply to acknowledge the filming process as it occurs.[97] For Odin, the family film has an effect at the moment of production that may in itself be sufficiently meaningful for family representation and ritual, but that also can be revisited, as necessary, through subsequent viewing. As an exercise in collective memory and re-performance, watching home movies is unlike watching other moving-image narratives. In the depiction of commonly experienced moments and events the film's participants and those close to them share a moment of mutual recognition. This may apply as much to Warhol's early repertoire of eating, cutting hair, sleeping and looking at the camera, as to later sound films such as *Camp*, *Afternoon*, *Kitchen* and *Mrs. Warhol* (all 1965), in which groups of people interact at the Factory or apartment spaces around loosely defined situations and circumstances. In drawing a comparison to Expanded Cinema, Odin remarks that

> Unlike fictional film screenings, interaction infuses the projection of a family film ... What transpires at the time of the showing forms an integral part of the text. To watch a home movie with the family is to collaborate in the reconstitution of a (mythical) family history.[98]

The process of viewing becomes the celebratory reassertion of community, or the charged moment that imperils it, yet for those viewers lying outside the circle the experience will produce no such effects. Instead, its collection of private events and banal moments will likely provoke mild curiosity or boredom, since, as Odin points out, 'the context resides in the experience of the Subject'.[99]

Contemporaneous accounts and later recollections of Warhol's exhibition practices reveal the significance of film screenings in the formation and functioning of his studio community. When art historian Patrick Smith asked Ondine, one of Warhol's most important superstars, 'How did [Warhol] show the movies – the early movies – at the Factory?' Ondine replied 'He'd just show them'. Pushed to elaborate, Ondine explained that 'There was a screen ... He pulled down the screen, or he'd get a sheet up, and we'd show them. That's all'. Ondine described the Factory as an enormous space, darkened by painted windows. 'You'd hang up big sheets off some of the pipes, and you'd show [films] on the sheets. And most of the areas in the Factory were cut off by screening. So, [you] could show films in the back or show films in the front.'[100] The improvised screens mentioned by Ondine move the projection experience away from theatre models into the realm of home-movie reception. While home-movie manuals of the time warned that 'few makeshift screens provide nearly as good a picture as the real article',[101] finding unconventional projection surfaces was part of the fun, especially given the relative mobility and spontaneity offered by portable projectors. 'Bed sheets, tablecloths, or window shades may be used in an emergency', *How to Make Good Home Movies* suggested.[102] Popular technology magazines from the 1930s through the 1960s regularly published tips for amateurs on crafting adequate projection surfaces from household objects as diverse as aluminium pans and card tables.[103] Warhol's varied Factory screens evoked the do-it-yourself strategies of middle-class homes, imbuing his deliberately amateurish filming techniques with familiar charm.

SCREENING THE SCREEN

In 'Experimental Screens in the 1960s and 1970s: The Site of Community', Tess Takahashi demonstrates that alternative and experimental cinema of those years employed a diversity of projection surfaces, including home-movie screens.[104] What distinguished Warhol's practice was the regular coupling of improvised screens with images that potentially depicted members of the audience, a combination that fostered strong connections to both the material and social frameworks of home-movie culture. The 'home' screenings at the Factory set the foundation of this experimentation. 'The projections at the Factory were always very casual', Mekas recalls, 'that is, with people milling around, walking in front of the screen, the music going on at the back'.[105] Once developed in the lab and returned to Warhol, a film could be a catalyst for, and component of, other social activities amid the sofas, chairs, fashion magazines, radios, record players and televisions of the roughly 50 x 100-foot Factory. For all the works made there – from paintings to sculpture to films – it was also a place to congregate, pop pills and generally kill time. Pat Hartley, who appeared in a couple of Warhol films, recalled her boredom in that environment. 'Sitting around in that sort of living room, I would get uneasy very quickly.'[106] Studio manager Billy Name, who lived in a back room, would later claim that 'The Factory was always open to anyone who came in and wanted to play with us and become a part of us'.[107]

Warhol set a relaxed mood in the studio with an improvised soundtrack of endless radio and record playing, from his preference for girl groups, Motown, and later the Rolling Stones, to Ondine and Name's collections of opera records. Visitors would bring records to play, like teenagers gathering in a rumpus room after school to spin 45s.[108] Once Warhol began making the films, the movie projector and screen became important components of Factory entertainment.[109] 'Projectors. Projectors. People. Lovely old furniture, couches, places to be comfortable' – such is Tally Brown's description of the Factory at its height.[110] Warhol relished this inviting atmosphere. 'It was a constant open house, like the format of a children's TV program', he explained, 'you just hung around and characters you knew dropped in'.[111]

The interpenetration of workplace and domestic space was securely established in Warhol's pre-Factory creative methods, as when he painted from opaque projectors in the various rooms of his Lexington Avenue townhouse before renting a studio. Geldzahler described the situation: 'Andy was playing phonographic records and was having T.V. sets running while people were sitting on the couch, talking to him while he was making a painting'.[112] Assistant Nathan Gluck explained that Warhol was not a 'come over to the house type' and never held parties at his home.[113] The transformation of the Factory into a welcoming social space alleviated the pressure to invite friends, collectors or colleagues home. Showing movies at the Factory – often from whatever canisters happened to be on hand – became an easy and effective way to engage, distract or entertain them.

'People would come by, and as soon as there was a crowd, [Warhol] or somebody would put on a movie and screen it', claimed Battcock. 'So maybe, if you happened to be there at the one time [a particular] film was screened, fine. But if you missed that one screening, the film was never retrieved, and God knows what happened to it.'[114] Battcock's further description demonstrates the integration of the projection event as an anchoring device within the daily activity of a social group:

> It seemed, mainly, you were hanging around and for some reason after a while the crowd would swell . . . Warhol would get the film on the machine, and everyone would sit or stand around and the film would go . . . The screenings were very informal. People were coming and going. The elevator was coming up with people getting in or out . . . It was really very amusing, and everyone would applaud very enthusiastically after these things.[115]

Stopping by the Factory in 1965, photographer Bob Adelman documented a screening (see Figure 2.1). About a dozen people were at the studio, among them Gerard Malanga, Edie Sedgwick, Dorothy Dean, Billy Name, Donyale Luna and Chuck Wein, all of whom participated in multiple Warhol films. As Adelman's group of photographs from the event demonstrate, the projector was placed on a steamer trunk such as one might find in a basement or attic home-movie viewing space, while those present gathered around it, sitting or standing, lying on the floor or reclining on the Factory's famous red sofa (Figure 2.6). The photographs reveal that the audience was neither stationary nor silent during the screening, but moved about the space, talked to each other, smoked and drank. Photographs by David McCabe of

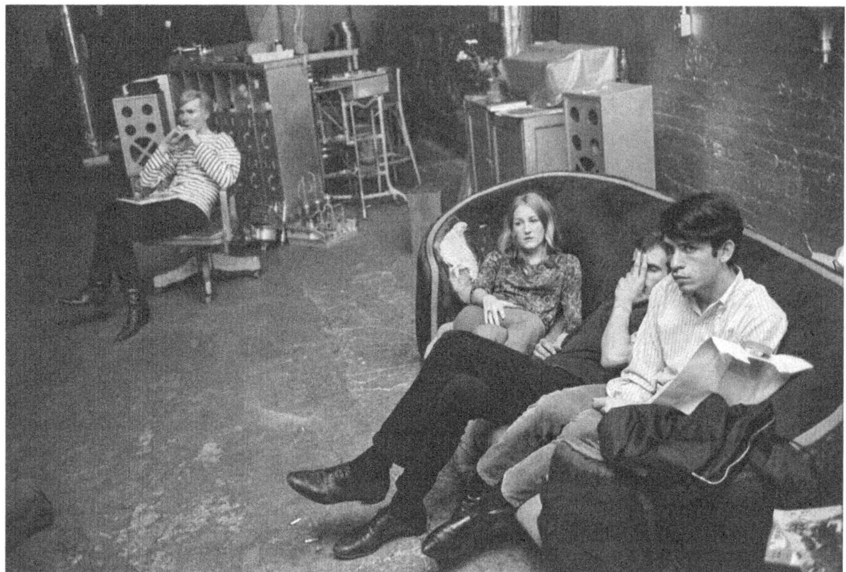

Figure 2.6 *Bob Adelman, Screening at Andy Warhol's Silver Factory, 1965. © Bob Adelman*

another screening from that year show a much larger crowd, but identical viewing practices.[116] The organisation of space, the variety of viewing positions and the audience's movements over the course of these screenings, not to mention the relative brightness of the space, strongly differentiate movie watching at the Factory from the circumstances of theatre-based screenings.

Other Factory screenings blurred the lines between home-movie viewing and practices more closely resembling stag parties and erotic film clubs. J. J. Murphy notes that Warhol enjoyed showing *Couch* – 'his sexually explicit home movie' of friends eating bananas and giving blow jobs on the couch seen in Adelman's photographs – in private screenings to Factory visitors. While *Couch* ends with multiple sex acts amid multiple partners, the first half of the film 'seems like a home movie, in which the participants largely sit around and mug for the camera' according to Murphy.[117] Fringe superstar Ultra Violet's recollections of the circumstances of a Sunday night Factory viewing of Warhol's other, more famous sex-related film, *Blow Job* (1964), demonstrate why private screenings were advantageous. Warhol's thirty-three-minute close-up of a man's face while he purportedly received off-screen fellatio was projected onto a bedsheet stretched between columns. The audience, which included Malanga, Ondine, Eric Emerson and Ingrid Superstar, began the screening quietly assembled 'on and around the battered couch, which [was] so piled with bodies it look[ed] like a lifeboat'. As the film's action slowly unfolded, however, viewers openly debated whether what was taking place was actual or simulated sex and the screening ended with Emerson giving a blow job to someone in the audience.[118] With a film like *Blow Job*, the projection onto a bedsheet and the bodies intertwined on the couch created a strong correspondence between screen action and audience conditions, perhaps precipitating Emerson's reaction. Even as audience members may have contested what took place in the film, its suggested event was repeated in their midst.

Art dealer Irving Blum described a very different experience at a Factory screening of *Empire*. Managing to watch only two hours of the film, Blum claimed that Warhol had organised this screening and others like it 'for people who came and went' during the projection. 'He was wanting the movie to be essentially background', Blum concluded.

> That was really an ideal of Andy's – that it could just *be there* always, and that you could come and go, and you could have lunch or do whatever, you could make an appointment, you could go to a department store, but you could come back and that film would still be there always, ever-present.[119]

Blum's examples of dining and shopping are extreme, as is the film that provoked his comments, yet his description maintains the basic element of casual and intermittent viewing attributed elsewhere to Warhol's screenings.

If the film was not always 'just there' to be had, it was never far away in those years, and Warhol described the situation by 1966 as a thorough integration of production, exhibition and existence. 'The Factory felt more strange to me than ever that summer', he would claim. At the Chelsea Hotel and elsewhere, he was shooting the scenes that would comprise *The Chelsea Girls*, his first theatrical release. But back at the Factory, he witnessed 'The mixture of mechanical sounds and the people sounds [that] made everything seem unreal and if you heard a projector going while you were watching somebody, you felt that they must be a part of the movie, too'.[120] To Warhol's mind, films, screenings and lived experience had become indivisible, leaving no distinction between the world the projector threw on the screen and the events that unfolded around it.

Warhol facilitated this proximity of film to everyday social experience in part by equipping the Factory with a mass-market, collapsible home-movie screen by 1964.[121] The portable tripod screen represented the constant dialogue between lived and filmed events in the Factory. Popping up in numerous photographs taken at the Factory from 1964 to 1966, his Radiant home-movie screen served as the concrete sign of the cinema's primary place and unifying role in the fragmented activity of Warhol's professional and social world.[122] Perhaps more importantly, this screen served not only in the exhibition of films, but also in their production. Warhol's

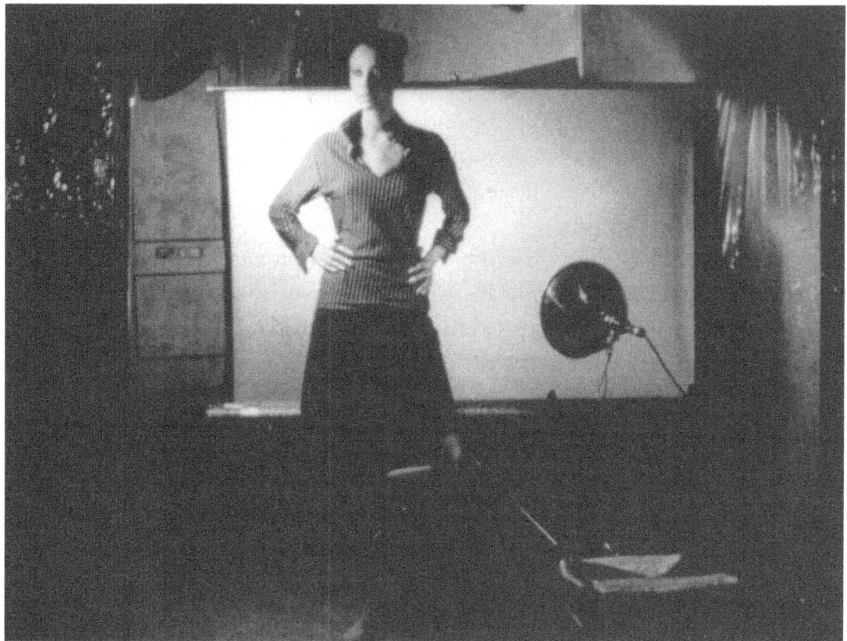

Figure 2.7   *Andy Warhol,* Screen Test, Donyale Luna, *1965, film frame. © The Andy Warhol Museum, Pittsburgh, PA, a museum of the Carnegie Institute, all rights reserved*

Screen Tests of 1964–6 regularly depict subjects before blank, white or off-white backgrounds that suggest a screen. Photographs documenting *Screen Test* sessions reveal a variety of backdrops, including paper rolls and paint-stained boards,[123] but several photographs – and even a film – confirm the deployment of the retractable home-movie screen as backdrop for multiple *Screen Tests*. Most striking in this regard is a 1965 *Screen Test* of young fashion model Donyale Luna, one of the few people of colour to appear in a Warhol film (Figure 2.7). Employing an atypical full-shot *mise-en-scène*, the *Screen Test* reveals Luna striking various poses under the otherwise customary *Screen Test* conditions of a home-movie screen backdrop with low-angled light reflecting off its bright surface.[124] While such lighting and composition techniques may appear far removed from home movies, in truth they resemble those suggested through minimalist illustrations found in home-movie manuals of the time (Figure 2.8).

By exposing the conditions of production and confirming the inclusion of the screen in the film frame, the *Screen Test* of Luna complicates readings of this celebrated film series. When projected, such *Screen Tests* superimpose the image of the screen onto the screen, inviting further interpretations of the series title as referring to the object and the act of exhibition. When these

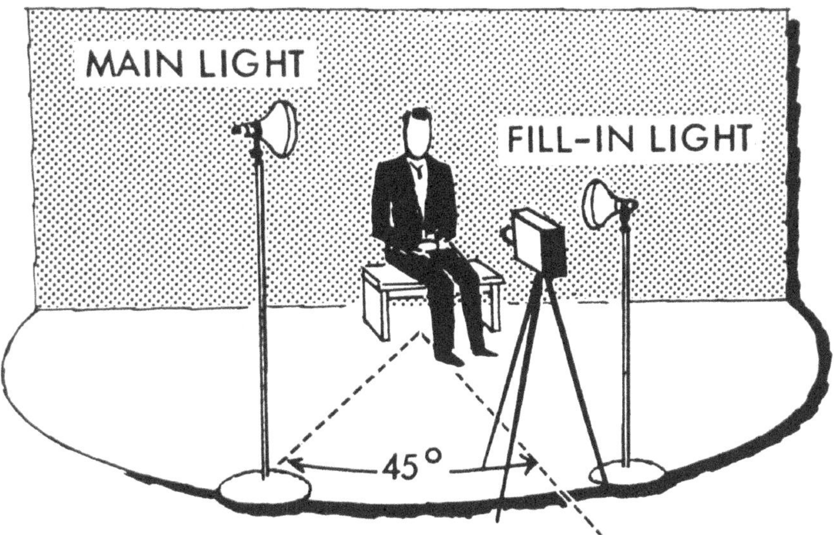

Figure 2.8 *Illustration from Eastman Kodak's* How to Make Good Home Movies, *1966.*
© *Eastman Kodak Company*

films were projected at the Factory, this doubling of screens would produce a confrontation between the original object and its filmic representation, a situation common to home-movie viewing (and these screenings) when the audience itself is often composed of those people seen on screen. In describing his experience as unofficial staff photographer at the Factory, Billy Name explains that 'It was almost as if the Factory became a big box camera – you'd walk into it, expose yourself and develop yourself'.[125] By appearing in production photographs and subsequently serving as the surface of visualisation, Warhol's portable home-movie screen was integral to this process. The site of entrance, exposure and development, the screen was the surface against which people would be filmed, only to re-emerge on that surface, sooner or later, as representation.

HOME VIEWING AND HOME WRECKING

In the 'collective game' of facing the camera – to reiterate Odin's claim for home movies – Warhol's nearly five hundred *Screen Tests* stand apart as a compendium of the personalities populating his world. Shot almost exclusively at the Factory as people paid social or business visits, the *Screen Tests* are the portrait of an extended family. 'Warhol presided over this alternative family like an inaccessible father figure', explains Taubin, who posed for two

Screen Tests in 1964.[126] For most *Screen Tests* Warhol or Malanga would start the camera and walk away as it filmed for three minutes. The sitter's awareness of the camera would be heightened by the single directive to stare at the camera without blinking. This action repeats, in a particularly sadistic and severe way, the common 'mistake' of the home-movie genre in the often awkward and even tense recognition of the camera by those being filmed. Under these circumstances, isolated between camera and screen backdrop, it is as though the sitter is already an image before an unseen audience. Yet, if these films are often interpreted in terms of the sitter staring at an unknown, anonymous, posterior audience, it must be remembered that participants from Warhol's entourage were also a regular presence in the audience for his films at the time they were made. The several *Screen Tests* of figures including Jane Holzer, Edie Sedgwick, Ivan Karp, Ivy Nicholson, Nico, Lou Reed, Ultra Violet, Mary Woronov and Gerard Malanga himself would also have been watched by these same people and their friends.[127] In a description of the power of home movies, Péter Forgács emphasises the place of private screenings depicting people close to, or in, the audience. 'The original context of the private film is the home screening rite, the celebration . . . of the nonverbal realm of communication and symbols. It is a recollection of the desired intimate vision and aims to immortalize the face of a lover, son, or father', Forgács explains. 'The meditation inspired by these screenings is: What has been revealed by making visible that which had remained imperceptible before?'[128] Indeed, Warhol's films included extended studies of lovers, including Giorno in *Sleep* and dozens of *Screen Tests* of Philip Fagan, and others close to the artist.[129]

Descriptions of a 'moviewatching party' in Holzer's Manhattan apartment in November 1964 provide a striking example of how Warhol would exploit this situation by blurring the boundaries between home-movie culture and other forms of film-making and viewing.[130] Among Warhol's first film muses, Holzer fêted the opening of Warhol's *Flowers* show at the Leo Castelli Gallery with a party that included projections of his films, among them *Screen Tests* of Holzer. Writer Jack Kroll attended the event and described it in *Newsweek*. 'At the party, Jane as usual ate nothing but candy. Warhol circulated among young wraiths from the worlds of fashion and frolic', he explained. He continued

> Jane's real-estate-broker husband watched impassively, like a character in a Mailer story, while on the screen Baby Jane's face in gigantic close-up chewed gum and brushed her teeth. A hypnotic pop tension built up, broken by Hollywood producer Sam Spiegel's wife shouting, 'We're all turned on to you, baby'. Such are the orgiastic climaxes of Warhol's world. It is a strange world; a chaos stylized against chaos.[131]

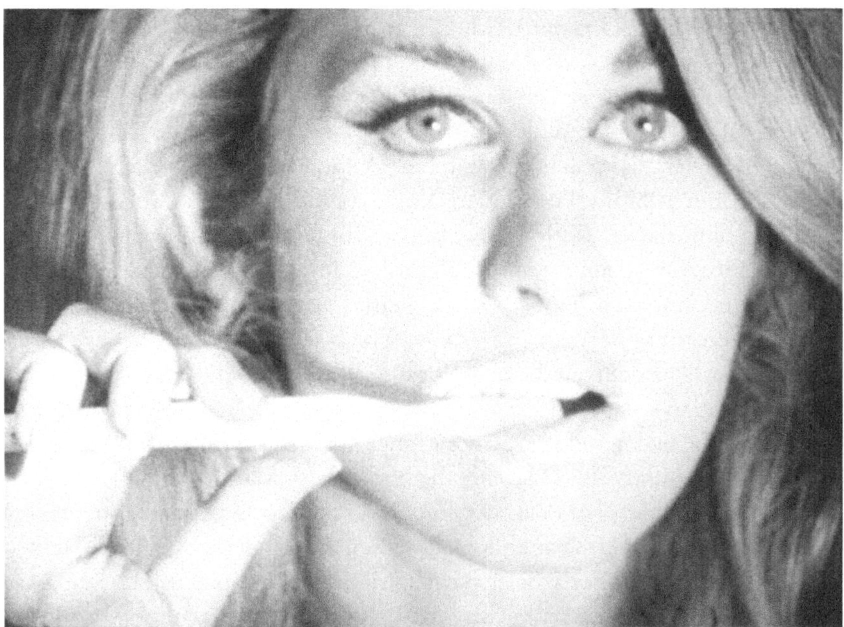

Figure 2.9   *Andy Warhol,* Screen Test, Jane Holzer (Toothbrush), *1964, film frame.* © *The Andy Warhol Museum, Pittsburgh, PA, a museum of the Carnegie Institute, all rights reserved*

While bearing all the attributes of an exclusive, celebrity event – Norman Mailer and Met curator Geldzahler attended – Holzer's party offered guests middle-class entertainment in home movies. Much like such movies at any party, Warhol's *Screen Test* of Holzer (Figure 2.9) did not dominate the event in Kroll's account, but rather functioned as a device promoting self-recognition and social participation of various sorts. Recalling Warhol's claims that his films permitted viewers to pursue other activities while engaging the projection completely, intermittently or not at all, Kroll's article describes differing levels of commitment. The artist 'circulated' during the proceedings, much like he did at Rainer's Judson Church event as described by Ronald Tavel. By contrast, Holzer's husband, developer Leonard Holzer, 'watched impassively' as his wife chewed gum and brushed her teeth into a frothy mess before New York high society, performances that crossed the home movie with the stag film by taking everyday activities and executing them with strong sexual over-tones. Meanwhile Betty Benson, the producer's wife, conflated the hostess and her filmic other by calling out to the silent, over-sized image.

Holzer's party marked a highpoint in Warhol's incorporation of home-movie culture into his film practice. These varied exhibition methods imme-diately preceded the Expanded Cinema movement's transformation of film exhibition, pushing film out of the theatre and into diverse environments. Expanded Cinema took form with the New Cinema Festival 1 and its performances of Nam June Paik's *Zen for Film* (1964), Carolee Schneemann's *Ghost Rev* (1965), Robert Whitman's *Prune Flat* (1965) and Claes Oldenburg's *Moveyhouse* (1965), as well as through Stan Vanderbeek's construction of the Movie-Drome in Stony Point, New York. At the same time, the affinity of Warhol's film-making with home movies became a common complaint in the mainstream denigration of Warhol's film career. In a *Life* report on underground cinema in January 1965, Shana Alexander described the world premiere screening of Warhol's *Harlot*, which marked a shift in his public practices, as '350 cultivated New York sophisticates who squeezed into a dark cellar . . . to see a single, grainy, wobbly shot projected onto a bedsheet'. Dismissing the event and its $2.50 entrance charge as gimmickry, Alexander said of underground films 'They are the home movies of the pop underworld, turned out for their own deadpan amusement'. This is perhaps a depiction Warhol himself would have endorsed. When Alexander visited the Factory for more material for her article, she experienced a 'sampler' of *Eat* and part of *Empire*. 'Underground movies are made for the kicks of making them', she astutely surmised after this alienating ordeal.[132] Her likening of underground films to home movies characterised them as unsophisticated and amateurish, but it also suggested that they remained inscrutable and insignificant to wider audiences. They were inside jokes, most relevant and meaningful to those who made and appeared in them.

In light of such readings of these films and their presentation by the popular press, Warhol's home-movie exhibition practices reached a dramatic conclusion in 1966 through two highly public events specifically intended to draw a wider, national audience: the commercial release of *The Chelsea Girls* and the creation of the Exploding Plastic Inevitable (EPI) multimedia concert tour. Steve Wurtzler claims that home movies 'quietly insist on a broadened definition of cinema as a representational technology'.[133] Warhol's *Chelsea Girls* and EPI resolutely upset any such calm. The three and a half-hour, double-screen *Chelsea Girls* built on the conceit of a voyeuristic glimpse into the rooms of the Chelsea Hotel. Even as its format challenged standard modes of theatrical exhibition, its simultaneous, side-by-side projections diverged from the home-movie model.[134] With Warhol's turn to commercial film-making, the audience, projection space and screen returned to the mainstream cinema context. As Battcock pointed out, '[*The Chelsea Girls*] takes place in a movie theater and the screen is where it belongs – up on the stage in front'.[135]

The Exploding Plastic Inevitable, built around concerts by the Factory's house band, The Velvet Underground, included Warhol's earlier films in a frenetic presentation meant to estrange audiences from representational content. EPI developed from Andy Warhol Up Tight, the group's multimedia performance for Mekas' Expanded Cinema series at the Film-Makers' Cinematheque in January 1966, and premiered in April at the Open Stage in the *Polsky Dom Narodny* in Manhattan. EPI offered performances during which Warhol and assistants projected films, slides and other lighting schemes at the band and audience from as many as ten projectors on the mezzanine. Still demonstrating his flair for converting any space into an effective screen, Warhol and his assistants took the time to give the place a fresh coat of white paint before the show opened.[136] Tally Brown, who assisted Warhol at these performances, recalled, 'I was flashing slides around, standing and holding a projector. I think that there were six projections, but it wasn't just in the performing area but all around – ceiling, walls . . ..'[137] Striking the band, the dancers and the audience while competing with strobes and slides of cut-out forms and coloured gels, the film images fragmented across the larger event. The hanging bedsheet, retractable screen or blank wall was replaced by innumerable uneven and moving surfaces. 'The Dom series of the Velvet Underground, with projections, were the most energy-charged performances I have ever seen', Mekas would claim twenty years later.[138] Excerpts from several films from 1963 to 1966 – including *Sleep*, *Banana*, *Couch* and the *Kiss* series – were included among the projections.[139] The insular Factory screenings for friends and acquaintances dissolved into this kinaesthetic psychedelic demonstration for the masses, first in New York, then in auditoriums, clubs and school gyms across the United States in what Gene Youngblood dubbed 'Andy Warhol's hellish sensorium'.[140]

With the commercial success of *The Chelsea Girls* and EPI, Warhol abandoned his prior film-exhibition practices. By 1968 – the year he barely survived an assassination attempt by Factory acquaintance Valerie Solanas, Warhol had withdrawn his pre-*Chelsea Girls* films from circulation to focus instead on his new film company, Andy Warhol Films, Inc., and the feature-length sexploitation films it produced with Paul Morrissey as director.[141] Annette Michelson suggests that this decision was 'linked to the marketing of a new product, coded with an eye to industrial norms'.[142] He would continue to shoot more intimate works of friends and acquaintances (including the aforementioned *Julia Warhola in Bed*) on video rather than film. The change of medium, combined with the Factory's move downtown to the more office-like setting of the Decker Building on Union Square, meant the end of informal, collective screenings.

Warhol claimed of the Factory of the mid-1960s that 'the truth was, we were all odds-and-ends misfits, somehow misfitting together'.[143] Zimmermann posits home-movie making as the film practice that has best accommodated marginalised populations throughout the history of cinema, seeing it as 'emerging out of dispersed, localized, and often minoritized cultures, not a practice imposed on them'.[144] To some extent the Factory activities that formed and sustained the sense of community implied in this chapter had been mainstreamed and commodified by the end of the decade. Bohemianism and countercultural antics – or at least their aesthetic – had become marketable to the mainstream. The nudity and straight or gay sexual activity that percolates in Factory films such as *Kiss*, *Couch*, *Blow Job* and *Haircut (No. 1)* ('an intricately choreographed striptease and peepshow', according to Murphy) became standard to the Warhol-Morrissey collaboration that brought *Nude Restaurant* (1967), *Flesh* (1968), *Blue Movie* (1969) and *Heat* (1972).

Asked in 1977 if he would ever release his earlier films on video, Warhol was uncharacteristically firm in resisting the idea. 'The old stuff is better to talk about than to see. It always sounds better than it really is.'[145] Whatever Warhol's reasons for rejecting the possibility, it is important to remember that by the mid-1970s the community these films had reflected and sustained was no longer together to experience them. Beyond the Factory's transformation into a business office *cum* studio after the assassination attempt, several previous Factory members had died, including Edie Sedgwick and Eric Emerson.

'Some might say that it's still discomforting to watch [Warhol's] films today', artist Philippe Parreno conjectured in 2006. 'Perhaps because the subjects are looking directly at us, perhaps it's because we know they are now dead or maybe it's just because the images are cruel and unforgiving.'[146] The preceding descriptions of Warhol's film exhibition strategies and the recollections of those who participated in the productions and their screenings suggest that the 'unforgiving' nature of these works becomes more acute with the passage of time. The direct gaze of the dead, which of course marks a permanent absence, places these images on a register far removed from the terms of their original use and impact. As Zimmermann claims, old home movies are 'always acts of mourning for those who have passed, markers of loss and trauma', in part because we see people, not characters.[147] Like finding someone else's home movies, however, the films lose their original significance before audiences not involved in their production, becoming spectacles of alienation rather than ritual objects of community.

This realisation is particularly important in light of prevailing methods for screening Warhol's works today, which present them as solemn works that transcend their material origins and demand careful, quiet contemplation. The Museum of Modern Art in New York exhibited selections of Warhol's *Screen Tests* in 2003 and 2010 by transferring them to digital video and presenting them either on embedded monitors or projected onto wall-mounted screens, in both cases circumscribing the images in black picture frames to emulate portrait paintings.[148] The one *Screen Test* presented on film during the 2010 show (projected onto a portable movie screen resembling Warhol's Factory model, no less) was not in the gallery, but near the entrance of the adjacent exhibition gift shop. 'The 16mm loop serves as a kind of synecdochic shoulder shrug for the exhibit, as if to say, what else can we do?' remarks Gregory Zinman.[149] A 2014 rehanging of the permanent collection at the Andy Warhol Museum in Pittsburgh, the repository of Warhol's archives and surviving Factory objects, fared little better in doing justice to the films and their screening history. Digital transfers of *Sleep*, *Haircut No. 1* and selected *Screen Tests* were retro-projected from behind a wall of semi-opaque plastic before a line of seats, but there was no sign of projector, film or make-shift, informal viewing conditions. Branden Joseph's contention, following Douglas Crimp, that the movies 'are best seen . . . in a darkened theater, on 16mm film, projected at the proper speed, in their full duration, and among an audience, however small', moves closer to the mark, yet like other recent exhibition strategies for Warhol's films it too abandons the ephemerality and contingency of Warhol's screening techniques.[150] Perhaps no presentation can adequately satisfy the needs of these films, however, whether screened in museum auditoriums or film societies, transferred to video, looped in gallery spaces or even placed in more historically informed situations. Away from the space and people of the Factory, and the incidental conditions they created, these works ultimately function like family movies without a family.

Notes

1. Andy Warhol and Pat Hackett, *POPism: The Warhol Sixties* (New York: Harcourt, 1980), p. 113.
2. Ibid. p. 203.
3. Mary Josephson, 'Warhol: The Medium as Cultural Artifact', *Art in America* 59:3 (May–June 1971): 40–6, p. 42.
4. Douglas Crimp found this term so accurate in describing the mechanisms of identity and subjectivity at work in these films, that he used it for the title of his book on Warhol's films. See Crimp, *'Our Kind of Movie': The Films of Andy Warhol* (Cambridge, MA: MIT Press, 2012).
5. Gillian Rose, 'How Digital Technologies Do Family Snaps, Only Better', in Jonas Larsen and Mette Sandbye (eds), *Digital Snaps: The New Face of Photography* (London: Tauris, 2014), p. 71; emphasis in text.
6. This is not to say that Warhol was the only artist working within a home-movie framework at that time. Jeff Keen, for example, incorporated Super-8 footage of his family into his works. However, Warhol's practices spanned both production and reception.
7. Warhol and Hackett, *POPism*, p. 89.

8. Gregory Battcock, as quoted in Patrick S. Smith, *Warhol: Conversations about the Artist* (Ann Arbor: UMI Research Press, 1988), p. 327.

9. Matthew Tinkcom, 'Warhol's Camp', in Colin MacCabe and Peter Wollen (eds), *Who Is Andy Warhol* (London: British Film Institute, 1997), p. 112.

10. Amy Taubin, '✶✶✶✶', in ibid., p. 29.

11. Ibid. p. 25. Additionally, one can cite claims that Warhol created a 'parody' of the Hollywood studio system. See Annette Michelson, '"Where Is Your Rupture?" Mass Culture and the *Gesamtkunstwerk*', in Annette Michelson (ed.), *Andy Warhol* (Cambridge, MA: MIT Press, 2001), p. 106; Yann Beauvais, 'Speed Reeling', in *3e Biennale d'art contemporain de Lyon: installation, cinéma, vidéo, informatique* (Paris: Réunion des Musées Nationaux, 1995), p. 59.

12. According to Tavel, Warhol told him, 'I don't want a plot, but I want a situation or situations'. See Smith, *Warhol: Conversations about the Artist*, p. 313.

13. Warhol's films did not perform well commercially before the release of *The Chelsea Girls*. In the summer of 1966, for example, rentals brought Warhol a net profit of $330. See Tony Scherman and David Dalton, *Pop: The Genius of Andy Warhol* (New York: Harper, 2009), p. 347.

14. Patricia R. Zimmermann, 'Introduction', in Karen L. Ishizuka and Patricia R. Zimmermann (eds), *Mining the Home Movie: Excavations in Histories and Memories* (Berkeley: University of California, 2008), p. 8.

15. Caroline A. Jones, *Machine in the Studio: Constructing the Postwar American Artist* (Chicago: University of Chicago Press, 1996), p. 265.

16. The *Screen Tests*, *Sleep*, *Eat*, *Haircut (No. 1)*, *Kiss* and *Couch* are some of the films presenting these actions.

17. Gerard Malanga, as quoted in Lynne Tillman, 'Like Rockets and Television II', in MacCabe and Wollen (eds), *Who Is Andy Warhol*, p. 146.

18. J. J. Murphy, *The Black Hole of the Camera: The Films of Andy Warhol* (Berkeley: University of California Press, 2012), pp. 7 and 104.

19. Péter Forgács, 'Wittgenstein Tractatus: Personal Reflections on Home Movies', in Ishizuka and Zimmermann (eds), *Mining the Home Movie*, p. 51.

20. John Wilcock, 'Andy as Moviemaker', in John Wilcock and Christopher Trela (eds), *The Autobiography and Sex Life of Andy Warhol*, 2nd edn (New York: Trela Media, 2010), p. 152.

21. According to Linda Williams, the stag film – unlike other types of pornography – preserves 'primitive styles and modes of address', a characterisation that is often made both of home movies and Warhol's early films. Linda Williams, *Hard Core: Power, Pleasure and the 'Frenzy of the Visible'*, 2nd edn (Berkeley: University of California, 1999), p. 60. In addition to depictions of oral sex in *Couch*, Emile de Antonio recalls that Warhol filmed an interracial *ménage à trois*, images of which appear in Jonas Mekas (ed.), *Andy Warhol: Filmmaker* (Vienna: Viennale, 2005). See Smith, *Warhol: Conversations about the Artist*, p. 191.

22. Charles Tepperman, *Amateur Cinema: The Rise of North American Moviemaking, 1923–1960* (Berkeley: University of California Press, 1997), pp. 1–2.

23. Brett Howard, 'Who's Afraid of Andy Warhol', *Adam Film Quarterly* 3 (n. d.): 88–9, p. 89.
24. Though decidedly different in outlook, tone and scope, Crimp's *Our Kind of Movie* and Murphy's *The Black Hole of the Camera* give greater attention to what can be called the home-movie characteristics of Warhol's production and exhibition practices than earlier books such as Michael O'Pray (ed.), *Andy Warhol Film Factory* (London: British Film Institute, 1989).
25. Stephen Koch, *Stargazer: Andy Warhol's World and His Films*, 2nd edn (New York: Marion Boyars, 1985), p. 20.
26. Giuliana Bruno, *Public Intimacy* (Cambridge, MA: MIT Press, 2007), pp. 194, 191. For a similar summation, see John G. Hanhardt, *The Films of Andy Warhol: An Introduction* (New York: Whitney Museum of American Art, 1988), p. 8.
27. *Sleep* was screened 17–20 January 1964 at the Gramercy Arts Theatre in New York and in June at the Cinema Theatre in Los Angeles. See David Bourdon, *Warhol* (New York: H. N. Abrams, 1989), pp. 176–8; Steven Watson, *Factory Made: Warhol and the Sixties* (New York: Pantheon, 2003), pp. 134–5; Jonas Mekas, 'Movie Journal: More on Warhol's Sleep', *Village Voice* (2 July 1964), reprinted in Jonas Mekas, *Movie Journal: The Rise of the New American Cinema, 1959–1971* (New York: Macmillan, 1972), pp. 146–7. Naomi Levine had earlier organised a screening of *Sleep* for Mekas at Wynn Chamberlain's loft at 222 The Bowery. See Victor Bockris, *The Life and Death of Andy Warhol* (New York: Bantam, 1989), p. 143. *Empire* premiered at the City Hall Cinema on 6 March 1965. According to Mekas, it started with an audience of 200 and ended with fifty or so enjoying themselves with beer and sandwiches. See Bourdon, *Warhol*, p. 188, and Jonas Mekas, *Anecdotes* (Paris: Scali, 2007), p. 206. *Empire* premiered at the Bridge Cinema in New York. 'Empire was a film where nothing happened except the audience's reaction', according to Gerard Malanga. See Bockris, *The Life and Death of Andy Warhol*, p. 155.
28. Parker Tyler, 'Dragtime or Drugtime: or Film à la Warhol', *Evergreen Review* 11:46 (April 1967): 27–31, 87–8, reprinted in Michael O'Pray (ed.), *Andy Warhol Film Factory* (London: British Film Institute, 1989), p. 97. Although Tyler recognises Warhol's projections outside the movie theatre, he sees them as striving toward theatre conditions, claiming that Warhol preferred 'art projection' that increased the image size to rival the theatre experience; ibid. p. 98. The question of time is particularly important in Warhol's silent films because of the 16 fps projection rate.
29. Warhol and Hackett, *POPism*, p. 124.
30. Jack Kroll, 'Saint Andrew', *Newsweek* (7 December 1964): 100–4, reprinted in Steven Madoff (ed.), *Pop Art: A Critical History* (Berkeley: University of California Press, 1997), pp. 278–80. Although unsigned, *Newsweek*'s table of contents attributes the article to Kroll, a senior editor at the magazine.
31. Callie Angell, *Andy Warhol Screen Tests: The Films of Andy Warhol Catalogue Raisonné* (New York: Whitney Museum of American Art/Abrams, 2006), p. 93.

32. These were Fairchild 400 projectors. Eugene Archer, 'Festival Bringing Pop Artist's Films to Lincoln Center', *New York Times* (12 September 1964), p. 15. The excerpted films were *Eat, Kiss, Sleep* and *Haircut (No. 2)*. An advertisement and set of instructions for the Fairchild 400 are preserved in Warhol's Time Capsule 65, Warhol Archives. Similar to the Lincoln Center presentation, in March 1965 a reel of Warhol's *Screen Tests* was continuously projected in the lounge of the Carnegie Hall Cinema, rather than on the theatre screen. See Angell, *Andy Warhol Screen Tests*, pp. 250–1.

33. David E. James, *Allegories of Cinema: American Film in the Sixties* (Princeton: Princeton University Press, 1989), p. 82.

34. Wilcock, 'Andy as Moviemaker', p. 155.

35. Sally Banes, *Greenwich Village 1963: Avant-Garde Performance and the Effervescent Body* (Durham, NC: Duke University Press, 1993), p. 90.

36. P. Adams Sitney, *Visionary Film: The American Avant-Garde, 1943–2000*, 3rd edn (Oxford: Oxford University Press, 2002), pp. 349–50. J. J. Murphy attributes the avant-garde and structuralist strain of criticism of Warhol's films to P. Adams Sitney and A. L. Rees, though Mekas contributed significantly to this understanding of Warhol's early films. See Murphy, *The Black Hole of the Camera*, pp. 10–12. A case may be made, of course, that avant-garde cinema often borrowed from the techniques and narrative codes of home movies. Paul Arthur is one of the few to identify the impact of home-movie making on 1960s avant-garde film, identifying what he calls the 'portrait film'. See Paul Arthur, *A Line of Sight: American Avant-Garde Film since 1965* (Minneapolis: University of Minnesota Press, 2005), pp. 24–44. While Warhol's work falls into this category, Arthur makes no mention of the artist's exhibition practices.

37. Zimmermann, 'Introduction', in Ishizuka and Zimmermann (eds), *Mining the Home Movie*, p. 1.

38. Warhol and Hackett, *POPism*, p. 29.

39. Patricia R. Zimmermann, *Reel Families: A Social History of Amateur Film* (Bloomington: Indiana University Press, 1995), p. 113.

40. Henry Geldzahler, as quoted in Smith, *Warhol: Conversations about the Artist*, pp. 182–3.

41. Kodak movie camera advertisement in *National Geographic* 104:4 (October 1953), p. 579.

42. Bell and Howell movie camera advertisement in *Life* (2 October 1944), p. 109; emphasis in text.

43. Warhol and Hackett, *POPism*, p. 180.

44. 'Crazy Golden Slippers: Famous People Inspire Fanciful Footwear', *Life* (21 January 1957): 12–13.

45. On Warhol's movie going, see Bockris, *The Life and Death of Andy Warhol*, pp. 124, 131 and Smith, *Warhol: Conversations about the Artist*, p. 175. Warhol's consternation over a missed opportunity to meet Jayne Mansfield is recorded in Warhol and Hackett, *POPism*, p. 152.

46. The practice continued into adulthood and this archive of movie memorabilia served as the source for several of his silkscreened paintings of actors.

47. Warhol and Hackett, *POPism*, p. 40.

48. John Warhola, as quoted in Bockris, *The Life and Death of Andy Warhol*, p. 18.

49. Charles Lisanby, as quoted in Patrick S. Smith, *Andy Warhol's Art and Films* (Ann Arbor: UMI Research Press), p. 380.

50. Georg Frei and Neil Printz, *Warhol 01, Paintings and Sculpture 1961–1963: The Andy Warhol Catalogue Raisonne* (London: Phaidon, 2002), pp. 468–9. Frei and Printz incorrectly give the projector's name as the 'Besemer Vue Lite'.

51. See Nathan Gluck's description in Smith, *Warhol: Conversations about the Artist*, p. 59.

52. Koch, *Stargazer*, p. 38.

53. For more on the genesis and construction of this film, see Branden W. Joseph, 'The Play of Repetition: Andy Warhol's *Sleep*', *Grey Room* 19 (Spring 2005): 22–53.

54. Jonas Mekas, 'Notes on Some New Movies and Happiness', *Film Culture* 37 (Summer 1965): 16–20, reprinted in Barbara Engelbach (ed.), *Jonas Mekas* (London: Koenig Books, 2008), p. 60.

55. Eastman Kodak Company, *How to Make Good Home Movies* (Rochester: Eastman Kodak Company, 1961), p. 18.

56. Fairchild movie camera advertisement in *Life* (5 May 1961), p. 19; emphasis in text.

57. Glenn O'Brien, 'Interview with Andy Warhol', in Mark Francis (ed.), *Andy Warhol: The Late Work* (Munich: Prestel, 2004), p. 58.

58. David E. James, 'Amateurs in the Industry Town: Stan Brakhage and Andy Warhol in Los Angeles', *Grey Room* 12 (Summer 2003): 80–93, pp. 87–8. According to Billy Name, Warhol was not satisfied with the results, finding it too derivative of Jack Smith's work. See John O'Connor and Benjamin Liu, *Unseen Warhol* (New York: Rizzoli, 1996), p. 40.

59. Murphy, *The Black Hole of the Camera*, p. 39.

60. Warhol and Hackett, *POPism*, p. 32.

61. Susan Sontag, *Against Interpretation* (New York: Delta, 1967), p. 228.

62. Tyler, 'Dragtime or Drugtime: or Film à la Warhol', in O'Pray (ed.), *Andy Warhol Film Factory*, p. 94.

63. Warhol and Hackett, *POPism*, p. 31.

64. For a study of Mekas' role in promoting independent cinema in New York, see Arthur, *A Line of Sight*, pp. 1–23.

65. As Jeffrey Ruoff explains, 'Just as Andy Warhol experimented with the long take in the early 1960s, Mekas rejects traditional notions of continuity editing in favor of a new realism borrowed from home-movie practice. Whereas Warhol experimented with the long take to foreground real time duration, Mekas explores a new synthetic form of pixilated editing, which incorporates shots as short as a single frame, 1/24 of a second long.' See Jeffrey K. Ruoff, 'Home Movies of the Avant-Garde: Jonas Mekas and the New York Art World',

Cinema Journal 30:3 (Spring 1991): 6–28, p. 16. Mekas has spoken about his work as home movies. See Jonas Mekas and Scott MacDonald, 'Interview with Jonas Mekas', *October* 29 (Summer 1984): 82–116, pp. 105–6.

66. While Annette Michelson argues that Brakhage's 'hyperbolic montage' seeks to create a present, 'one image succeeding another at a pace that allows no space or time for recall or anticipation', his choice of events like the birth of his first child in *Window Water Baby Moving* (1958) strains this reading by evoking family, memory and possibility. See Michelson, '"Where Is Your Rupture?"', in Michelson (ed.), *Andy Warhol*, pp. 105–6.

67. Jonas Mekas, 'The Experimental Film in America', reprinted in P. Adams Sitney (ed.), *Film Culture Reader* (New York: Praeger, 1970), pp. 21–6.

68. Sontag, *Against Interpretation*, p. 228.

69. Reva Wolf makes the argument that the Warhol film that is most closely related to the film poem is the Hollywood-influenced *Tarzan and Jane . . . Sort of*, since it includes poet-film-maker Mead and relates to the Beats. See Reva Wolf, '"The Flower Thief": The "Film Poem", Warhol's Early Films, and the Beat Writers', in Wheeler Winston Dixon and Gwendolyn Audrey Foster (eds), *Experimental Cinema, The Film Reader* (London: Routledge, 2002), pp. 192–4.

70. Jonas Mekas, 'Sixth Independent Film Award', in Sitney (ed.), *Film Culture Reader*, p. 427.

71. Warhol and Hackett, *POPism*, p. 166.

72. David Antin, 'Warhol: The Silver Tenement', *Art News* 65:4 (Summer 1966): 47–8, 58–9, reprinted in Madoff (ed.), *Pop Art*, p. 290.

73. Peter Gowland, *How to Take Better Home Movies* (Greenwich, CT: Fawcett Publications, 1956), pp. 53, 56; emphasis in text.

74. Ibid. p. 55.

75. Eastman Kodak Company, *How to Make Good Home Movies*, p. 7.

76. Ibid. p. 9.

77. Tally Brown, as quoted in Smith, *Warhol: Conversations about the Artist*, p. 250; emphasis in text. Other Factory regulars, like Gregory Battcock, also would describe their being filmed unawares. See ibid. pp. 323–4.

78. Warhol and Hackett, *POPism*, p. 110.

79. Eastman Kodak Company, *How to Make Good Home Movies*, p. 99.

80. Battcock's description certainly applies to his participation in films that include *Horse* (1965), a 'western' shot in the Factory with a rented horse taking up much of the frame. Battcock, as quoted in Smith, *Warhol: Conversations about the Artist*, p. 323.

81. Vincent Canby, '"Chelsea Girls" in Midtown Test', *New York Times* (1 December 1966), p. 56.

82. Warhol and Hackett, *POPism*, p. 124.

83. Parker Tyler, *Underground Film: A Critical History* (New York: Da Capo, 1995), p. 47.

84. Warhol met Naomi Levine and Tally Brown at Happenings at the Living

Theater in 1963 and 1964, for example. At the Cinematheque in December 1965 he saw *Prune Flat*, Robert Whitman's stage and film piece presenting actors interacting and overlapping with their projected image. See Smith, *Warhol: Conversations about the Artist*, p. 250 and Richard Kostelanetz, 'The Discovery of Alternative Theater: Notes on Art Performances in New York City in the 1960s and 1970s', *Perspectives of New Music* 27:1 (Winter 1989): 128–72, p. 163.

85. Warhol and Hackett, *POPism*, p. 65.

86. Ibid. p. 54. Among the future Factory collaborators Warhol met there were dancers Freddy Herko and Eric Emerson. In spring 1964, Herko appeared at Judson Church in *Home Movies*, a musical play by Rosalyn Drexler. See Sontag, *Against Interpretation*, pp. 158–9. For background on the Judson Dance Theater, see Sally Banes, *Democracy's Body: Judson Dance Theater, 1962–1964* (Durham, NC: Duke University Press, 1993).

87. Ronald Tavel in Smith, *Andy Warhol's Art and Films*, p. 480. *Screen Test #1* paralleled another film project by Warhol, *Six Months* (1964–5), made from over six-months' of daily *Screen Tests* of Fagan. See Angell, *Andy Warhol Screen Tests*, pp. 217–8.

88. Joan Adler, as quoted in Watson, *Factory Made*, p. 86.

89. Jérôme Sans and Jonas Mekas, 'Just Like a Shadow', in Patrick Remy (ed.), *Jonas Mekas: Just Like a Shadow* (Göttingen: Steidl, 2000), [p. 27]. For Mekas' description of the loft and its function, see Mekas, *Anecdotes*, p. 267.

90. Kodak movie camera advertisement in *The Literary Digest* (5 March 1932), p. 31.

91. Kodak movie camera advertisement in *Life* (12 May 1952), p. 75; emphasis in text.

92. Gretchen Berg, 'Andy Warhol: My True Story', in Kenneth Goldsmith (ed.), *I'll Be Your Mirror: The Selected Andy Warhol Interviews* (New York: Carroll & Graf, 2004), p. 92.

93. Jonas Mekas, 'Notes after Reseeing the Movies of Andy Warhol', in O'Pray (ed.), *Andy Warhol Film Factory*, p. 31.

94. The police raid of a *Flaming Creatures* screening at the New Bowery Theater in March 1964 had a deleterious effect on public presentations of underground work. As J. Hoberman points out 'The Underground nearly went underground during the spring of 1964. There were no more public screenings, as Jonas Mekas devoted his energies to a series of court battles.' J. Hoberman, *On Jack Smith's* Flaming Creatures *and Other Secret-Flix of Cinemaroc* (New York: Granary Books/Hips Road, 2001), p. 133.

95. Chuck Wein, quoted in Roger Vaughan, 'Superpop or a Night at the Factory', in Madoff (ed.), *Pop Art*, p. 286.

96. Tyler, *Underground Film: A Critical History*, p. 45.

97. Roger Odin, 'Reflections on the Family Home Movie as Document: A Semio-Pragmatic Approach', in Ishizuka and Zimmermann (eds), *Mining the Home Movie*, pp. 256–7; emphasis in text.

98. Ibid. pp. 259–60.

99. Ibid. p. 260.
100. Ondine, as quoted in Smith, *Andy Warhol's Art and Films*, p. 448.
101. Eastman Kodak Company, *How to Make Good Home Movies*, p. 83.
102. Ibid. p. 83.
103. See 'Short Cuts and Tips from *Popular Science* Readers', *Popular Science* (September 1959), p. 170; 'Home-Movie Screen from Aluminum Baking Pan', *Popular Mechanics* (December 1931), p. 124; 'Window-Shade Movie Screen Mounted on Back of Television Set', *Popular Mechanics* (October 1955), p. 207; 'Solving Home Problems', *Popular Mechanics* (January 1953), p. 178; 'How to Build a Rear-Projection Cabinet for a Home Movie Theater Wall', *Popular Science* (September 1961), p. 194.
104. Takahashi cites the examples of screenings at the homes of Amos Vogel and Ken Jacobs, as well as Canyon Cinema's 'backyard screenings on bedsheets in the early 1960s'. Tess Takahashi, 'Experimental Screens in the 1960s and 1970s: The Site of Community', *Cinema Journal* 51:2 (Winter 2012): 162–6, p. 165.
105. Mekas, 'Notes after Reseeing the Movies of Andy Warhol', in O'Pray (ed.), *Andy Warhol Film Factory*, p. 31.
106. As quoted in Stephen Shore and Lynne Tillman, *The Velvet Years: Warhol's Factory, 1965–1967* (New York: Thunder's Mouth Press, 1995), p. 58.
107. Billy Name, as quoted in *Andy Warhol: A Documentary Film*, directed by Ric Burns (Arlington: PBS Home Video, 2006), DVD.
108. Billy Name explains, 'Eventually I installed one of Andy's hi-fi set-ups in the Factory and I would bring records, or Henry [Geldzahler] or Ondine would bring theirs over'. See Collier Schorr, 'A Talk with Billy Name', in Dave Hickey (ed.), *All Tomorrow's Parties: Billy Name's Photographs of Andy Warhol's Factory* (London and New York: Frieze/DAP, 1997), p. 21.
109. The television makes an important appearance, however, in Warhol's 1965 film, *Outer and Inner Space*.
110. Brown, as quoted in Smith, *Warhol: Conversations about the Artist*, p. 257. Contrary to common belief, very few parties took place at the Factory, but one of those that did, the Fifty Most Beautiful People party of spring 1965, has become legendary. Attended by Judy Garland, Montgomery Clift, Tennessee Williams, Brian Jones and other celebrities, it featured films of Warhol's entourage. Producing a correspondence between the Factory regulars in the audience and on screen as the 'in' crowd, Gerard Malanga claimed that with this event 'the stars went out and the superstars came in . . . There were more people staring at Edie than at Judy.' Malanga, as quoted in Warhol and Hackett, *POPism*, p. 105.
111. Ibid. p. 75.
112. Geldzahler, as quoted in Smith, *Warhol: Conversations about the Artist*, p. 183. Victor Bockris states, 'Andy kept painting on the floor, surrounded by the television set, radio, and phonograph all playing at the same time, stacks of teen, movie, and fashion magazines, and a telephone', Bockris, *The Life and Death of Andy Warhol*, p. 100.

113. Gluck, as quoted in Smith, *Warhol: Conversations about the Artist*, p. 69.
114. Battcock, as quoted in Smith, *Andy Warhol's Art and Films*, p. 323.
115. Battcock, as quoted in ibid. p. 325.
116. See David McCabe, *A Year in the Life of Andy Warhol* (London and New York: Phaidon, 2003).
117. Murphy, *The Black Hole of the Camera*, pp. 42–3. Only the first half of the film, where the sexuality remains a subtext, was shown in screenings outside the Factory.
118. Although Ultra Violet dates the screening to autumn 1964, the participation of Emerson and Superstar makes late 1965 or early 1966 a more likely date. Ultra Violet also describes a screening of *Sleep* that purportedly induced sleep in her, Emerson and Ondine. Ultra Violet, *Famous for 15 Minutes: My Years with Andy Warhol* (San Diego: Harcourt Brace Jovanovich, 1988), pp. 31–3, 110. For another example of sex during a Factory screening, see Mary Woronov, *Swimming Underground: My Years in the Warhol Factory* (London: Serpent's Tail, 1995), pp. 77–8.
119. Blum, as quoted in Smith, *Warhol: Conversations about the Artist*, p. 199; emphasis in text.
120. Warhol and Hackett, *POPism*, p. 172.
121. This date is based on photographs taken during the filming of a *Screen Test* of Jane Holzer in 1964.
122. For example, the screen is centrally placed in Jerry Schatzberg's 1966 portrait of Warhol reflected in a mirror surrounded by the tools and wares of his trade and it turns up rather unexpectedly in a 1965 photograph by Fred W. McDarrah of Warhol shooting *Camp*. See Catherine Millet, *L'art contemporain: histoire et géographie* (Paris: Flammarion, 2009) and Germano Celant (ed.), *SuperWarhol* (Milan/London: Skira/Thames and Hudson, 2003), vol. 1, pp. 134–5. The Radiant screen was one of two found among Warhol's affairs after his death, the other being a twelve-foot collapsible screen. Unlike Warhol's cameras and projectors, unfortunately, these screens were not considered worth preserving by the Andy Warhol Foundation for the Visual Arts and have been lost. Email correspondence with Matt Wrbican, 29 June 2010.
123. Consider the examples of multiple *Screen Tests* of John Cale, Isabel Eberstadt, Jane Holzer, Lou Reed, Edie Sedgwick and Susan Sontag. See Angell, *Andy Warhol Screen Tests*, pp. 47–8, 67–8, 95–6, 159–60, 179–80, 188.
124. This *Screen Test* is catalogued as ST196 in Angell, pp. 118–19. Photographs by Nat Finkelstein confirm the same folding-screen set-up for *Screen Tests* of another model, Kellie, made at the Factory the same day as Luna's, and a 1965 *Screen Test* of Holzer. See Angell, *Andy Warhol Screen Tests*, pp. 24–5, 94.
125. Billy Name, as quoted in Schorr, 'A Talk with Billy Name', in Hickey (ed.), *All Tomorrow's Parties*, p. 18.
126. Taubin, '★★★★', in MacCabe and Wollen (eds), *Who Is Andy Warhol*, p. 28. For more on Warhol as father figure in the Factory, see Jones, *Machine in the Studio*, p. 265.

127. It is not hard to imagine that viewing these images may have informed their subsequent sittings, adding yet another layer to our interpretation of these short films as tests.

128. Forgács, 'Wittgenstein Tractatus', in Ishizuka and Zimmermann (eds), *Mining the Home Movie*, p. 49.

129. Angell, *Andy Warhol Screen Tests*, pp. 217–41.

130. This was one of several examples of Warhol screening his work in private homes. Screenings were also held in a number of Philadelphia homes at the time of Warhol's 1965 exhibition at that city's Institute of Contemporary Art. See Scherman and Dalton, *Pop*, p. 284.

131. Kroll, 'Saint Andrew', in Madoff (ed.), *Pop Art*, p. 280. The films Kroll describes are catalogued as ST146 and ST147 in Angell, *Andy Warhol Screen Tests*, pp. 94–8.

132. Shana Alexander 'Report from Underground', *Life* (29 January 1965), p. 23. The screening took place on 10 January 1965, at the Cafe au Go Go on Bleecker Street.

133. Steve Wurtzler, 'Sound and Domestic Screens', *Cinema Journal* 51:2 (Winter 2012): 153–6, p. 153.

134. Projectionists at the film's first New York screenings were encouraged to improvise by presenting reels in any order, but a standard sequence was established before the film was released elsewhere. See Scherman and Dalton, *Pop*, pp. 345–6.

135. Gregory Battcock, 'Notes on *The Chelsea Girls*: A Film by Andy Warhol', *Art Journal* 26:4 (Summer 1967): 363–5, p. 364.

136. Warhol and Hackett, *POPism*, pp. 162–3, 156. See also Branden W. Joseph, '"My Mind Split Open": Andy Warhol's Exploding Plastic Inevitable', *Grey Room* 8 (Summer 2002): 80–107.

137. Tally Brown, as quoted in Smith, *Warhol: Conversations about the Artist*, p. 253.

138. Mekas, 'Notes after Reseeing the Movies of Andy Warhol', in O'Pray (ed.), *Andy Warhol Film Factory*, p. 32.

139. Warhol and Hackett, *POPism*, p. 163.

140. Gene Youngblood, *Expanded Cinema* (New York: E. P. Dutton, 1970), p. 103.

141. The *Film-Makers' Cooperative Catalogue Supplement* for 1968 alerted clients that all Warhol titles previously available for rental had been withdrawn and could be ordered only '*directly* from Warhol Films, 33 Union Square West, New York, New York, 10003'. *Film-Makers' Cooperative Catalogue Supplement* (New York: Film-Maker's Cooperative, 1968), p. 5; emphasis in text.

142. Michelson, '"Where is Your Rupture?"', in Michelson (ed.), *Andy Warhol*, p. 93.

143. Warhol and Hackett, *POPism*, p. 219.

144. Zimmermann, 'Introduction', in Ishizuka and Zimmermann (eds), *Mining the Home Movie*, p. 1.

145. Warhol, as quoted in O'Brien, 'Interview with Andy Warhol', in Goldsmith (ed.), *I'll Be Your Mirror*, p. 247. Perhaps because of the disappearance of these early films or the choices of his later film career, by the1970s Warhol's name

was often left out of exhibitions and histories of avant-garde film. See, for example, The American Federation of Arts, *A History of the American Avant-Garde Cinema* (New York: The American Federation of the Arts, 1976).

146. Philippe Parreno, 'After Affects', in Rachel Thomas (ed.), *All Hawaii Entrées/Lunar Reggae* (Milan and Dublin: Charta/Irish Museum of Modern Art, 2006), p. 38.

147. Zimmermann, 'Introduction', in Ishizuka and Zimmermann (eds), *Mining the Home Movie*, p. 24.

148. Wayne Koestenbaum, 'Andy Warhol: Screen Tests', *Artforum* 42:2 (October 2003): 166, 198; Amy Taubin, 'Andy Warhol: Motion Pictures', *Artforum* 49:7 (March 2011): 260–1.

149. Gregory Zinman, 'Not Fade Away: What Are We Seeing When We Look at an Andy Warhol *Screen Test?' Moving Image Source* (29 December 2010), http://www.movingimagesource.us/articles/not-fade-away-20101229 (accessed 1 September 2015).

150. Although Joseph stresses theatre screenings, the studio context is evoked in the title of the article within which he makes his claim. Branden W. Joseph, 'Factory Setting: Branden W. Joseph on Two Studies of Warhol's Films', *Artforum* 51:2 (October 2012): 59–60, p. 60.

CHAPTER 3

Private Dis-Pleasures: Mona Hatoum, Mediated Bodies and the Peep Show

The commercial viability of independent cinema at the start of the 1970s, heralded by the success of Dennis Hopper's *Easy Rider* (1969) as an example of what would be called 'New Hollywood', diminished the market for aesthetically unconventional soft- and hardcore films made by Warhol Films and others. Depictions of drug use, nudity and sex no longer attracted the vice squad, but qualified for Academy Award nominations and trophies. This turn obviated the need for an avant-garde moniker to facilitate distribution.[1] As expanded-cinema groups such as the London Film-makers Cooperative tested the material and ontological limits of film and the cinema apparatus, a flood of low-budget genre films – from blood-and-guts exploitation films for drive-ins to hardcore pornographic features for dying urban theatres – capitalised on the recent dismantling of long-standing obscenity laws and censorship codes in North America and Western Europe. Following the increased availability and visibility of porn magazines in public places such as newsstands, pornographic films previously mail-ordered for home projection or viewed in unlicensed bars or clubs began to appear in more conspicuous public settings. New porn theatres (usually once-venerable single-screen movie theatres squeezed out of the first-run market by multiplex theatres) and storefront peep-show parlours sprang up in most North American and Western European cities, spreading to post-communist Eastern Europe in the 1990s. 'To struggling [American theatre] owners, it seemed like a miracle when in 1969 the Production Code was repealed', states Jack Stevenson, 'There was suddenly easy money to be made screening porn.'[2] Urban areas previously known for other forms of legal and illegal entertainment – New York City's Times Square, Paris' Pigalle, London's Soho – became centres of porn distribution and exhibition, providing consumers with rows of sex shops filled with magazines, books, films and live shows.

The principal formats for moving-image pornography – film and videotape – were increasingly absorbed into artistic practice during this period. In the 1970s and 1980s, video co-ops and collectives such as Videofreex in New York, Raindance and TVTV (Top Value Television) in California and TVX in London, developed alongside – or replaced – art-film groups. Like 8-mm and 16-mm film before it, consumer-grade video proved an inexpensive and effective weapon for challenging an ever-more pervasive mass-media culture. Women and ethnically underrepresented artists in particular used film and video to expose and undermine established patriarchal forms and institutional structures, not only in art but also within popular culture and its fascination with the moving image. The video work of Dara Birnbaum, VALIE EXPORT, Joan Jonas, Nam June Paik, Adrian Piper and Martha Rosler, among many others, belongs to this trend. By the 1990s, artist production in film and video prompted many museums and galleries to exhibit both media on a regular basis, often in spaces already dedicated to more traditional media. Some institutions would take the additional step of designing galleries specifically for moving-image works. These became known as 'black boxes', due to their reduced lighting levels and minimal décor.

Mona Hatoum's career as a performance and video artist in Britain was formed amid these cultural and technological shifts. Intensely focused on the role and representation of the body in contemporary culture, this London-based British artist of Palestinian descent created a series of pieces in the 1980s that combined live performance, photography and video. Often exploring the dynamics of surveillance and the gaze, the violence and eroticism of these works addressed conditions of repression and abjection. Hatoum's shift from performance to installation in the 1990s continued the trajectory, replacing the live, performing body with its recorded image. Her presentation of *Corps étranger*, an installation of video projections first exhibited at the Centre Georges Pompidou in Paris in 1994, and since appearing in numerous exhibitions worldwide, marked a critical moment in this journey.[3] Still among her best-known works, *Corps étranger* intersects art centred on identity issues, moving images created specifically for the gallery space, and late twentieth-century transformations in popular and institutional representations of the body as a visual and material object. In this way, it builds on Rauschenberg's and Warhol's earlier investigations into audience-as-performer within visual spectacle. Nevertheless, where those artists engaged moving-image cultures oriented toward inclusive, shared experiences (widescreen and home movies), Hatoum's work draws on the visual regimes of imaging systems that isolate the body, while also encompassing forms of participation marked as abnormal or deviant. This chapter considers this turn in two ways. First, it relates *Corps étranger* and other 1990s video installations by Hatoum to her earlier performance works. Second, it considers them in relation to two seemingly opposed visual apparatuses for institutional authority and bodily commodification that emerged between 1965 and 1985: computer-aided medical-imaging devices and the pornographic peep show. As means of isolating, regulating and circulating the body, these apparatuses find their

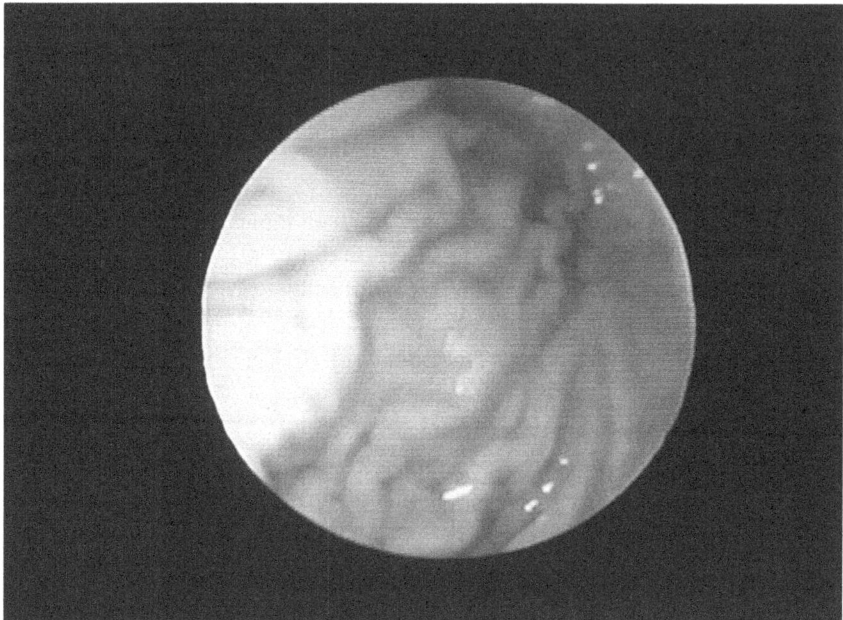

Figure 3.1 *Mona Hatoum,* Corps étranger *(detail), 1994. Video installation with cylindrical wooden structure, video projector, video player, amplifier and four speakers, 137¹³/₁₆ x 118⅛ x 118⅛ in. (350 x 300 x 300 cm). © Mona Hatoum. Courtesy White Cube*

formal and phenomenological reiteration in the conception, construction and exhibition of *Corps étranger*. Hatoum's pivotal 1994 piece therefore represents an important example of popular and non-theatrical moving-image formats re-emerging with new-found significance in art contexts.

FOREIGN BODIES

Corps étranger presents an alien world. Like a space probe's transmissions back to Earth, its colour video images reveal pulsating topographies and voids with surfaces smooth or textured, glistening or dry (Figure 3.1). Scale has no place in these fields devoid of recognisable objects. Upon extended and careful viewing, however, these disparate terrains may coalesce in the spectator's mind as varying regions of the human body. Slopes and craters, textures and lines transmogrify into skin, membranes and orifices. Through this montage, Hatoum renders alien and unfamiliar what is always nearest at hand. The distancing processes of *Corps étranger*'s technological mediation – bound up in magnification, cropping and editing – destroy proportion and render the body as scattered fragments. However, stepping back to consider the space

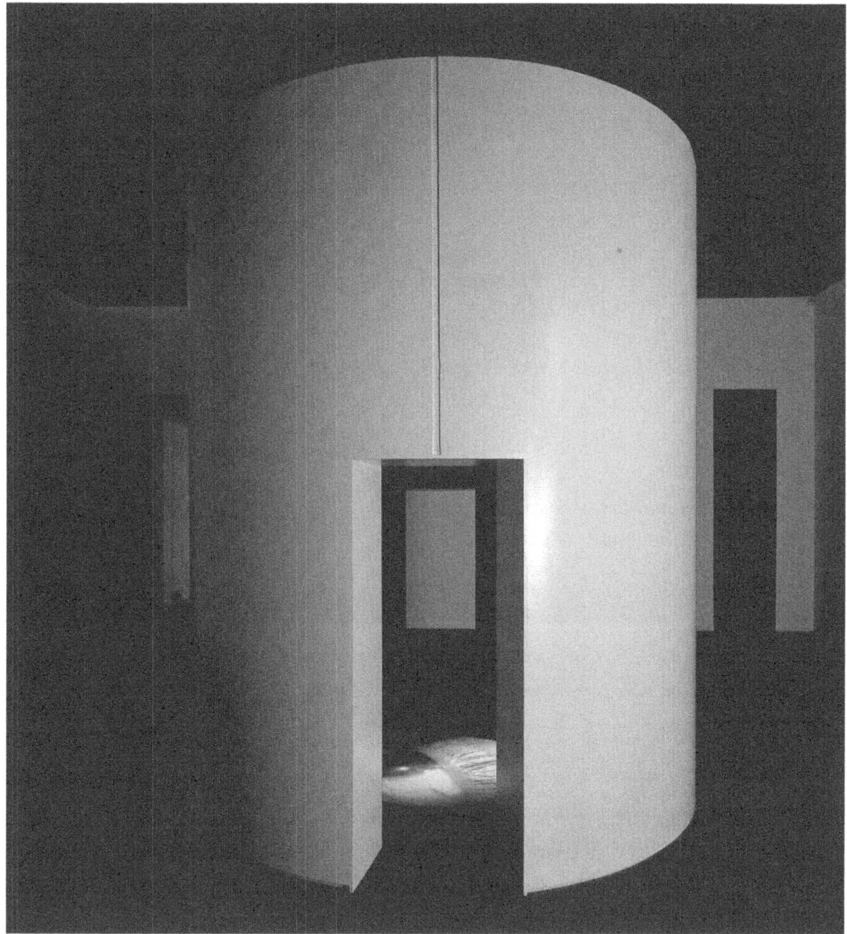

Figure 3.2 *Mona Hatoum,* Corps étranger, *1994. Video installation with cylindrical wooden structure, video projector, video player, amplifier and four speakers, 137¹³/₁₆ x 118¹/₈ x 118¹/₈ in. (350 x 300 x 300 cm). © Mona Hatoum. Courtesy White Cube*

of exhibition itself reveals how this work's process of disorienting spectators begins upon their approach, before any images can be seen. Projected onto the floor of a narrow cylindrical chamber, the video cannot be seen until spectators enter the smooth, white, 11½-foot-high enclosure through one of the two passageways that bisect it (Figure 3.2). At twenty-two inches wide and six feet high, these opposing passageways are significantly smaller than a standard household doorframe, forcing gallery visitors to enter one at a time. Tall people must duck their heads. These passageways provide access to the equally cramped seven-foot, ten-inch-wide interior of smooth, upholstered

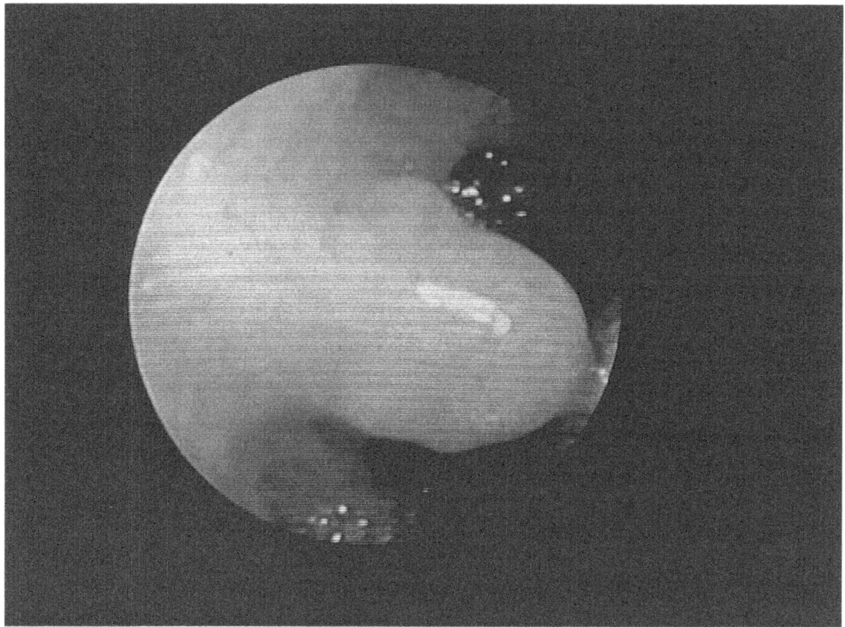

Figure 3.3   *Mona Hatoum,* Corps étranger *(detail), 1994. Video installation with cylindrical wooden structure, video projector, video player, amplifier and four speakers, 137¹³/₁₆ x 118⅛ x 118⅛ in. (350 x 300 x 300 cm). © Mona Hatoum. Courtesy White Cube*

black walls that can accommodate only a handful of people. A 4¼-foot white disc marks the centre of the floor, leaving only a twenty-two-inch band of floor space around it. The atypical design of Hatoum's viewing machine has generated diverse descriptions in response to the work. It has been called a 'cell', a 'cylinder', a 'room', a 'booth', a 'space partially closed upon itself', 'a sort of shelter' and even 'a sort of mausoleum'.[4]

However it is described, an overhead projector points directly downward on the central axis of this space to project a twelve-minute looped video of bodily images on the disc-screen. Though nothing demarcates the start of the video, for those who stay long enough it seems to begin with extreme close-ups of the body's surface that subsequently cede to dark and aimless underlying visceral voids. Images of skin, hair follicles, an eyeball, mouth, ear, vagina and anus make way for the oesophagus, intestinal track, cervix and rectum (Figure 3.3). Speakers mounted at ear level behind the fabric walls emit muffled echographic sounds of a heartbeat as recorded from different points in the body. As the camera explores the body's surface, these sounds are intermingled with recordings of breathing. Wall text outside the installation informs viewers that the body on display is that of the artist.

In structure and action, *Corps étranger* creates a complex relationship between image, frame and spectatorship. It interrogates the body in three ways that provoke conflict and opposition. First, it represents corporeality through images of the body that are unfamiliar and possibly unsettling. Second, it encloses these images in a narrow darkened structure that mimics the smooth, soft bodily passages seen in the video. Third, the unusual orientation of its image display can cause physical discomfort for spectators, who must negotiate both physical and psychological barriers to view the projection at their feet in this claustrophobic setting. Through the dynamics of these three vectors of visual and haptic experience, the imaged body and the spectatorial body enter into an ambivalent relationship of fluctuating hierarchies imposed by the apparatus. 'The boundaries between object and subject are less marked', notes Desa Philippi. 'We incorporate as we are incorporated, and while visually penetrating the inside of the body we are also swallowed up by that body.'[5]

Corps étranger's conceit of a journey over and through the human body can be interpreted as an abject reworking of corpo-centric science fiction films like *Fantastic Voyage* (Richard Fleischer, 1966) and *Innerspace* (Joe Dante, 1987). The installation also bears affinities to amusement park rides, such as Walt Disney World's defunct Body Wars, and interactive educational attractions common to science museums, such as the interactive film *Vital Space* (Michael Coulson, 2000). In its unusual frame for the performance of spectatorship, however, the work fuses multiple and sometimes opposing theories and practices in the visual culture of the body from the 1970s to 1990s. These include the aesthetics and mechanisms of medical imaging, abstract and formalist art production, film theory, feminist performance art, and pornography exhibition. As art historian Ewa Lajer-Burcharth explains, *Corps étranger* instantiates an 'anatomical theatre' composed of 'the aesthetic gaze (video projection); the clinical gaze (endoscopy); and the pornographic or voyeuristic gaze (the peepshow)'. In this triple exposure 'these different gazes displace one another and mutually thwart their own regulatory effects'.[6]

Through its association of bodily isolation with the institutional and affective mechanisms of medical and pornographic visuality, this installation addresses 'the major lines of combat of every invasion by media', as formulated by media theorist Friedrich Kittler: 'the three fronts of war, disease, and criminality'.[7] The medical imaging and pornography industries together objectify the human body. They do so toward different ends, of course, yet both adhere to methods of restricting or regulating access to the images they produce in relation to larger socio-disciplinary systems. *Corps étranger* exposes the material terms of social control by mimicking the imaging and exhibition conditions employed by both. The installation's medicalised gaze pushes to an extreme pornography's increasingly 'clinical' and 'abject' gaze most prevalent in the straight porn industry's female 'beaver' shot but also present in straight and queer subgenres of scatological and medical porn. The exploration of the visual and haptic terms of abjection, reinforced by the image's downward orientation on the gallery floor, is facilitated by the viewing structure's crossing of the sleek, sterile design common to medical imaging equipment such as MRI machines, with the cramped, darkened environs typically found in the peep-show arcades of adult bookstores and porn shops in London and other cities. Through this synthesis, *Corps étranger* opens a liminal space in the public sphere of the museum, where occlusion and concealment battle with access and exposure. The visitor must navigate not only the atypical architecture and unfamiliar images that comprise the work, but also the attendant social and psychological conflicts raised by sharing this constricted space with strangers. Where Lajer-Burcharth might perceive its similarities to peep-show culture as indicative of solely repressive systems for policing the body, however, one may also argue that the work's structural affinity to spaces and practices situated at the periphery of social acceptability contributes decisively to its unbinding of such 'regulatory effects'. In other words, those properties of *Corps étranger* that appear to isolate and alienate also produce a liminal space opening onto new possibilities of interaction.

By recalling both the strong emphasis on the regulation of public spaces found in Hatoum's early performance practices and the history of the peep show as a potential refuge from normative sexual ideologies that faced constant political threat of restriction and elimination, this chapter demonstrates how *Corps étranger* articulates the place of projection as a space of corporeal, sexual and social subversion. The fundamental properties of *Corps étranger* – a small, dark enclosure offering explicit views of the female body – derive from visual systems that typically reinforce gender difference and hierarchy. Yet the work creates a powerful trap, both physically and conceptually, by laying bare this machinery of objectification and fetishisation. The closeted, peephole view of the naked body retraces voyeuristic fantasies of control and possession historically linked to male social dominance and colonial subjugation. The work's relationship to issues of exile, geo-political imbalance and state violence is present in its title, but emerges more fully when its mechanisms of visuality are considered alongside Hatoum's personal circumstances and the conceptual direction of her work in the early 1980s.

Born of Palestinian exiles in Beirut in 1952, Hatoum found herself extending a short trip to Britain in 1975 into the migration of an exile after the outbreak of civil war in Lebanon. While a student at the Slade School of Art at University College London from 1979 to 1981 and as a London-based performance artist thereafter, Hatoum created art events exploring issues of difference and suffering that were motivated in part by her personal experiences of social injustice and Western perceptions of her as a foreign body (or *corps étranger*).[8] Performances including *Under Siege* (1982), *The Negotiating Table* (1983) and *Variations on Discord and Divisions* (1984), in addition to the installation *A Thousand Bullets for a Stone* (1988), were informed by continuing unrest in the Middle East, not only in Lebanon but also the West Bank, as Hatoum strove to underscore the inhumanity and suffering – as well as acts of resistance – playing out in sectarian and state-supported violence worldwide. 'In the performance work, I was trying to make general statements about the relationship between the Third World and the West, and I was trying to keep my own story out of it', Hatoum explains.[9] While attempting to keep her personal history at arm's length, Hatoum often placed her body at the centre of performance, where it might be bandaged, bound, bagged or otherwise confined as it struggled to free itself amid paint, blood, mud and animal entrails. As art critic Guy Brett points out, 'Although some of these early performances do make specific reference, either through the sound track or photographic images, to the war in Lebanon, these references tend to be secondary to the primary presence of the body as a metaphor for oppression in a wider and more universal sense'.[10]

By 1988, Hatoum realised that she had been pigeonholed as a 'political artist'. This brought 'the beginning of the end of working in an overtly political way', she would later acknowledge, as she shifted her efforts to creating sculptural installations with titles such as *Short Space* and *Light Sentence* (both 1992) that make use of hanging bed springs or stacked wire-mesh lockers to create spaces evoking institutionalisation and imprisonment. She also produced the video *Measures of Distance* (1988), which explores her long-distance relationship with her mother, who continued to live in Beirut.[11] While *Corps étranger* draws implicitly and explicitly on the linking of politics and violence in Hatoum's performance pieces, it also engages a corollary strain in her work that involves surveillance, gender and body politics. Beyond the title's link to Hatoum's personal history as a double exile (from Palestine and Lebanon), *Corps étranger* generates three foreign bodies: the spectator's body as it penetrates the enclosed installation space, Hatoum's imaged body made unfamiliar by the endoscopic perspective, and the endoscopic camera as an outside agent intervening between them.[12]

Hatoum's interest in the body and authority, in fact, predates her overt artistic engagement with Middle East politics and the consequences of war, figuring most prominently in her earliest art performances. In works such as *Video Performance* and *Don't smile, you're on camera!* (both 1980), *Look No Body!* and *Waterworks* (1981), Hatoum united cameras, live feeds and images of nudity with attempts to disrupt common divisions of public space arising from entrenched hierarchies of bodily function and etiquette. 'I would like to challenge the hierarchical structure which is placed on the different orifices of the body', Hatoum wrote in her proposal for *Waterworks*, which entailed placing cameras in the toilet stalls of London's Institute of Contemporary Arts and displaying live feeds of those spaces in the adjoining bookstore. 'The upper orifices [are] considered more respectable than the lower ones', the artist explained, 'and all the functions related to the lower ones [are] completely screened-off and tabooed'.[13] This perspective on the regulation of public space along distinctions of bodily processes and conduct not only signals the underlying logic of *Corps étranger* (which Hatoum had planned by that time), but also overlaps with contemporaneous struggles in London to confront the proliferation of porn peep-show booths as spaces that – depending on one's position in the debate – liberated or desecrated the body both as image and participant in commodified spectacle. Before examining the details of those struggles in relation to Hatoum's moving-image work, however, it is enlightening to consider the properties and regulatory effects of the other major influence on the form and function of *Corps étranger*: medical imaging technologies emergent in the late twentieth century.

PENETRATING GAZES

In the early 1980s, MRI devices and peep shows represented the extremes of national pride and shame in British visual culture. One was hailed as exemplary entrepreneurship and ingenuity that benefited both nation and humanity by potentially boosting a sagging British economy while curing the sick. The other was decried as both a symptom of, and conduit for, British society's decent into sexual and psychological pathologies. By merging the forms and dynamics of MRI and the peep show in a hybrid, ambivalent structure, *Corps étranger* creates an environment synthesising apparatuses for the body's submission to – and defiance of – the mechanisms of authority. According to Hatoum, the idea for *Corps étranger* struck her in 1980, when it was included in a funding request submitted to the projects committee at Slade.[14] 'It was in the context of a number of other works I was making at the time which had to do with surveillance', she explains. 'Surveillance cameras, being observed, the eye of Big Brother . . .'[15] In her performances of that time, which intermingled live feeds of the performance space with pre-recorded or live body imagery, she 'pretended [she] had a "penetrating gaze"', producing what she describes as the 'eery [sic] feeling that the camera could penetrate the layers of clothes and flesh'.[16] It is unsurprising that Hatoum would resort to X-ray images in the early 1980s to represent the camera's penetration of the body. Up to that time, X-rays were virtually the sole means of photographing the body's interior without resorting to the scalpel. Much in the same way that the cinema relies on projection to exhibit images, standard (pre-digital) X-rays produce transparencies rendered visible when light passes through them. Processing X-rays through computer programs in the 1970s allowed for computed tomography (or CT and CAT scans) that can furnish sectioned images of the body on a monitor. In the early 1980s, however, nuclear magnetic resonance imaging – a revolutionary new form of corporeal visualisation better known as MRI – was being developed by Oxford scientists and engineers for widespread application. The first commercial MRI devices would appear in hospitals by mid-decade. MRI – then also known as NMR – produces images that, unlike X-ray photography, can illustrate bodily processes. Employing high-powered magnets to measure differences in atomic activity in compound substances, NMR had been in use in laboratories since the 1950s to analyse materials in small amounts. In 1980 – the year Hatoum devised *Corps étranger* – the first MRI commercial machines were manufactured outside London at Osney Mead, Oxford. As *The Times* reported, converting NMR for medical application represented a major step forward for the medical gaze. 'Doctors have always dreamed of a machine that will let them see what is going on inside the human body without having to cut into it', the newspaper stated in 1981. MRI offered 'a completely different technique for "looking"' into the living body, one that would be 'a non-invasive method for seeing what is happening in the body'. In terms that foreshadow the visuals of *Corps étranger*, *The Times* explained that 'fluids and wet tissues show up clearly, and bones are invisible' in MRI imaging.[17]

The conversion of MRI from table-top spectrometers with magnets measuring less than a foot into multi-ton hospital devices capable of imaging an entire human body required a major design overhaul (Figure 3.4). *The Times* described the resulting device as 'an instrument capable of accommodating the whole body . . . [housing] a four-ton superconducting magnet with a 60 centimetre bore, which will encompass normal-sized but not obese patients'.[18] The smooth, white, cylindrical housing of *Corp étranger* strongly resembles one of these machines turned on end. In fact, original patent drawings of the MRI device do not depict it as the horizontal cylinder that would eventually become standard, but rather as a vertical chamber within which the patient would stand.[19] The installation's shiny, white, cylindrical surface, its thick walls and hollowed centre all match the basic form of the devices as they were first manufactured by Oxford Instruments at about £500,000 apiece. The circular screen at the centre of Hatoum's installation, in fact, is a near-identical match for the bore meant to accommodate 'normal-sized' bodies. By 1994, the look and intended uses of an MRI machine would have been familiar to museum goers, whether through

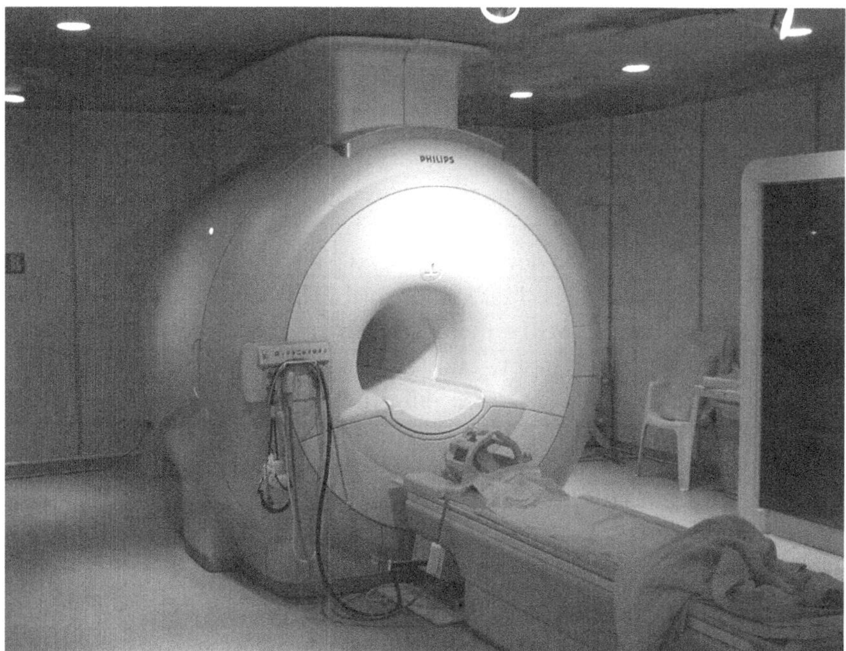

Figure 3.4   *A magnetic resonance imaging (MRI) machine for use in hospitals and clinics, 2006. Photo courtesy Kasuga Huang, Creative Commons Attribution-Share Alike 3.0 Unported licence*

news photographs and TV medical dramas or their own experiences of hospital and clinic. In organising *Corp étranger*'s space such that spectators may enter the structure but skirt the circular screen on the floor, however, the artist creates a viewing situation that, unlike the MRI, can accommodate one person (or more) while imaging another body. Spectators' bodies are therefore both inside and outside the process. They are engulfed within the objectifying device and, while not the bodies that the device images, spectators can become acutely aware of their bodies as objects within the awkward architecture of the installation. The event performs the 'invasive medical gaze', as Gannit Ankori points out, while for Hatoum the body 'becomes vulnerable in the face of the scientific eye, probing it, invading its boundaries, objectifying it'.[20]

Although MRI was being publicised as a major breakthrough in medical technology when Hatoum conceived *Corps étranger*, it nevertheless remained in the research phase. Conversely, endoscopy, another body imaging technique based on the insertion of a small tethered camera into bodily orifices, was by then a common medical procedure. While still a Slade student, Hatoum unsuccessfully petitioned University College Hospital to undergo endoscopy for her installation project. She did manage to secure echographic recordings of her heartbeat and digestive system at that time, however, and she would first employ them in 1981 in *Look No Body!* before they became the basis for the soundtrack of *Corps étranger*.

POLITICS OF A BOOTH

'When I speak of works . . . as making a reference to some kind of institutional violence', Hatoum has stated, 'I am speaking of encountering architectural and institutional structures in Western urban environments that are about the regimentation of individuals, fixing them in space and putting them under surveillance'.[21] Certainly the development of MRI and other medical technologies derive from, and reinforce, such structures. At the same time that Hatoum developed *Corps étranger* in the shadow of these inventions, and performed works challenging hegemonic disciplinary measures that divided public space along bodily functions, a drag-out battle over the presence and function of sex shops in London was reaching its peak. After years of raids, fines and unsuccessful prosecution of businesses by local governing bodies amid revolving shop owners and changing addresses, Parliament passed special licensing measures in 1981 that granted local councils wide latitude in regulating and closing these enterprises.

The most visible target was Soho's booming sex trade, in London's West End, where porn had turned the neighbourhood 'into one of the nasty places of the Western world', according to a reporter for the *Observer*.[22] Located only a mile from the Slade classrooms where Hatoum was finishing plans for *Look No Body!* and *Waterworks*, Soho harboured over one hundred and sixty sex shops within a few city blocks (Figure 3.5).[23] Another *Observer* reporter explained that the porn shops of the period were 'run supermarket style' with 'the bulk of the goods cater[ing] for odd tastes'. Magazines, books and various sex accessories would fill most of a shop, but often there was an additional area set-off from the main retail space. 'At the back of many of these parlours [were] booths showing coin-in-the-slot "explicit Continental films"', the reporter wrote, with differential pricing for sound and silent films at '50p with grunt and 10p without'.[24]

A place of prostitution dating back to the nineteenth century, Soho's conversion to organised sex entertainment and porn retail did not begin until 1959, with the passage of the Street Offences Act allowing strip clubs amid the area's theatres, restaurants and book shops.[25] Cinemas dedicated to 'blue films' and naturist documentaries soon joined them, along with film clubs like the Compton Cinema Club, which showed movies sometimes deemed obscene by authorities.[26] The West End sex trade became a cat-and-mouse

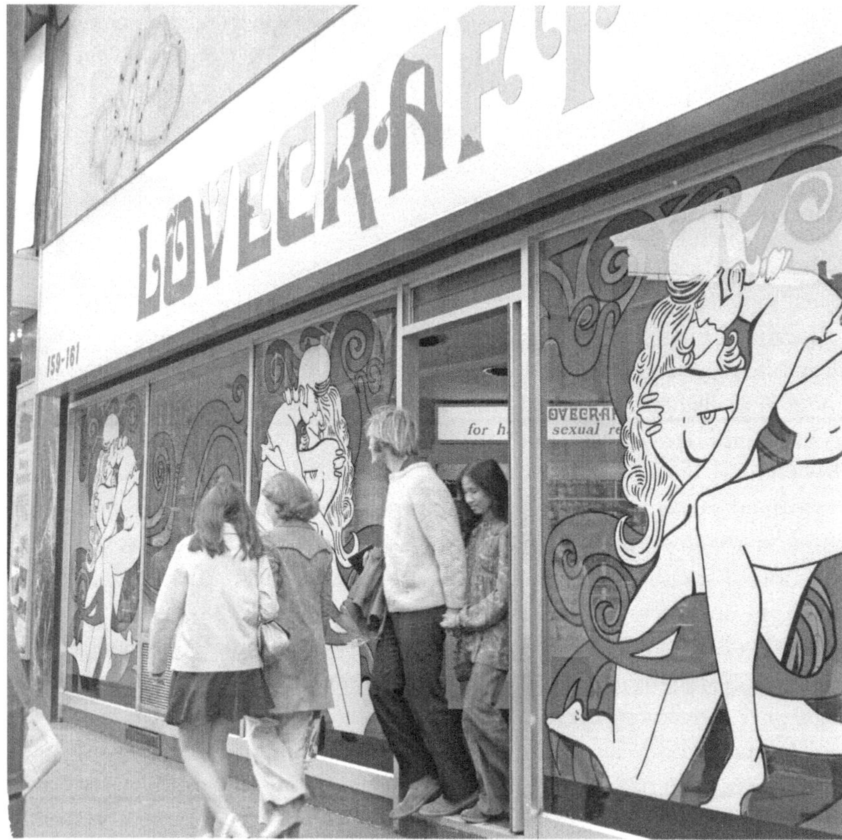

Figure 3.5   *Henry Grant, A couple leaving a London sex shop, 1975. © Museum of London*

game involving pornographers, distributors and government agencies, producing what Laurence O'Toole calls 'windows of semi-freedom and hardcore exposure in Soho bookshops and cine clubs during the early seventies, or the short-lived loophole of hardcore video of the early eighties, before the new technology got properly wrapped up in legal controls'.[27]

Throughout the 1970s local and national authorities had sought ways to curb the proliferation of businesses offering sex shows and pornographic materials. In 1978 the Home Office created the Committee on Obscenity and Film Censorship, headed by Cambridge moral philosopher Bernard Williams, to study porn's impact on British society. To the chagrin of conservative reformers, the Williams Committee reported no measurable harmful effects from the circulation of pornography and recommended no attempts to restrict it among adults, as long as those who might find it offensive were not inadvertently exposed to it. The committee noted images of violence and cruelty as potentially offensive, as well as those depicting 'sexual, faecal or urinary functions or genital organs'.[28] Framing the spread of porn as a national crisis, Conservative politicians vowed that 'sex shops' would be 'driven back to the sewers where they belong'.[29] Parliamentary debates compared their spread to a 'poisonous fungi all over the country'. Since 'pornography relied for its effect on the degradation of women', one Member of Parliament claimed, 'it was specifically designed to undermine society'.[30]

Significantly – though not surprisingly, given the normative terms of Parliamentary debate – two fundamental aspects of the porn industry were consistently ignored amid the inflammatory rhetoric. First, for as much as there may have been a 'strong and growing [negative] reaction' among the population, if sex shops were spreading like a pestilence in Great Britain – as authorities contended – that growth required a large consumer base of ordinary citizens. Second, while heterosexual pornography may have been prominent, sex shops also offered significant amounts of bisexual and homosexual content that complicated convenient patriarchal arguments casting all pornography as necessarily degrading to women.[31]

While peep-show clientele was overwhelmingly male, these viewing spaces offered opportunities for non-normative behaviour that troubled standard ideological frameworks of gender and subject. The motivation for curbing the visibility and accessibility of sexual material by shutting down the spaces devoted to it contained the implicit desire to preserve what Lauren Berlant and Michael Warner call 'heteronormativity'. Berlant and Warner – building on Michel Foucault's work on cultural constructions of sexuality and its policing – explain that society promotes heteronormativity through narratives of heterosexuality, private intimacy and reproduction that create a 'privatized sexual culture [that] bestows on its sexual practices a tacit sense of rightness and normalcy. This sense of righteousness – embedded in things and not just sex – . . . is produced in almost every aspect of the forms and arrangements of social life.'[32] Sex shops, especially those that include diversified spaces for social and sexual interaction, would pose a threat to such narratives. In this regard it is worth quoting Berlant and Warner at length:

> Heterosexual culture achieves much of its metacultural intelligibility through the ideologies and institutions of intimacy . . . Although the intimate relations of private personhood appear to be the realm of sexuality itself, allowing 'sex in public' to appear like matter out of place, intimacy is itself publicly mediated, in several senses. First, its conventional spaces presuppose a structural differentiation of 'personal life' from work, politics, and the public sphere. Second, the normativity of heterosexual culture links intimacy only to the institutions of personal life, making them the privileged institutions of social reproduction, the accumulation and transfer of capital, and

self-development. Third, by making sex seem irrelevant or merely personal, heteronormative conventions of intimacy block the building of nonnormative or explicit public sexual cultures.[33]

The result, Berlant and Warner conclude, is that 'the heteronormative culture of intimacy leaves queer culture especially dependent on ephemeral elaborations in urban space and print culture', which would include the peep show and the images it contains, as well as more common examples such as parks and public toilets.[34]

Corps étranger brings views such as those of Berlant and Warner to bear on the liminal public space of the museum by carving out an alternative space for viewing and interacting within its normative framework rooted in the historical project of empire and subjugation. Through the intersection of allusions to the form and functioning of medical and pornographic imaging machines, the installation suggests an interdependence of normativity and deviance – the one determining the other – as underpinning such institutional frameworks. The terms of the pornography fight in Britain in the early 1980s and its concomitant crisis over sexuality and space – in addition to synchronous developments in medical imaging – therefore provide a rich social and historical backdrop to Hatoum's performances of that era, her creation of *Corps étranger* and the first deployment of that work a decade later.

While the legal battles embroiling authorities and sex-shop owners did not hinge on weakened obscenity laws, but rather on the use of general retail licenses to sell materials off-limits to minors, the wider war involved issues of access and visibility. Between 1974 and 1981 Parliament launched a half-dozen attempts to curb the industry through the regulation and policing of public and commercial space. It was only with the passage of the Indecent Displays Act and new licensing requirements at the end of 1981 that the government gained the upper hand. Armed with these, London authorities would successfully shut down 70–80 per cent of Soho's sex shops within two years.[35] In a subsequent effort to parse the widening range of commodified sexual activities available for public consumption in Soho, in 1986 – or mid-way between Hatoum's idea for *Corps étranger* and its eventual realisation – the Greater London Council created licenses for 'sex encounter establishments'. These were shops where 'entertainments which are not unlawful are provided by one or more persons who are without clothes or who expose their breasts, genital, urinary or excretory organs during the entertainment'.[36] Whether on video, film or in live 'sex encounters', such entertainment was often exhibited in peep-show booths at the back of a shop, beyond racks of magazines and accessories.

Drawing on the centuries-long history of peep shows as optical boxes containing views and scenes accessible through a small hole or viewfinder, peep-show booths in the UK and elsewhere were small and cheaply constructed partitioned enclosures dividing retail space into private viewing rooms. According to Laurence O'Toole, the 'self-contained peepshow machine' was invented by Swedish porn film-maker Lasse Braun and American distributor Reuben Sturman in 1971, though peep shows based on existing exhibition machines were in use by the 1940s.[37] Steve Rudnick, who assembled peep-show booths for North American porn distributor Reuben Sturman in the mid-1970s, describes them as plywood and wood-grain panelling stapled together. 'One [panel] would be a wall, and another one would be a door or something like that. Incredibly sloppy.'[38] Booths would contain a coin-operated Super-8 projector that retro-projected films onto a small screen. Some included a small, waist-level opening to an adjacent booth. Known as a 'glory hole', a term borrowed from the oil and mineral industries, this opening allowed the possibility of physical contact between patrons during visits. The relative privacy and anonymity of the booth allowed patrons to 'pay and spray', either in masturbating to the images or engaging in sexual contact through the glory hole.[39] A photograph by Lucinda Devlin of the interior of an American peep-show booth in the 1980s demonstrates that the structure had changed little by the time Hatoum conceptualised *Corps étranger* (Figure 3.6). In Devlin's photo a narrow, panelled enclosure contains a metal stool set before a small screen, a coin-drop box and a channel switch. Barely visible on the right wall is a glory hole, placed at about the height of the lower edge of the screen. The only significant difference from earlier booths is the screen, which is a video monitor rather than a projection screen. True to the 'pay and spray' claim, the booth's floor bears several splatter stains.

In a 1979 exposé of Leicester Square's live peep shows, *Guardian* reporter Andrew Veitch described booths there as 'wooden cells [with] black walls, tissues on the floor, and flimsy doors with locks, some of which don't work'. Each booth was fitted with a metal shutter that, for fifty pence, would draw back for two minutes to expose a narrow eye slit. 'You can see the girl from breast bone to mid[-]thigh', Veitch recounted. 'Across the room another shutter opens, a pair of eyeballs swivel, following her around the room. They flick towards you. Involuntarily you duck.' When the shutter descended, adding another fifty pence in the slot reversed its action to reveal a pair of buttocks 'inches away. And the eyes across the room.'[40] Perhaps inadvertently, Veitch's account describes a complex encounter of varying relationships. The body of the woman on display draws the disembodied gazes surrounding her, yet these train not only on her, but also on each other. For as much as the peep show isolates the dancer from the customers and the customers from each other, this arrangement of black boxes encircling the body

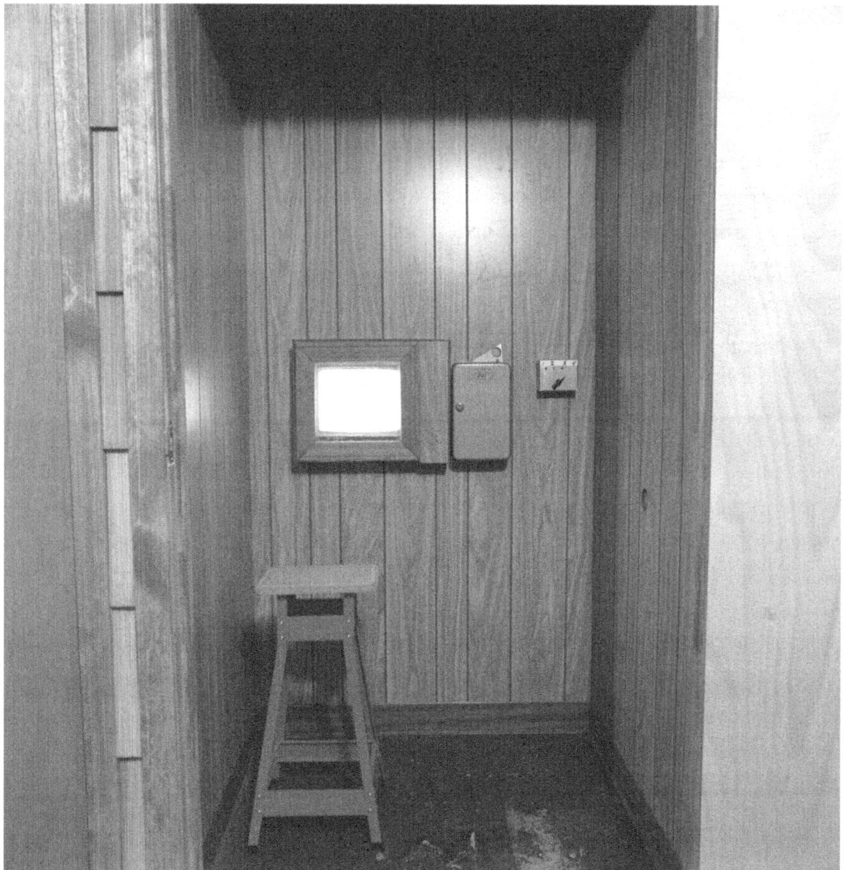

Figure 3.6 *Lucinda Devlin,* Peep Show, Boulevard Books, Dewitt, New York, *1985.*
© *Lucinda Devlin*

on view becomes the frame for a network of recognition among patrons, initiated in the exchange of gazes. While promising isolation and privacy, the London peep show also opened up a potential space for non-normative encounter, straining the heteronormative 'conventions of intimacy' described by Berlant and Warner through a structure that permitted public contestation of sexual norms even as it seemed to reinforce them. As an instrument ostensibly designed to support the straight male gaze, the Leicester Square peep show allowed for its disruption and unpinning in the visual exchange between viewers across the field of the female body as presumed object of desire.

Because they could function as a readily accessible space for such interactions, peep-show booths were considered particularly hazardous to moral and civic order. For regulators, the booth posed a major challenge in the dual desire to limit the availability of pornographic imagery and police sexual inter-actions. The differing systems of carefully placed curtains, blinds, doors and screens that would separate back-wall peep shows from the rest of a shop – not to mention separating peep-show viewers from each other – became the material intersection of the competing forces of government ordinances, social norms and sexual desires.[41] Indeed, the peep-show booth appeared to present such a grave threat to normative sexuality that campaigns against porn often focused as much or more on the configuration of its space as the images it housed. This was especially true in the United States. The report of the Attorney General's Commission on Pornography, a commission organ-ised by President Ronald Reagan in 1985 and popularly known as the Meese Commission after Attorney General Edwin Meese, identifies the peep-show booth as 'a haven for sexual activity' creating serious hazards to hegemonic culture and public health. With 'enough room for two adults to stand shoul-der to shoulder', the peep-show booth's threat lay not only in the images it presented but the activities it could house and conceal. 'The inside of the booth is dark, when the door is closed, except for the light which emanates from the screen or enters from the bottom of the door', the commission's report details.

> Many booths are equipped with a hole in the side wall . . . The holes are used for oral and anal sexual acts. Sexual activity in the booths involves mostly males participating in sexual activities with one another. However, both heterosexual and homosexual men engage in these activities. The anonymity provided by the 'glory holes' allows the participants to fantasize about the gender and other characteristics of their partners.[42]

Although the report raises other issues throughout this description – from graffiti to prostitution – its conclusion crystallises the space's greatest threat to any ideological base for regulating bodily functions in the public sphere. While 'anonymous sexual relations' were already problematic to policing public space, the report's writers project onto the booth a far greater danger to normative sexual roles in the potential 'fantasiz[ing]' of gender and 'other characteristics of their partners' presumably made available to patrons through the booth's design and placement. In an article on historical viewing conditions for pornography, Gertrud Koch concludes 'It may be that films' effects are more directly related to the social environments in which the films are presented than to the films' form and content. In other words, the audi-ence's sexual orientation defines the way the product is consumed.'[43] The Meese Commission's statements sustain this view, finding in the booth's material and spatial conditions a far more insidious peril to hegemonic heter-onormativity than any image that might appear on the screen.

As Amy Herzog confirms in her pioneering examination of peep-show exhibition culture, 'The peepshow is in fact one of the few areas within cinema culture where the activities of spectators receive greater attention than the content of the films'.[44] Herzog interprets the potential instabilities raised by the Meese Commission report as one of the format's defining features. For her, the peep show's emergence in the 1970s for the exhibition of pornography stems from its differentiation from the movie theatre in constructing visual and social conditions based on new understandings of the body's relation to public space. Herzog calls the peep-show arcade an 'anomalous space' where 'public and private become enfolded'.[45] 'The apparatus of the peepshow subjects the body of the patron to a highly individualized and intimate mode of address, compelling in return an active and equally intimate corporeal response.' However, Herzog warns, 'At the same time, this exchange takes place in public, with the patron's body rendered visible as it circulates through the arcade (to greater or lesser degrees, depending on the architecture of the venue and the booths)'.[46] The peep show is shaped in its material and spatial terms by the social as well as sexual needs of consumers. Herzog explains that within that framework

> Interior spaces, both corporeal and domestic, are opened to view, while the exterior realm of the public foyer is enveloped within the enclosed space of the booth. Just as the filmed bodies exist in a suspended yet politically charged space between exposure and intimacy, the bodies in the arcade enact a self-conscious performance that is at once personal and socially contingent.[47]

Susan Stewart goes further still, arguing that public-private performance of visibility remains only one aspect of the operation, bound to a parallel performance of incorporating and incorporation. Recalling Veitch's 1979 description of Soho peep-show booths as 'wooden cells' with sometimes faulty locks, Stewart describes the peep-show booth as the 'perfect form for serving this need for privacy and accessibility, confinement and violation. The symbolics of the lock, the "glory hole", and the "screen" work out the problematics of hiding and display, fantasy and realizability in the remarkable merging of pornographic form and function.'[48]

The Meese Commission report notes that 'The booth is sometimes equipped with a lock on the door. Many patrons intentionally leave the door unlocked. Some patrons look inside the booths in an attempt to find one already occupied. It is commonplace for a patron to enter an occupied booth, close the door behind him, and make advances toward the occupant.'[49] Facing this possibility, the commission argued for increasingly severe steps to regulate peep-show booths. These included removing doors, plastering over glory holes to eliminate 'inter-booth sexual contact', requiring official inspections and licenses, and making illegal 'any form of indecent act by or among' patrons, thereby classifying as a crime nearly any physical contact considered sexual, whether done individually or with others.[50] Other methods of policing these spaces included mandating minimum surface areas, lighting levels, and maximum occupancy. In San Diego, California, in 1971, lawmakers pointed to health and safety concerns in requiring that aisles between peep shows be at least forty-two inches across and light levels be at least ten foot-candles throughout. There was to be no more than one person per thirty square feet 'in any room or partitioned portion of a room where a peepshow device is located'.[51] As the Meese Commission reported, in the early 1980s peep-show booths averaged 3 x 5 feet, but could be as large as 4 x 8 feet.[52] These measures for distancing, isolation and confinement demonstrate once again the extent to which the architecture of the peep show, rather than its imagery, remained the primary target of regulators and reformers throughout its brief history.

PERFORMING ORIFICES

The floor area of *Corps étranger* is just under the eight-foot maximum noted for booths in the Meese Commission report. Lined in black, the installation's space is consistently much darker than the surrounding gallery. Like the peep show, its screen and small passageways are the only sources of light. The darkness and limited space of *Corps étranger* create an unusual and potentially uncomfortable situation for the gallery visitor, regardless of the images presented. 'In contrast to the visual complexity of the video sequence the housing of the work is of the utmost simplicity', Frances Morris remarks. 'Movement is severely restricted, and the communal proximity to other viewers also complicates the experience of intimacy.'[53] Christine Ross goes further, deeming the space 'a sort of shelter that also serves as a meeting place for other viewers' by allowing bodies to brush against each other, consciously or unconsciously.[54]

If the space of *Corps étranger* can be deemed constrictive, it can also be understood as intimate and communal. Large enough to accommodate multiple spectators, it nevertheless places them in close proximity. Its cylindrical layout leaves no corner for retreat. Visitors must be willing to rub shoulders and bump into each other in negotiating both the screen and each other's presence as impediments to free circulation. They must be willing to exchange gazes, and be caught in the gaze of others as they gaze downward at the projected image. Like the peep-show booth, the chamber of *Corps étranger* becomes a space of potential that is only partially predicated on the content of its projected images. *Corps étranger* and the peep show (and, indeed, many public film-exhibition formats, including the movie theatre and the drive-in) offer multiple potential experiences of spectacle that merge visual image with immediate tactile circumstances. These possibilities have been described to varying degrees and in differing terms by those writing on *Corps étranger*. As Volker Adolphs describes it, in the tight confines of *Corps étranger*, 'the spectator . . . becomes a prisoner of the body viewed inside . . . gazing into an abyss that threatens to swallow you'. He continues, 'we sense that this journey into the depths of another body is destabilizing the very ground beneath our feet'.[55] In words that strongly recall the fantasies evoked by the peep show's combination of screen and glory hole, Hamid Naficy claims that the installation's pulsating images 'hypnotize' viewers and 'urge them to give into the imminent engulfment and plunge in'.[56] Hans-Jürgen Buderer presents an account that suggests resistance to such temptations, however. 'In the video *Corps étranger*, 1995 [sic], Mona Hatoum penetrates her own body. She inserts an endoscope and records the pictures of her body cavities on a video tape. With these results of her research, she then approaches the spectator very intimately', Buderer explains. 'The recorded video is projected onto the floor in the middle of a dark room. The viewer stays close to the wall in order not to step onto the living shapes moving on the floor at his feet, but also not to be touched by them.'[57] Desa Philippi similarly elaborates on a perceived threat: 'By ostentatiously directing and confining movement, and by making the danger of touch potentially real in a culture which tends to notice the body only when it is in pain, [Hatoum's] work makes a claim for physicality beyond the disembodied eye which we tellingly call the spectator or the viewer'.[58]

These differing interpretations demonstrate a surprisingly wide range of psychological and physical interactions with the work, all tied to ideas of intimacy, sexuality and contamination. The flexibility *Corps étranger* presents within these categories, despite (or because of) its restrictive space places it on par with the peep show as an enclosure opening onto the possibility of unbinding codes of sexual and subjective being. Hatoum has claimed that the potential for physical contact is an integral aspect of the piece. 'It is a complex work. It is both fascinating to follow the journey of the camera and quite disturbing. On one hand, you have the body of a woman projected onto the floor. You can walk all over it. It's debased, deconstructed, objectified. On the other hand, it's the fearsome body of the woman as constructed by society.'[59]

While *Corps étranger* brings some of the conditions of the pornographic peep show to bear on the art gallery, its roots in gendered bodily spectacle and the visuality of institutional authority extend to Hatoum's performances at the time of the work's conception in 1980 and their relationship to feminist art and media theory. Just as Helen Potkin has claimed that feminist performance art has carried the compound burden of addressing narcissism and 'other traditions of women on stage – such as the stripper', Hatoum's performed pieces turned spectacle and camera back onto the artist's body in an exploration of corporeal processes within the performance of public life.[60] *Video Performance*, *Look No Body!*, *Don't smile, you're on camera!* and *Waterworks* specifically involved the camera's mediation of the body and the spectator's relation to the production and negotiation of space. These tendencies not only inform *Corps étranger* as a performance across represented and viewing bodies but also set into place that installation's evocation of intimacy and abjection as grounding factors.

In *Video Performance*, staged in July 1980 at the London Film-makers Co-op Summer Show, Hatoum carefully panned the audience with a hand-held, closed-circuit camera that generated live, close-up images on a monitor beside her. She then sat on the floor of the low-lit space, drawing a circle around herself and pointing the camera at her body from above. Anticipating the vertical gaze of *Corps étranger*, the angle offered images of her scalp and hair on the monitor, images that would subtly and inexplicably change to (previously recorded) close-ups of Hatoum's naked body. Like X-ray vision, buttons and clasps appeared in images of her bare skin, as though the camera could penetrate her clothes. Video artist Catherine Elwes, who was in the audience, describes the effect. For Elwes, being caught in the camera's gaze 'to become the focus of public attention in a situation that is controlled by another individual fills me with a kind of terror I find hard to define . . .' She explains, 'I feel trapped. If I get up and move out of the camera's range, I draw attention to myself. If I stay where I am, I become exposed to this electronic voyeurism.'[61] The discomfort provoked by this turn of observer becoming observed is similar to the effect of *Corps étranger*, where the spectator risks being trapped by the limited privacy of the enclosure as it is accessed by others, potentially creating uncomfortable group viewing experiences of fragmented images of the human body caught in the vertical beam of the camera.

Don't smile, you're on camera!, first performed at the Battersea Arts Centre in March 1980, extended this voyeurism in multiple directions (Figure 3.7). For this piece, Hatoum turned the camera on the audience, panning slowly over the spectators, stopping here and there. Two unseen assistants nearby produced live images of their own naked bodies, while a third assistant mixed the images from the two cameras on a monitor facing the audience so that it appeared Hatoum's camera was able to penetrate clothing. Hatoum pushed these explorations deeper into the spaces of public life with *Look No Body!* by installing a camera in the toilet adjacent to her performance space, again linked to a monitor facing the audience. A year later, she performed *Look No Body!* at The Basement in Newcastle (Figure 3.8). The performance involved

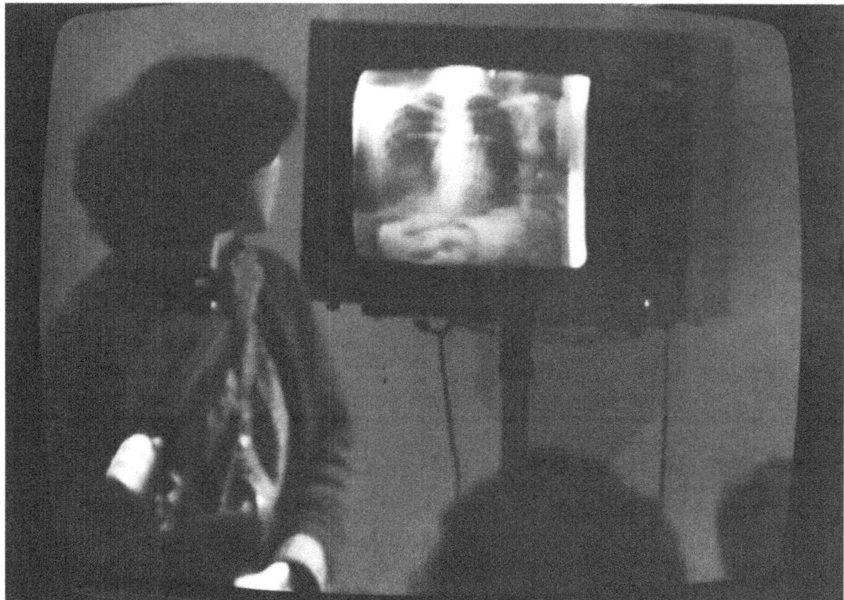

Figure 3.7   *Mona Hatoum,* Don't smile, you're on camera!, *1980. Black-and-white video with sound; duration: 11 minutes, 15 seconds. © Mona Hatoum, courtesy White Cube*

the artist drinking prodigious amounts of water and offering every other cup to audience members with the hope that it would force them to use the toilet under video surveillance. Only Hatoum went to the toilet, however, her urinating accompanied by a soundtrack combining the recitation of scientific descriptions of urination with the echographic recordings that would later accompany *Corps étranger*. 'With *Look No Body!* I was considering the body in terms of its orifices', Hatoum explains, 'and how some of the orifices and the activities associated with them are considering socially acceptable and some not . . . It was like looking inside the body while keeping the "correct" distance.'[62] *Waterworks*, a related (but unrealised) installation referenced earlier in this chapter, entailed abolishing that distance by installing cameras in the toilet stalls of the ICA in London, with links to monitors mounted above their doors to the adjoining bookshop. Hatoum's proposal for the work emphasises 'our general negative attitudes to the body and its natural processes, which socialization teaches us to keep under control in order to maintain a formal social distance'.[63] As she later explained, 'I wanted to look into the taboos around bodily functions, and how the body's orifices have been organized in a hierarchical structure'.[64]

These works, like *Corps étranger*, all represent an approach to the screened body where corporeal presence rests upon an oppositional genealogy of

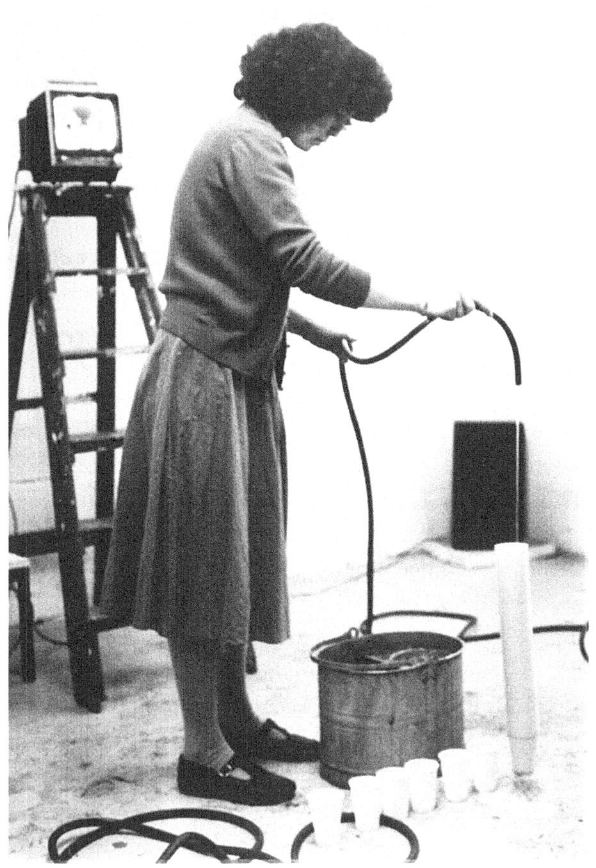

Figure 3.8   *Mona Hatoum,* Look No Body!, *28 March 1981. Live action with video monitor, sound tape, water hose and a stack of plastic cups. Performed at The Basement Gallery, Newcastle-Upon-Tyne. Duration: 40 minutes. © Mona Hatoum, courtesy White Cube*

feminist, body-centred performance. Hatoum's interventions evince the influence of artists such as VALIE EXPORT and Carolee Schneemann, who in the 1960s and 1970s contested and overturned the neat, seamless depictions of femininity and fantasy found in the peep show, the movie theatre and the museum. EXPORT's 1968 street performance *TAPP und TASTKINO*, for example, involved a cardboard box covering the artist's bare chest and the solicitation of passers-by to 'experience' the cinema haptically by reaching inside. In Schneemann's 1975 'Interior Scroll', the artist appeared naked before an audience and slowly unwound a long strip of printed text from her vagina. The text recounted a conversation between a male and female film-maker and the elision between film and body.[65]

Recalling the cinema-centric tactile exercises of interior-exterior found in such works, *Corps étranger* plumbs Hatoum's body with the miniature endoscopic camera that paradoxically enacts and disturbs male fantasies of woman as object for pleasure and spectacle as challenged not only by artists but also by feminist film scholars. Working from apparatus and reception theories that emphasise cinema's voyeuristic gaze as facilitated – or imposed – by the paradigm of the movie theatre, Mary Ann Doane, Laura Mulvey, Kaja Silverman and others have explored the contradictory, yet entrenched situation of the gendered gaze in cinema. Doane's account is particularly germane in the present context. 'Spectatorial desire, in contemporary film theory, is generally delineated as either voyeurism or fetishism, as precisely a pleasure in seeing what is prohibited in relation to the female body', she claims. 'The image orchestrates a gaze, a limit, and its pleasurable transgression . . . To "have" the cinema is, in some sense, to "have" the woman.' Referencing Mulvey's work, Doane notes the importance of 'opposition between proximity and distance in relation to the image' in this transaction.[66] The male gaze is one predicated on distance – the woman-image being as unattainable as it is desirable, while the female gaze is narcissistic in recognising itself. 'Female specificity is thus theorised in terms of spatial proximity', and the woman's ability to distance herself, Doane posits, is through the masquerade of excessive femininity. 'The masquerade, in flaunting femininity, holds it at a distance . . . The masquerade's resistance to patriarchal positioning would therefore lie in its denial of the production of femininity as closeness, as presence-to-itself, as, precisely, imagistic.'[67] Collectively, Hatoum's performances subvert such structures by offering images of the body that trouble these distancing psychological mechanisms. Proximity and distance become entangled as spectators become aware of being 'taken in' by the structure even as they take in the spectacle set before them. As Morris notes, Hatoum's performance pieces had the ability to move from a situation 'in which the spectator was empowered – often as voyeur – to a situation in which the spectator was entrapped'.[68]

In the peep show, orifices implied or exhibited in the image may open physically within the booth's architecture in the form of the glory hole. By means of this orifice, the eye's penetration of the screen image can be supplemented with, or supplanted by, physically penetrating (or being penetrated in) one bodily orifice or another. The glory hole enacts a double penetration: that of the wall itself and that which may lie behind it. However explicit and 'depraved' the peep-show's exhibited images may be, they remain safely confined to celluloid and screen, dependent on projection mechanisms to lurch into action. The glory hole, by contrast, represents human sexual contact stripped of the normative heterosexual social armature of intimacy, emotional dependency and monogamy. The glory hole circulates uncertainty and fantasy: *Who* or *what* is that on the other side of the wall?

Immediately after *Corps étranger*, Hatoum would embark on another projection installation that raises that question by closely resembling a glory hole. *Testimony* (1995–2002) has been called 'the male counterpart to *Corps étranger*'.[69] It projects a two-minute, thirty-seven-second loop of a circular, extreme close-up of a scrotum onto the wall of 'a separate room that acts as a vestibule to the gallery' (Figure 3.9).[70] With only the elastic twitching of this rough, wrinkled surface visible within the one-foot, seven-inch circle placed low and within arm's reach, the installation and its 'rosy skin of an anonymous scrotum' bears the greatly magnified formal properties and attendant mystery of a glory hole.[71] As the sign of non-normative ideologies and

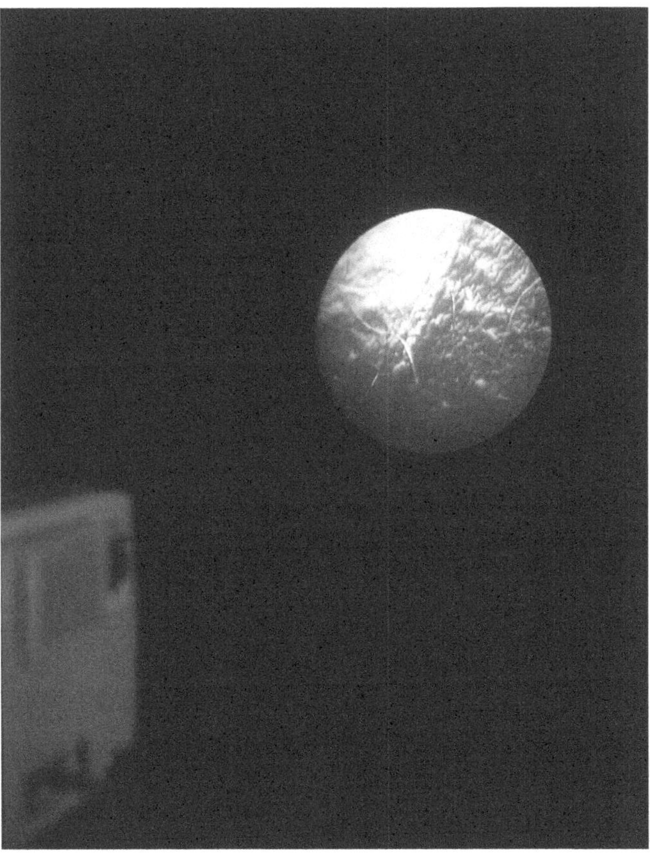

Figure 3.9　*Mona Hatoum, Testimony, 1995–2002. DVD projection, dimensions variable; duration: 2 minute, 37 second loop. © Mona Hatoum. Photo © Arturo González de Alba, courtesy Laboratorio Arte Alameda, Mexico City, Mexico*

practices threatening hegemonic stability, the glory hole as invoked in *Corps étranger* and *Testimony* can serve as a locus for Hatoum's long-sought breakdown of hierarchies. The two greatest threats of the peep show, as identified by the Meese Commission report, are abjection and gender troubling, both of which are mediated by the peep show in general and the glory hole in particular. Abjection and gender troubling inhere in *Corps étranger*. If abjection is a primary aesthetic category of *Corps étranger*, with its ground-based orientation, then gender trouble is the central action of its imagery. The stream of images does not easily read along the standard codes of gender, but it evokes the abjection of physiological processes and bodily fluids at every turn. While voyeurism remains significant to this play of gender and abjection enveloping the viewer in *Corps étranger*, it can become almost secondary by comparison.

Frances Morris claims of *Corps étranger* that 'At first sight it is "outside" culture, timeless, primitive, unchanged – virgin territory for the camera's "imperialistic" eye. However the intrusion of medical equipment, the "framing" of the sophisticated viewing chamber, establish co-ordinates that are modern, social, cultural and political: the terminology of colonialism is unavoidable. So too is the language of Gender.'[72] She explains that

> As the camera [in *Corps étranger*] encounters an orifice, it enters, and the interminable forested landscape of the surface gives ways to glowing subterranean tunnels lined with pulsating animate tissue, moist and glistening. The camera slowly lurches on downwards until it can go no further. Emerging once again onto the surface of the body, it seeks another way in. All orifices are explored in turn.[73]

Rainald Schumacher explains it thus: '*Corps étranger* shows the body in image sequences, never in its entirety, presenting all the parts as being of equal value, without making any distinction between Inside and Outside. The hierarchy of orifices, which is a construct of social conventions, rules and taboos, no longer applies here.'[74] For her part, Ewa Lajer-Burcharth contends 'While the space of projection may have recalled the [peep-show] booths of the pornographic industry, it obviously did not accord the spectator the same position of externality and distance from the viewed body. Hatoum made you step *inside* the body . . . transformed you into a kind of internal anatomical voyeur.'[75] In other words, once inside the chamber that is *Corps étranger*, spectators already find themselves *under* the skin in this piece. Their hypodermic entrance exacerbates the confusion of the screen's own hyper-hypo split as the video projection cuts back and forth from exterior images of skin, hair follicles, sclera and cornea to interior views of rectum, oesophagus, cervix and auditory canal.

Spectators find themselves hopelessly in-between, and commentators on the work often return to the threat that its inside-out play poses to the spectator's spatial stability.[76] 'Without warning[,] the camera enters each orifice it approaches: tunnels of wet, soft, tubular forms follow until the lens surfaces through another orifice to the exterior of the body, only to reenter again', Jessica Morgan comments.[77] In such descriptions, gender is rarely invoked, identified or established. It is more often *the* body, rather than a *male* or *female* body. In collapsing distances – the distance of the comprehensive view and the distance of cultural apparatuses of visuality such as the gendered viewing theorised by Doane, not to mention the physical distance between spectator and screen – the projected body is stripped of most cultural and anatomical indicators of gender. The images are shot in such extreme close-up, and often depict such (visually) unfamiliar zones of the body that at first glance it may not be possible to identify the object as a human. In its predominantly genderless performance, the body remains unfixable and alien. Depending on what moment in the loop spectators begin viewing, even once the images are identified as constituting a body there may be a considerable interval before anyone hazards to assign it a gender. 'The images projected could belong to any human body. Even the gender of the body is of secondary importance', observes Volker Adolphs.[78] The gendered gaze, instrument of tremendous power in assuring societal social hierarchy, is placed at risk by the chamber.

Hatoum's descriptions of the work, however, reflect an attempt to make gender legible for the audience. She 'wanted to give the feeling that the body becomes vulnerable in the face of the scientific eye, probing it, invading its boundaries', she notes. 'On the other hand ... when you enter the room, in places, you feel like you are on the edge of an abyss that can swallow you up, the devouring womb, the vagina dentata, castration anxiety ...'[79] Although Hatoum's description involves signifiers of female gender, her emphasis on psychoanalytic terms in describing the installation's effect presents the possibility of gender identification deriving just as easily from a lack of determinate evidence of gender – and female as representing lack – as from the presence of any physical markers of gender. The perception of a brink mentioned by Hatoum originates in part from the spectator's wait for a marker that may or may not present itself. Gender ambiguity may indeed be the most troubling outcome to the spectator because it situates gender as mere projection (whether that projection originates with the viewer or is communicated by an outside authority). Like the peep show, *Corps étranger* therefore offers a space wherein culturally fixed gender – and all the behavioural assumptions it entails – may come unhinged.

ABJECTION

Josh Alan Friedman's account of a sex shop at lunchtime in New York City's Times Square in the late 1970s echoes that of the Meese Commission report, minus the latter's censorious tone. 'There are twenty occupied booths', Friedman writes. 'Cocks of every age, race and size are being drawn out in the booths. Some will spurt onto the walls, some into Kleenex, some will even discharge into fifty-cent French tickler condoms from the store's vending machine. These will be discarded on the floor.'[80] For authorities faced with such conditions, Susan Stewart concludes, peep-show booths 'horrifyingly mime[d] the contamination of bodily orifices' by materialising presumed non-normative fantasies.[81]

As mentioned above, Schumacher notes that *Corps étranger* – much like the peep show – breaks down divisions between inside and outside and overturns the hierarchy of parts and orifices. Just as the peep show can represent both orifice and contamination through design features and the physical and visual orientation of the spectator, *Corps étranger* establishes conditions for vacillation between inside and outside, though in the very different context of the museum (Figure 3.10). In this ambiguity, the intersection of images of bodily passages and constricted spaces that increase the likelihood of a spectator's contact with wall, screen, projection and other spectators can raise the fear – or fantasy – of contaminating and being contaminated. This potential renders in physical terms abjection as it has been theorised by Julia Kristeva. In Kristeva's well-known formulation, the abject is 'what disturbs identity, system, order. What does not respect borders, positions, rules. The inbetween, the ambiguous, the composite.'[82] Elsewhere, she explains that

> I insist on the privative aspect: 'ab-ject', which means for me that one is neither subject nor object. When one is in a state of abjection, the borders between the object and the subject cannot be maintained . . . This crisis of person, which I call abjection and which is a state of dissolution, can be experienced either as suffering or as rapture.[83]

In *Bodies that Matter*, Judith Butler applies Kristeva's theory of the abject to the formation of the normative subject. For Butler, abjection is the 'threatening spectre' whose rejection allows the normative subject to emerge. 'The subject is constituted through the force of exclusion and abjection', Butler argues, producing 'a constitutive outside to the subject, an abjected outside, which is, after all, "inside" the subject as its own founding repudiation'. For Butler, within heterosexual hegemony 'abjected or delegitimated bodies fail to count as "bodies"'.[84] As she states

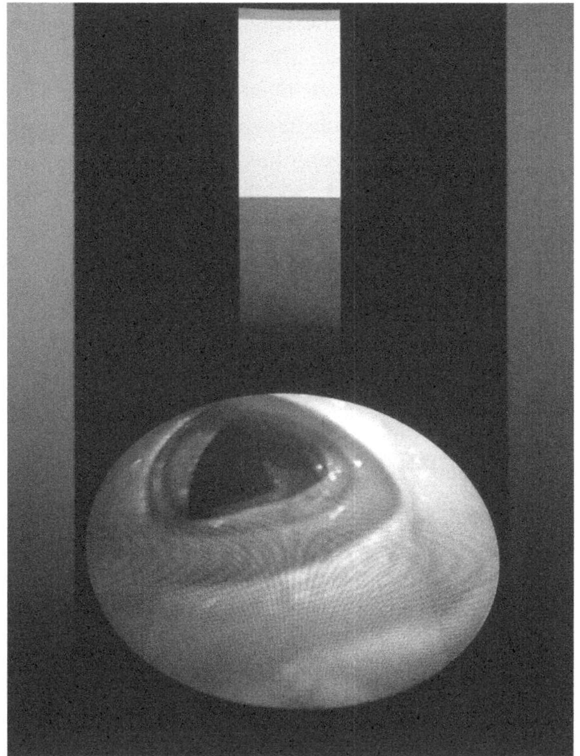

Figure 3.10   *Mona Hatoum,* Corps étranger, *1994. Video installation with cylindrical wooden structure, video projector, video player, amplifier and four speakers, 137¹³/₁₆ x 118¹/₈ x 118¹/₈ in. (350 x 300 x 300 cm). © Mona Hatoum. Photo © Philippe Migeat, courtesy Centre Pompidou, Paris*

in another context, it is through this process that 'Others become shit'.[85] Spectacularising this problematic formation of subject-from-abjection, *Corps étranger* serves both reactionary and radical understandings of abjection, which by 1994 had been influenced by a decade of coping with AIDS and the public panics the virus had unleashed. In speaking of the 1995 *Rites of Passage* exhibition that included *Corps étranger*, Kristeva notes that the sense of abjection evoked by some of the works displayed would allow for two reactions:

> There are those who repress this state of crisis, who refuse to acknowledge it, in which case they either don't come or they find the works disgusting, stupid, insipid, insignificant, and wonder why the curators bothered. Others may be looking for a form of catharsis. When they look at these objects, their ugliness and their strangeness, they see their own regressions, their own abjection, and at that moment what occurs is a veritable state of communion.[86]

The dark walls, the holes and the sticky floors of the peep-show booth create an environment that raises 'the terrifying possibility of a return to, and absorption in, the sexual orifices'.[87] *Corps étranger* is another dark environment, yet extraordinarily clean when matched against accounts of peep shows. The installation's possibilities for befouling and contaminating, whether physical or psychological, are not through bodily emissions but rather the possibility of contact with the floor-based screen and the projector beam that transmit and render images of bodily tissues moist with fluids. '[*Corps étranger's*] whole scenario brings the spectators to stare down, down, into a tunnel of churning viscera unfolding at their feet and threatening to swallow them', Guy Brett states.[88] Placing these potentially troubling images on the floor to produce such an effect was the artist's single, major change to the work's design between 1980 and 1994. Hatoum has said that she 'wanted it to be a circular projection on the floor so you could actually walk on it'.[89] Just as the peep show offered fantasies of intimacy and proximity 'compelling in return an active and equally intimate corporeal response', this floor-based projection surface literally encroaches on the spectator's ground while grafting the imaged body onto the presumed site of bodily contamination – the peep-show floor as receptive surface of bodily fluids.[90]

Screen contamination represents a two-fold process in *Corps étranger* by placing the spectator in the paradoxical situation of contaminating while being contaminated. At the physical level, stepping on the plastic laminate of the work's bright, white screen transforms spectators into agents of contamination as the screen risks scuffing, staining and marking underfoot.[91] Psychologically, spectators may feel contaminated as their bodies cross into the space of projection and the glistening cavities of the imaged body move across skin and clothing. Spectators' bodies become temporally absorbed in the supposedly abject body placed under them or, as Nadia Tazi describes it, they are 'sucked up into abjection'.[92]

Just as one can question the extent to which the contents of the video read as female, particularly for those spectators who do not remain for the nearly twelve minutes of the entire loop, the possibility of contact and the inevitably of contact represent very different propositions.[93] Where several of the foregoing accounts recognise potentiality, Christine Ross has stressed inevitability. In her detailed account of the phenomenological consequences of *Corps étranger*, Ross claims abjection is rooted in an unavoidable tactility built into the work's architecture. According to Ross, the spectator cannot escape physical contact with either the screen or fellow spectators. 'Abjection is and remains a constant. Why? Because in *Corps étranger* the viewer never ceases to enter into contact with the other, even if he or she often does so in an unconscious or involuntary manner', she states. The exhibition of the imaged body becomes the opportunity for bodily encounters between spectators. 'If the installation problematizes the body and sexuality as models of depth and absence, if it attempts to bring about a transformation of the body into surface, it does so by employing a tactility performed by the viewer who thereby becomes engaged in a meeting of surfaces (between her or his shoes and the screen or her or his skin and that of others in the same space)', Ross explains.[94] 'In the first instance', she maintains

> the body is represented as incorporated (as much by the camera that penetrates it as by the viewer who follows its movement); in the second instance, the body becomes an incorporating power to the extent that, by following the intrusive action of the camera, viewers feel themselves absorbed by what they are so intently looking at, as if they themselves were being pulled down into the profound darkness of the body's cavities.[95]

Merging physical contact and visual perception, Ankori's reading of *Corps étranger* supports Ross' claims. She similarly asserts that 'Hatoum forces the viewers to trespass upon her body and experience a disturbing "voyage" through her entrails'.[96]

Despite these descriptions, it is important to note that *Corps étranger* does not *force* contact – whether between spectators or between spectator and screen – any more than it forces spectators to enter or remain within its structure. In placing too much regulatory power in the work's parameters, commentators such as Ross and Ankori may discount the range of actions available to the spectator, thereby diminishing the important role of agency and desire. It is this range, in fact, that makes the installation a powerfully disruptive space on par with peep-show booths or other liminal sites facilitating non-normative social behaviour. If the actions described by Ross and Ankori were inevitable, *Corps étranger* would be far less complex and challenging. It is as much the spectator's power to choose to deliberately touch the screen – resting in close proximity to the foot but relatively removed from the eyes of museum guards and surveillance cameras – that contributes to the transgressive power of this work. Each spectator's decision – to touch, to avoid touching, to stay or go when others enter, to rub elbows or cross the screen in the presence of others – hinges on a recognition of the space as lying just beyond the standard social structures imposed by public places like the museum gallery. As Morris points out, 'The cylinder creates a space that is both inside and part of, yet also separate from[,] the space of the museum'.[97] No matter where spectators stand in *Corps étranger*, the surrounding gallery remains within view, yet there is no spot that allows a full view of the entryways. Spectators may either face one entryway with their backs to the other or accept angled views of both. Like the descriptions of peep-show booths with faulty locks, doors ajar, and holes or slots for viewing or other activity, the spectator will always have within view a glimpse onto another space, but the view is always limited, suggesting that any view in from that other space is equally restricted.

Untangling the Tingle

Within *Corps étranger*'s constricted space, the compounded signifying charges of peephole, glory hole and bodily passage all converge on the white disc at its centre. The projection screen holds all the promise and danger of a hole for seeing, touching, penetrating and evacuating. While some may be repulsed by its images and uncomfortable within its dark confines, *Corps étranger* opens up a space of subversive potential. As it evokes the institutional eye in its mimesis of medical imaging, its appropriation of peep-show design can read as respite from – or reinforcement of – the authoritarian gaze of the institution. That *Corps étranger* takes pornography and its exhibition as a reference to mimic, explore and deconstruct – in addition to the work's links to medical imaging, exile and Otherness – is confirmed by Hatoum's recycling of the installation's images in a subsequent work, *Deep Throat* (1996).

Deep Throat directly invokes commercial pornography by appropriating the title of the 1972 hit porn film by Gerard Damiano, which placed hardcore pornography at the centre of mainstream society for the first time.[98] This follow-up installation employs the intestinal tract footage of *Corps étranger*, displayed on a video screen embedded into a dinner plate placed on a simple, yet elegantly set dining table (Figure 3.11). Damiano's film depicts a young American woman in the suburbs who claims to be ready to marry and 'settle down', but once she discovers her only means of sexual climax is stimulating the inside of her throat she embarks instead on a multi-partner oral-sex spree. 'How far does a girl have to go to untangle her tingle?' the film's original poster provocatively asked moviegoers. The plot suggested she had to go everywhere and nowhere as she put herself in different spaces and situations in search of a sensation felt well within the body.

Integrating images of bodily passages into a décor of quintessential domesticity, Hatoum's *Deep Throat* ingeniously renders in material terms the movie plot's central conflict (Figure 3.12). However, when Hatoum's installation appeared among such objects as Jake and Dinos Chapman's mannequins of mutant children with penis noses in the exhibition *Sensation: Young British Art from the Saatchi Collection* at the Royal Academy of Arts in 1997, the porn film it invoked must already have seemed a quaint

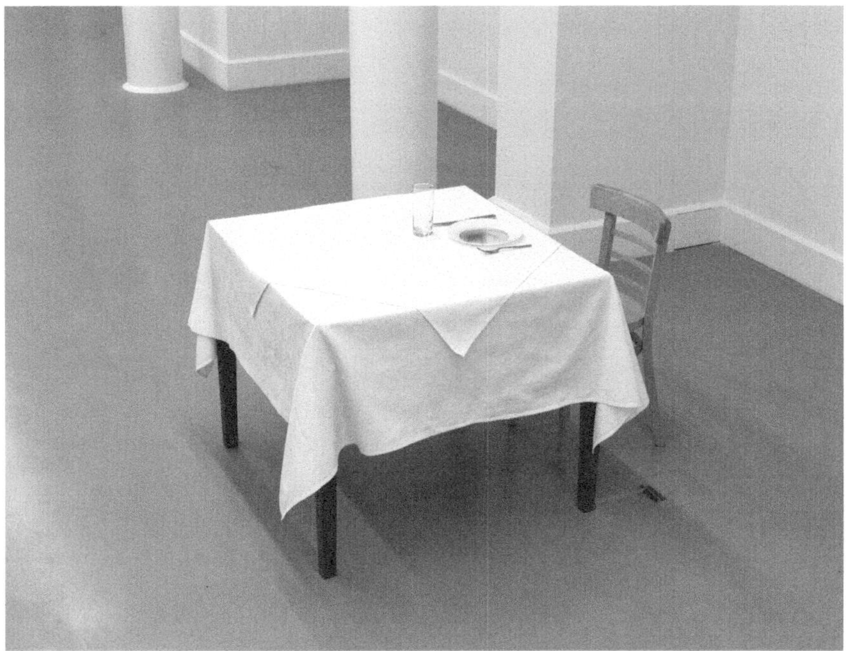

Figure 3.11   *Mona Hatoum*, Deep Throat, *1996. Table, chair, tablecloths, plate, fork, knife, water glass, monitor and DVD player, 35¹/₁₆ x 33⁷/₁₆ x 51³/₁₆ in. (89 x 85 x 130 cm). © Mona Hatoum. Photo © Hadiye Cangökçe, courtesy Arter, Istanbul and White Cube*

memory.[99] The integration of pornographic films into mainstream movie-theatre culture had been short-lived as other means of distribution and exhibition – first the peep show, then home video – offered more suitable conditions for intimate interactions among spectators. As *Corps étranger* and *Deep Throat* circulated through gallery and museum exhibitions in the late 1990s, not only was the peep show on its way out – diminished by the era of AIDS and definitively replaced as an exhibition model by cable TV and internet porn – but the viability of cinema itself was being called into question as film reached its centenary. Pressured by cable, satellite and digitisation, some wondered whether cinema could survive and, if so, under what circumstances. The question would open the door to a range of artistic responses, as artists and curators recognised the *zeitgeist* and seized the opportunity to mine a century of movies and movie going – already suggested in Hatoum's renaming of the *Corps étranger* footage for her *Deep Throat* installation – in what would become a flood of activity around film in the museum space. In that rush to recognise cinema, the diversity of its forms throughout the twentieth century would be overlooked frequently.

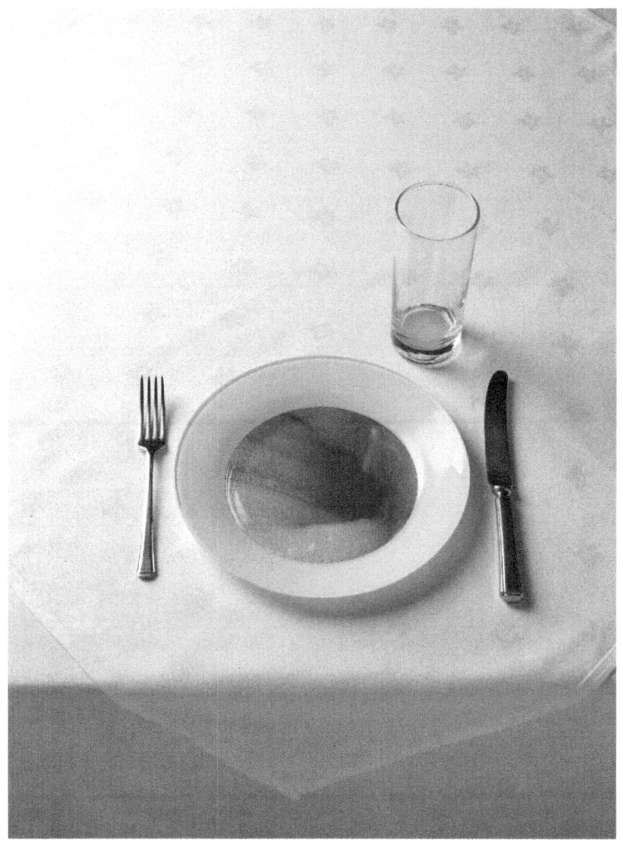

Figure 3.12	*Mona Hatoum,* Deep Throat, *1996. Table, chair, tablecloths, plate, fork, knife, water glass, monitor and DVD player, 35¹/₁₆ x 33⁷/₁₆ x 51³/₁₆ in. (89 x 85 x 130 cm). © Mona Hatoum. Photo © Hadiye Cangokçe, courtesy Arter, Istanbul and White Cube*

Notes

1. *Midnight Cowboy* (John Schlesinger, 1969) was nominated for several Academy Awards and won in the Best Picture, Directing and Writing categories. *Last Tango in Paris* (Bernardo Bertolucci, 1972) was nominated in the Best Actor and Directing categories. Both were released with an X rating from the Motion Picture Association of America.
2. Jack Stevenson, 'Grindhouse and Beyond', in John Cline and Robert G. Weiner (eds), *From the Arthouse to the Grindhouse: Highbrow and Lowbrow Transgression in Cinema's First Century* (Lanham: Scarecrow Press, 2010), p. 132.
3. *Mona Hatoum*, Musée national d'art moderne, Centre Georges Pompidou, 8 June–22 August 1994.

4. Gannit Ankori, *Palestinian Art* (London: Reaktion Books, 2006), p. 134; Mona Hatoum, as quoted in Janine Antoni, 'Mona Hatoum Interviewed by Janine Antoni', in Laura Steward Heon (ed.), *Mona Hatoum: Domestic Disturbance* (North Adams: Massachusetts Museum of Contemporary Art, 2001), p. 29; Claudia Spinelli, 'Interview with Mona Hatoum', *Das Kunst-Bulletin* 9 (September 1996): 16–23, reprinted in Michael Archer, Guy Brett, M. Catherine de Zegher and Mona Hatoum, *Mona Hatoum* (London and New York: Phaidon Press, 1997), p. 138; Frances Morris, 'Mona Hatoum', in Stuart Morgan and Frances Morris (eds), *Rites of Passage: Art for the End of the Century* (London: Tate Gallery, 1995), p. 102; Hans-Jürgen Buderer, 'Between Shock and Banality: Examples of a Topical Art Scenery', in Hans-Jürgen Buderer and Thomas Köllhofer (eds), *Dimensions: Fünf Künstler aus Großbritannien* (Mannheim: Städtische Kunsthalle Mannheim, 1996), p. 81; Christine Ross, 'To Touch the Other: A Story of Corpo-electronic Surfaces', in Amelia Jones (ed.), *The Feminism and Visual Culture Reader* (London and New York: Routledge, 2003), p. 516; Giorgio Verzotti, *Mona Hatoum* (Milan: Charta, 1999), p. 29; Ewa Lajer-Burcharth, 'Real Bodies: Video in the 1990s', *Art History* 20:2 (June 1997): 185–213, p. 195; Michael Archer, 'Mona Hatoum', in Buderer and Köllhofer (eds), *Dimensions*, p. 87.
5. Desa Philippi, 'Mona Hatoum: Some Any No Every Body', in M. Catherine de Zegler (ed.), *Inside the Visible: An Elliptical Traverse of 20th Century Art in, of, and from the Feminine* (Cambridge, MA: MIT Press, 1996), p. 17.
6. Lajer-Burcharth, 'Real Bodies', p. 199.
7. Friedrich A. Kittler, *Gramophone, Film, Typewriter*, trans. Geoffrey Winthrop-Young and Michael Wutz (Stanford: Stanford University Press, 1999), p. 128.
8. Hatoum comments, 'In general my work is about my experience of living in the West as a person from the Third World, about being an outsider, about occupying a marginal position, being excluded, being defined as "Other" or as one of "Them"'. Sara Diamond, 'An Interview with Mona Hatoum', *Fuse* 10:5 (April 1987): 46–52, reprinted in Archer, Brett, de Zegher and Hatoum, *Mona Hatoum*, p. 127.
9. Hatoum, as quoted in Spinelli, 'Interview with Mona Hatoum', in Archer, Brett, de Zegher and Hatoum, *Mona Hatoum*, p. 138.
10. Guy Brett, 'A Hatoum Chronology', in Mona Hatoum, Desa Philippi and Guy Brett, *Mona Hatoum* (Bristol: Arnolfini, 1993), p. 17.
11. Michael Archer, 'Interview: Michael Archer in Conversation with Mona Hatoum', in Archer, Brett, de Zegher and Hatoum, *Mona Hatoum*, p. 13.
12. Hatoum explains, 'I called it *Corps étranger*, which means "foreign body", because the camera is in a sense this alien device introduced from the outside. Also, it is about how we are closest to our body, and yet it is a foreign territory, which could, for instance, be consumed by disease long before we become aware of it. The "foreign body" also refers literally to the body of a foreigner.' Mona Hatoum, as quoted in Antoni, 'Mona Hatoum Interviewed by Janine Antoni', in Heon, *Mona Hatoum*, p. 29.
13. Mona Hatoum, 'Proposal for the New Contemporaries 1981: "WATERWORKS"

(Video Installation)', reproduced in Archer, Brett, de Zegher and Hatoum, *Mona Hatoum*, p. 116.

14. Email correspondence with Mona Hatoum, 28 August 2015.

15. Hatoum, as quoted in Spinelli, 'Interview with Mona Hatoum', in Archer, Brett, de Zegher and Hatoum, *Mona Hatoum*, p. 137.

16. Ibid. p. 137.

17. Clive Cookson, 'Technology: "Magnets that Look Inside the Body"', *The Times* (2 October 1981), p. 21; Pearce Wright, 'Science Report: A New Aid in the Fight Against Cancer', *The Times* (18 June 1981), p. 2.

18. Cookson, 'Technology: "Magnets that Look Inside the Body"', p. 21.

19. Raymond Damadian, 'Apparatus and Method for Detecting Cancer in Tissue', US patent 3789832 A, 17 March 1972.

20. Ankori, *Palestinian Art*, p. 135; Hatoum, as quoted in Spinelli, 'Interview with Mona Hatoum', in Archer, Brett, de Zegher and Hatoum, *Mona Hatoum*, p. 138.

21. Mona Hatoum, as quoted in Antoni, 'Mona Hatoum Interviewed by Janine Antoni', in Heon, *Mona Hatoum*, p. 21. This recalls Michel Foucault's theorisation of the clinic and medical diagnosis as modern means to control populations by classifying, identifying and treating abnormality. See Michel Foucault, *The Birth of the Clinic: An Archaeology of Medical Perception*, trans. A. M. Sheridan (New York: Pantheon Books, 1973).

22. Patrick O'Donovan, 'Furtive Soho Lives in Plastic', *The Observer* (15 February 1981), p. 6.

23. Michael Horsnell, 'Soho Sex Establishments Proliferate Despite Promises', *The Times* (29 January 1981), p. 4; O'Donovan, 'Furtive Soho Lives in Plastic', p. 6.

24. David Hunn, 'When Porn in Soho is an Obscene Rip-off', *The Observer* (2 December 1979), p. 2.

25. It is worth noting that *Peeping Tom*, the well-known 1960 Michael Powell film about a serial killer who films the stalking and murder of his victims, is set in Soho. Powell's treatment of misogyny, violence and filmic mediation perfectly fits the West End's post-war image as a center of commodified sex and depravity. The protagonist's use of the camera lens as literally both viewing device and weapon has made *Peeping Tom* a prime case study in scholarly explorations of cinematic voyeurism and gender issues. The operations at work in this film, both narratively and meta-narratively, foreshadow Hatoum's engagement with the camera as agent for the subjugation and violation of the body from her 1980s performances through the creation of *Corps étranger*.

26. For example in 1977, or two years after Hatoum's arrival, London police raided the Compton for projecting Pier Paolo Pasolini's *Salo, 120 Days of Sodom*. See Ed Glinert, *West End Chronicles: 300 Years of Glamour and Excess in the Heart of London* (London: Allen Lane, 2007), p. 113.

27. Laurence O'Toole, *Pornocopia: Porn, Sex, Technology and Desire* (London: Serpent's Tail, 1998), p. 101.

28. As quoted in Brian Smart, 'Offensiveness in the Williams Report', *Philosophy* 59:230 (October 1984): 516–22, p. 516.

29. This statement is attributed to Bernard Brook-Partridge, spokesman for the Conservative-controlled Greater London Council. 'Sex Film Raids in Soho', *The Guardian* (6 October 1977), p. 22.

30. These remarks are attributed to Bernard Braine, a Conservative MP from south-east Essex, in 'Protests at Sex Shop Proposals: Pornography', *The Times* (4 February 1982), p. 4.

31. For example, an *Observer* reporter mentions copies of *AC/DC*, an American bisexual magazine, on sale at a Soho shop. Hunn, 'When Porn in Soho is an Obscene Rip-off', p. 2.

32. Lauren Berlant and Michael Warner, 'Sex in Public', *Critical Inquiry* 24:2 (1998): 547–66, p. 554.

33. Ibid. p. 553.

34. Ibid. p. 562.

35. O'Donovan, 'Furtive Soho Lives in Plastic', p. 6; Denis Herbstein, 'Tough Laws Halve Soho Sex Shops', *The Observer* (13 February 1983), p. 2; Shyama Perera, 'Soho's Shops State a Case', *The Guardian* (2 August 1983), p. 2.

36. Shiranikha Horbert, "Law Report: No Let-out for the Peepshow," *The Guardian* (23 March 1990), p. 39.

37. Erotic peep shows had developed by World War II, when distributors converted Panoram projection boxes meant for viewing short musical and instructional films to use with burlesque and cheesecake shorts by masking off the display window and fitting it with a viewfinder for more personalised viewing. 'Gorgeous glamour lovelies in full color behind protective glass make an artistic presentation', reads a 1944 *Billboard* ad for Hollywood Peep Shows. 'Imagine the "come on" feature of this artistic display', it urges readers, illustrating a box bearing a 'For art students only' warning above the window. Amy Herzog notes that several invention claims exist, citing Martin Hodas' installation of booths in a Times Square bookstore in 1967. Herzog claims that the peep show had been 'a fairly continuous presence', at least in North America, since the invention of film, but that the 'modern-day' peep show dates to the 1960s. Amy Herzog, 'In the Flesh: Space and Embodiment in the Pornographic Peep Show Arcade', *The Velvet Light Trap* 62 (Fall 2008): 29–43, pp. 31–2. See also Amy Herzog, 'Fetish Machines: Peep Shows, Co-optation, and Technological Adaptation', in Jillian Saint Jacques (ed.), *Adaptation Theories* (Maastricht: Jan van Eyck Academie, 2011).

38. As quoted in Legs McNeil, Jennifer Osborne and Peter Pavia, *The Other Hollywood: The Uncensored Oral History of the Porn Industry* (New York: Regan Books, 2005), p. 106.

39. O'Toole, *Pornocopia*, p. 103.

40. Andrew Veitch, 'Girls, Girls, Girls', *The Guardian* (21 May 1979), p. 11.

41. One could relate this to Roland Barthes' and Jean-Louis Baudry's theorisations of the cinema space as a multi-layered apparatus separating the viewer from the street. See Barthes, 'Upon Leaving the Movie Theater', trans. Bertrand Augst and Susan White, in Theresa Hak Kyung Cha (ed.), *Apparatus, Cinematographic*

Apparatus: Selected Writings (New York: Tanam Press, 1980); Jean-Louis Baudry, 'Ideological Effects of the Basic Cinematographic Apparatus', trans. Alan Williams, *Film Quarterly* 28:2 (Winter 1974–5): 39–47.

42. Attorney General's Commission on Pornography, *Attorney General's Commission on Pornography: Final Report* (Washington, DC: US Government Printing Office, 1986), pp. 1473–5.

43. Gertud Koch, 'The Body's Shadow Realm', trans. Jan-Christopher Horak and Joyce Rheuban, *October* 50 (Fall 1989): 3–29, p. 8.

44. Herzog, 'In the Flesh', p. 36.

45. Ibid. p. 30.

46. Ibid. p. 29.

47. Ibid. p. 41.

48. Susan Stewart, *Crimes of Writing* (New York: Oxford University Press, 1991), p. 243.

49. Attorney General's Commission on Pornography, *Attorney General's Commission on Pornography*, p. 1476.

50. Ibid. pp. 457–8.

51. Antonello *et al.* v. City of San Diego, 16 Cal. App. 3d 162 (1971). See http://law.justia.com/cases/california/calapp3d/16/161.html (accessed 1 September 2015).

52. Attorney General's Commission on Pornography, *Attorney General's Commission on Pornography*, p. 1471. Gordon Hawkins and Franklin Zimring note elsewhere that 'booths are partitioned, four-sided cubicles generally made out of wood or plaster with dimensions on the average of about three by five feet.' Movies 'may last from ten to twenty minutes'. Gordon Hawkins and Franklin E. Zimring, *Pornography in a Free Society* (Cambridge: Cambridge University Press, 1988), p. 44.

53. Morris, 'Mona Hatoum', in Morgan and Morris (eds), *Rites of Passage*, p. 103.

54. Ross, 'To Touch the Other', in Jones (ed.), *The Feminism and Visual Culture Reader*, p. 519.

55. Volker Adolphs, 'The Body and the World', in Mona Hatoum and Christoph Heinrich, *Mona Hatoum* (Ostfildern-Ruit: Hatje-Cantz, 2004), p. 48.

56. Hamid Naficy, *An Accented Cinema: Exilic and Diasporic Filmmaking* (Princeton and Oxford: Princeton University Press, 2001), p. 119.

57. Buderer, 'Between Shock and Banality', in Buderer and Köllhofer (eds), *Dimensions*, p. 81.

58. Desa Philippi, 'Do Not Touch', in Hatoum, Philippi and Brett, *Mona Hatoum*, p. 13.

59. Hatoum, as quoted in Antoni, 'Mona Hatoum Interviewed by Janine Antoni', in Heon, *Mona Hatoum*, p. 29.

60. Helen Potkin, 'Performance Art', in Fiona Carson and Claire Pajackzkowska (eds), *Feminist Visual Culture* (New York: Routledge, 2001), pp. 76–7.

61. Catherine Elwes, 'Notes from a Video Performance by Mona Hatoum', in Rhea Anastas and Michael Brenson (eds), *Witness to Her Art: Art and Writings by Adrian*

Piper, Mona Hatoum, Cady Noland, Jenny Holzer, Kara Walker, Daniela Rosell, and Eau de Cologne (New York: The Center for Curatorial Studies, Bard College, 2006), p. 118.

62. Mona Hatoum and Michael Archer, 'Michael Archer in Conversation with Mona Hatoum', in Archer, Brett, de Zegher and Hatoum, *Mona Hatoum*, p. 10.

63. As quoted in Guy Brett, 'Itinerary', in Archer, Brett, de Zegher and Hatoum, *Mona Hatoum*, p. 38.

64. Hatoum and Archer, 'Michael Archer in Conversation with Mona Hatoum', in Archer, Brett, de Zegher and Hatoum, *Mona Hatoum*, pp. 10–11. The work was refused by the ICA as an invasion of privacy, despite prior acceptance by the institute's New Contemporaries exhibition committee. The ICA told Hatoum that 'the toilets are in a public space, where people have not made a conscious decision to be confronted by art'. It was subsequently banned from Hatoum's graduation show at Slade. Ibid. p. 11.

65. In addition to these two works, New York artist Anita Steckel created a visual piece entitled *Feminist Peep Show* in 1972–3 that appeared at several arts events in that city in the mid-1970s. See Ruth Gilbert, 'In and Around Town', *New York* (25 February 1974), p. 29.

66. Mary Ann Doane, 'Film and the Masquerade: Theorising the Female Spectator', *Screen* 23:3–4 (September –October 1982): 74–87, pp. 76–7.

67. Doane notes Christian Metz's observations that voyeurism remains at the top of the social hierarchy of the senses. Socially accepted arts – like theatre or cinema – rely on senses at a distance, while the lower arts – culinary, perfumery – require proximity. Doane, 'Film and the Masquerade', pp. 79, 81–2.

68. Morris, 'Mona Hatoum', in Morgan and Morris (eds), *Rites of Passage*, p. 103.

69. Ursula Panhans-Bühler, 'Being Involved', in Christopher Heinrich (ed.), *Mona Hatoum* (Ostfildern-Ruit: Hatje Cantz, 2004), p. 21.

70. This is the description of the work as it was exhibited in Mexico City in 2002. Francisco Reyes Palma, '"Drink Me", "Eat Me"', in Mona Hatoum, *Mona Hatoum* (Mexico City: Laboratorio Arte Alameda, 2002), p. 71.

71. Adolphs, 'The Body and the World', in Hatoum and Heinrich (eds), *Mona Hatoum*, p. 50.

72. Morris, 'Mona Hatoum', in Morgan and Morris (eds), *Rites of Passage*, p. 105.

73. Ibid. pp. 102–3.

74. Rainald Schumacher, 'Mona Hatoum', in Rainald Schumacher and Matthias Winzen (eds), *Just Love Me: Post/Feminist Positions of the 1990s from the Goetz Collection* (Cologne: Walther König, 2003), p. 65.

75. Lajer-Burcharth, 'Real Bodies', p. 200; emphasis in text.

76. See for example Dan Cameron, 'Boundary Issues', in Mona Hatoum, Jessica Morgan and Dan Cameron, *Mona Hatoum* (Chicago: Museum of Contemporary Art, 1997); Adolphs, 'The Body and the World', in Hatoum and Heinrich (eds), *Mona Hatoum*.

77. Jessica Morgan, 'The Poetics of Uncovering', in Hatoum, Morgan and Cameron, *Mona Hatoum*, p. 2.

78. Adolphs, 'The Body and the World', in Hatoum and Heinrich (eds), *Mona Hatoum*, p. 48.

79. Hatoum, as quoted in Spinelli, 'Interview with Mona Hatoum', in Archer, Brett, de Zegher and Hatoum, *Mona Hatoum*, p. 138.

80. Josh Alan Friedman, as quoted in James Traub, *The Devil's Playground: A Century of Pleasure and Profit in Times Square* (New York: Random House, 2004), p. 191.

81. Stewart also notes that elsewhere in the report peep-show booths are described as 'filthy beyond description.' Stewart, *Crimes of Writing*, p. 243.

82. Julia Kristeva, *Powers of Horror: An Essay on Abjection*, trans. Leon S. Roudiez, (New York: Columbia University Press, 1982), p. 4.

83. Charles Penwarden and Julia Kristeva, 'Of Word and Flesh: An Interview with Julia Kristeva', in Morgan and Morris (eds), *Rites of Passage*, p. 22.

84. Judith Butler, *Bodies That Matter: On the Discursive Limits of 'Sex'* (New York and London: Routledge, 1993), pp. 3, 15.

85. Judith Butler, *Gender Trouble: Feminism and the Subversion of Identity* (New York and London: Routledge, 1990), p. 134. Butler's conclusion here derives from an exploration of the work of Iris Young and Kristeva.

86. Penwarden and Kristeva, 'Of Word and Flesh', in Morgan and Morris (eds), *Rites of Passage*, p. 23.

87. Stewart, *Crimes of Writing*, p. 243.

88. Brett, 'Itinerary', in Archer, Brett, de Zegher and Hatoum, *Mona Hatoum*, p. 70.

89. Hatoum, as quoted in Spinelli, 'Interview with Mona Hatoum', in Archer, Brett, de Zegher and Hatoum, *Mona Hatoum*, p. 138.

90. Herzog, 'In the Flesh', p. 29.

91. This was the author's experience of the work during its presentation in the Centre Pompidou's *elles@centrepompidou* exhibition (27 May 2009–21 February 2011). On multiple visits during the exhibition's two-year run, the screen bore signs of having been trod upon.

92. Nadia Tazi, 'Duelle', in Centre Georges Pompidou, *Mona Hatoum* (Paris: Centre Georges Pompidou, 1994), p. 21. 'transgression cathartique . . . du pur et de l'impur, du dedans et du dehors tels qu'ils ne se séparent plus, mais s'aspirent dans l'abjection'. Author's translation.

93. The precise duration of the video is eleven minutes, forty-nine seconds.

94. Ross, 'To Touch the Other', in Jones (ed.), *The Feminism and Visual Culture Reader*, p. 519.

95. Ibid. p. 517.

96. Ankori, *Palestinian Art*, pp. 135–6.

97. Morris, 'Mona Hatoum', in Morgan and Morris, *Rites of Passage*, p. 103. Such considerations remain an issue for exhibiting projections in gallery and museum spaces. While improvements in projector technology allow for adequate display in relatively bright spaces, darkened rooms remain the norm. The most common solutions for cutting out gallery light are curtains, doors or narrow corridors into the projection space. Unlike *Corps étranger*, these options often create spaces completely outside the gallery guard's view.

98. *Deep Throat*'s success marks a brief period in the early 1970s when legalised hard-core porn had become fashionable. The film's star, Linda Lovelace, appeared on the covers of *Time* and *Newsweek*, and *The New York Times* called the film 'porno chic'. Ralph Blumenthal, 'Porno Chic', *New York Times Sunday Magazine* (21 January 1973), p. 28.

99. Hatoum laments 'I didn't want to be part of that. [Saatchi] managed to get hold of a couple of works and that was why I was in Sensation.' Michael Hutak, 'Exile from Main Street', *The Bulletin with Newsweek* 123:12 (22 March 2005), p. 62.

CHAPTER 4

A Monument in Ruins: Douglas Gordon, Screen Archaeology and the Drive-in

In a bare patch of the Mojave Desert in the Bullion Mountains of California, 150 miles east of Los Angeles near the town of Twentynine Palms, a white screen rose under the late-summer sun in September 2001. Like a white-washed billboard, or the abandoned screen tower of a drive-in movie theatre, this uncanny structure evoked the neglected remains of modern culture, caught between interstate freeways and networks of new routes in the recently declared digital 'superhighway' of the World Wide Web.[1] As the sun set on the desert, an image began to emerge across the surface of this mute, material testimony to the voracious speed of contemporary consumerism and technological obsolescence. The image slowly filled the screen's empty spaces like a photographic print bathed in developer (Figure 4.1). It would reveal cowboys on horseback fording a river, or a family gathering for dinner in their rough-hewn cabin, or the iconic eroded buttes of Monument Valley lying 500 miles to the northeast. The image hovered, silent and still, its glowing Technicolor hues contrasting sharply with the scoured sand and brush of the desert. Its changes were imperceptibly slow, even when compared with the quiet surroundings, lingering like a memory, present but incomplete. A passer-by or spectator might set about piecing together the image's narrative from the mind's palimpsest of innumerable Hollywood westerns seen in theatres and on late-night TV. In its nearly geological pacing, however, the evolving image would resist the particulars of its filmic past to appear as immobile and seemingly 'dead' as the desert landscape that was simultaneously represented within its frame and stretching in all directions around the screen. In this moment the cinematic 'monuments' of America's geological wonders, the near-motionless images of John Ford's monumental western *The Searchers*, and the cinema apparatus itself all converged in an event that embedded cinema within trans-historical and natural processes, as though it were a fossil or ruin. This event was *5 Year Drive-By*, a projection-installation by Douglas Gordon that had taken about as long to create as it would take the film to play out if it had stood in the desert for the duration prescribed by the work's title.

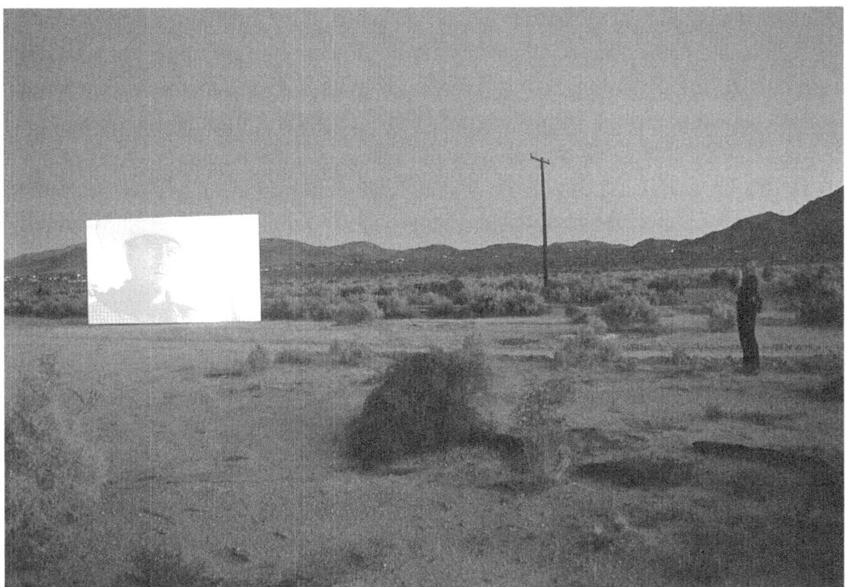

Figure 4.1   *Douglas Gordon,* 5 Year Drive-By, *1995. Video installation, dimensions variable,*
installation view Twentynine Palms, 2001. © Studio lost but found / VG Bild-Kunst, Bonn 2015,
© Douglas Gordon / SODRAC (2015), photo Studio lost but found / Kay Pallister, courtesy Studio lost
but found, Berlin. From The Searchers, *1956, USA. Directed by John Ford. Produced by Merian C.*
Cooper, Patrick Ford and C. V. Whitney. Distributed by Warner Bros. © Time Warner Entertainment
Company, L.P.

CINEMA'S PASSING

Film's 1996 centenary – celebrated amid growing anxieties of a coming
millennium – elicited alternately panicked and adamant declarations of the
'death' of the medium. 'Pronouncements of the "death of cinema" have
permeated popular discourses on film . . . where they fit comfortably into the
fin de siècle zeitgeist', Michael Witt commented in 1999.[2] By the 1990s, the sale
and rental of films on videotape, laserdisc and DVD, the spread of cable and
satellite television distribution of pay-per-view channels and movie networks
such as Home Box Office and Showtime, in addition to the rise of digital
production, all suggested that film-based production and movie-theatre exhibition might be nearing the end of their life cycles.[3] 'Our prior theorizations
of cinema have been burst asunder', Anne Friedberg alerted film scholars in
1991 as the video cassette (among other things) 'turns film experience into
a book-size, readily available commodity'.[4] The development of internet distribution, both authorised and illicit, further eroded the theatre's place as the

primary frame for film exhibition and consumption. Exposing and developing light-sensitive strips of plastic to then project light through them in dark rooms had begun to appear an overly complex and anachronistic means of visual communication. Film culture itself was fading into the nostalgia and sentiment that before had been confined primarily to stories on screen.[5] 'It's also interesting to see', film artist Matthew Buckingham would observe as late as 2003, 'how incredibly long "the death of cinema" is taking'.[6]

Some among those announcing cinema's commercial demise saw its potential 'survival' in the refuge of the art gallery.[7] To an extent, the idea of film's extinction made it not only a viable medium for artists and curators, but also one worthy of celebration and exultation in spaces where it had previously been shunned. In its embattled state, film became eminently museological. 'In an obligatory return of the repressed', critic Yann Beauvais remarked in 1995, 'cinema has been invading the field of contemporary art in an unavoidable way for several years now'.[8] The centenary of cinema and the decade that followed saw a spate of museum and gallery exhibitions on film and its kinship with art, among them *Hall of Mirrors: Art and Film Since 1945* at the Museum of Contemporary Art in Los Angeles, *Spellbound: Art and Film* at the Hayward Gallery in London and *Scream and Scream Again: Film in Art* at the Museum of Modern Art in Oxford (all 1996), *Cinéma Cinéma: Contemporary Art and the Cinematic Experience* at the Stedelijk Museum in Eindhoven (1999), *Between Cinema and a Hard Place* at the Tate Modern in London (2000), *Into the Light: The Projected Image in American Art 1964–1977* at the Whitney Museum of American Art in New York (2001), *X-Screen: Film Installations and Actions in the 1960s and 1970s* at the Museum Moderner Kunst Stiftung Ludwig Wien in Vienna and *Image Stream* at the Wexner Center for the Arts in Columbus, Ohio (both 2003), *Cut: Film as Found Object in Contemporary Video* at the Milwaukee Museum of Art (2004), and *Le Mouvement des Images* at the Centre Pompidou in Paris and *Beyond Cinema: The Art of Projection* at the Hamburger Bahnhof in Berlin (both 2006).

Kerry Brougher, curator of *Hall of Mirrors*, believes this trend was an inevitable step in the medium's long progression. 'Somewhere near the mid-twentieth century, film's evolutionary history seems to have crested', he explains in the exhibition's catalogue, '[and] film began to turn back in on itself'. Accordingly, Brougher claims, 'From the opposite side of this evolution, from the perspective of postwar, post-classic film, post-Hollywood culture, film can be investigated and deconstructed'.[9] Detecting a 'reign of salvage and recycling' in the 1990s, Beauvais similarly predicted that 'only the retreatment of the image holds meaning, in a veritable fulfilment of postmodernism', an action that applied 'as much to the arrangement of shots as to their presentation in space'. 'To push cinema to the extreme', he declared, 'all the way to its destruction, so as to confirm its necessity in the face of the all-devouring media which see it as no more than a nostalgic pastime: such remains the only possible attitude for filmmakers today'.[10] Within these conceptualisations, the projected image's presence in art spaces is akin to an aged, terminally ill body retreating to the clinic in anticipation of its autopsy.[11]

No one participated in this transition with as much perspicuity as Scottish artist Douglas Gordon, whose first decade as a professional in the art world fits squarely within this trajectory. 'Just as it approached its 100th birthday', Gordon has intoned, 'cinema was quietly transferred from the critical ward and onto a permanent life-support machine. So, technically it may not be dead, but it's an artificial life.'[12] Elsewhere he has gone further, envisioning his generation 'Standing at an open grave wherein lies the ever-young corpse of cinema. Having seen the full burial postponed, we enjoy the wake.'[13] Beginning with his single- and multi-projection gallery installations of the 1990s and ending with the partial realisation of his monumental outdoor work, *5 Year Drive-By*, in California in 2001, Gordon presented moving-image art as a performative undertaking that encompasses not only the image and its projection, but the screen and its relationship to the environment. His appropriationist attitude, redeploying classic feature films and found scientific and medical footage under distressed or attenuated operating conditions, has regularly strained the material and temporal conditions of exhibition. Through a combination of reduced image speeds and precarious screen placements, his works have presented cinema as an archaeological artefact caught within larger temporo-historical registers. Cinema functions like fragments of a modern ruin in Gordon's installations not only through its compromised physical and temporal aspects, but also through the ruin's affective ties to nostalgia, memory and longing.[14] 'The buried fears are those things which need to be exhumed', Gordon proclaims. 'Forgotten beliefs "will" be remembered. They are around every psychological corner, and hidden in every nook and cranny in the cellars and attics of our heads.'[15] As he continued to enact cinema's presence in art spaces into the twenty-first century as a constant archaeology of a haunting cinematic imaginary, much was made of the temporal aspect of these works, and for good reason. In some cases the titles alone – *24 Hour Psycho*, *5 Year Drive-By* – plainly point to this preoccupation. The belief that many of Gordon's projected works are entirely about time, rather than space, ran so strongly that a critic could claim that 'Gordon's ideas are often more interesting to hear than to see'.[16] Similarly, a curator could comfortably publish a discussion with Gordon about key works such as *24 Hour Psycho* based not on her first-hand experience but 'on [her] own fantasies of what *Psycho* must look like when slowed down to near stasis'.[17]

Gordon himself has claimed that his pieces can be more important as ideas than as phenomenological experiences, stating that 'The realization and presentation of an idea are of secondary or tertiary interest to me'.[18] But elsewhere he has defended the necessity of experiencing his works as material and spatial entities. 'The context, which contributes for 50 per cent to the significance of a work, is vital', he told Simon Sheikh in 1997.[19] Environmental conditions and spatial concerns do play a critical role in these works, as the physical conditions of cinema are taken as potentially destabilising factors. Measuring the impact of this frequently overlooked '50 per cent' requires consideration of architecture, environment and the screen as narrative agents. Gordon's attention to these becomes clear in his description of the evolution of *Between Darkness and Light (After William Blake)*, a double projection on a screen in a pedestrian underpass in Münster in 1997. 'Once I had decided to pursue the idea of using the material then I had to start thinking about the form, how people might approach the work, where I could install a screen, and so on', Gordon states, adding

> The form of the work – certainly in my case – is rarely spoken about, or rarely discussed. And this is strange for me because the form and the context in which the work is seen are very important in establishing a relationship by which the viewer can start thinking about what they are experiencing.[20]

This chapter responds to Gordon's complaint, emphasising the physical form and placement of his projected-image works over a ten-year period to demonstrate how these reframe the modernity of film and its exhibition models around themes of archaeology, the ruin and geological processes. It recognises Gordon's practice as one strongly contoured by the interdependence of space and time in the effectiveness of the projected image. From *24 Hour Psycho* to *5 Year Drive-By*, this ultimately ties film narrative and memory to the historical, material and spatial conditions of the projection event itself. In particular, his work retraces through its material components and spatial contexts the diverging paths of popular film in the second half of the twentieth century by invoking the movie theatre and the drive-in. Just as commercial film exhibition ventured into the landscape in the 1950s and 1960s (particularly in America, but also in Europe and elsewhere) to convert unused or open spaces into drive-in theatres, Gordon embarked on an archaeological pursuit at the end of the twentieth century that transferred cinema from the magnetic residue of the VCR cassette to the halls of the museum as a partially preserved artefact, only to re-situate it subsequently as an abandoned, ruined monument in the desert landscape in *5 Year Drive-By*.

SCREEN ARTEFACTS

'I think that ways of looking are determined more by the circumstances in which a film is seen than the commercial or "alternative" intent of the director', Gordon has said.[21] Indeed, the film installations he produced throughout the 1990s configure the screen within gallery spaces in ways that emphasise its material presence and reinforce its potential physical and affective weight. Gordon literally lowered the screen from its fixed position on the wall – where it had remained for nearly all forms of film viewing for over a century – to stand it on the floor. Sometimes in a free-standing leaning position, other times set to rest against the architectural features of the exhibition space, these screens are seemingly damaged or contingent objects that deny tranquil viewing. In his multi-projection works, screens may appear to lean together, each seemingly propping up the image borne by its neighbour. As he customarily slows the images to move at extremely reduced speeds – from nearly two frames per second in *24 Hour Psycho* to a frame every quarter-hour in *5 Year Drive-By* – the temporal resistance of the image can appear to further weigh upon or wear down the material conditions of the projection apparatus itself.

Gordon's first moving-image installation, *24 Hour Psycho*, not only remains his best-known work, but also is regularly invoked to represent a generation of contemporary artists working through, and under, the influence of cinema.[22] Slowing Alfred Hitchcock's 109-minute psychological thriller to project over an entire day, the film is presented (in video transfer) at less than a tenth its normal speed. Gordon claims the idea sprang from his late-night toying with films on a VCR. 'I started watching and then rewatching scenes from [*Psycho*] in slow motion. The more I looked at it, the more I realized I didn't know what was going on.'[23] By activating the machine's frame-advance mode, Gordon discovered a 'micro-narrative' of details that would escape perception at normal speed. 'It was as if the slow motion revealed the unconscious of the film', he claims. Gordon's account recalls an archaeologist's close excavation of the field. He strips away the layers of the film's *mise-en-scène*, sweeping over small portions of this ground again and again, to find new fragments surfacing like mysterious chips of ancient pottery. As Richard Flood writes, upon viewing *24 Hour Psycho* he observed 'Details that previously slipped by unnoticed suddenly loom large: an uneaten sandwich, neatly folded clothes; the excuse and the routine'. Flood notes, 'Obviously, all of this information was available in the original but there it was just a blip on the scanner . . .'[24]

The slowed film becomes an opportunity to unearth a tale fixed in the idea of the artefact's ability to trigger memory and association. 'In a slow motion film everything takes so long to happen that you have forgotten where it started. It detaches itself, so to speak', Gordon explains.[25] The image acts as a fragmentary artefact torn from its original cultural context, around which the viewer seeks to restore its historical function by setting it within a narrative chain of related fragments. While Michael Newman claims that this extraction transforms every frame, such that 'Each moment of the film, including those that remain marginal to the core narrative, becomes monumental', Gordon suggests it places both image and story in limbo.[26] 'The past is a confusion of memory', he contends. 'The images follow in such slow sequence that it is impossible to remember. The past keeps going and the future never happens, so everything is presence.'[27] Laura Mulvey finds that the crippling slowness of this installation's images opens a temporal overlap of past and present in the spectator's mind. 'While the flow of the image at 24 frames a second tends to assert a "now-ness" to the picture, stillness allows access to the time of the film's registration, its "then-ness"', she claims. 'This is the point, essentially located in the single frame, where the cinema meets the still photograph, both registering a moment of time frozen and thus fossilized.'[28] Recalling André Bazin's claim that cinema is 'change mummified',[29] these descriptions emphasise the relationship between duration, narrativity and memory. Whether understood as a monument or fossil, the work would force a consideration of the past as significant and immense, suggesting the past 'keeps going'. As with Gordon's subsequent projected works of the 1990s, the deceleration of action and lack of sound in *24 Hour Psycho* can transform the film image into a totem for the death of cinema by 'a kind of slow asphyxiation', according to Eric Mézil, while presenting the body of cinema in an 'extended frame-by-frame autopsy'.[30]

Gordon initially soft-pedalled the material and spatial specificities of this process of petrifaction or mummification, suggesting that anyone could recreate his work on their home VCR and television.[31] If such flexibility were integral to the work, like Robert Rauschenberg's insistence that his *White Paintings* could be copied or altered where and when necessary, then there would be great incentive to exhibit *24 Hour Psycho* on monitors or as straightforward wall projections. For the most part, however, Gordon has resisted these possibilities, instead relying on projection screens placed away from the wall. 'Working in galleries and museums there's no point in giving people the cinema experience', Gordon explains

> what I want to do is maybe isolate aspects of it, and isolate them in such a way that people realize that something's missing, that they're having to do a wee bit extra work, but maybe they're not absolutely sure what it is that's missing.[32]

Despite differing spaces, institutions and social contexts, *24 Hour Psycho* is regularly projected onto a screen hung or erected within the viewer's space, allowing movement around the object. Seating is rarely available, eliminating safe anchors and pushing viewers to contend more actively and consciously with the body's physical relationship to the screen-object. The first exhibition of *24 Hour Psycho* at Tramway in Glasgow in 1993 established these parameters in a presentation dominated by spatial, as much as temporal, issues. 'I just kept thinking about the space, made a wee model of the space, this kind of thing', Gordon claims of the year between receiving an invitation to create a work for Tramway and proposing *24 Hour Psycho*. '[I] couldn't come up with an idea, really the architecture of the space was so dominant', he says of this art gallery housed in a former tram depot.[33] In this seminal incarnation of the work, and its subsequent exhibition history in dozens of shows worldwide, Gordon sought to 'take away the convention of theater', insisting that 'Most of [my] installations should look quite informal'.[34]

Gordon has produced two basic configurations for *24 Hour Psycho* since 1993, both emphasising the 10 x 13-foot semi-translucent screen as fundamental to the work's physical and psychological functioning. The first configuration presents the projection on a screen suspended more or less at the centre of the exhibition space, often placed diagonally in relation to existing architecture. This was the case at Tramway and has been reproduced multiple times, including exhibition appearances at the Hayward Gallery in London in 1996 and 2002, the Musée d'Art Moderne de la Ville de Paris in 2000, Gordon's first American survey at the Geffen Contemporary for the Museum of Contemporary Art in Los Angeles in 2001, his retrospective at the Museum of Modern Art, New York, in 2006, and at the Royal Scottish Academy in Edinburgh in 2007.[35] The second, less-common configuration, involves a standing, slightly inclined screen. It sometimes rests against an element of existing architecture, such as a column. This alternate version of the work was first presented at the Kunste-Werke in Berlin in 1993 and repeated at the Hauptbahnhof Leipzig in 1995 and the Akademie der Bildenden Künste in Vienna in 1996.[36]

In both versions, the temporality of the seemingly fixed moving image is transferred to the screen-object in its provisional and precarious posture, contributing to what Gordon calls 'the distress of the films, both physically and metaphorically'.[37] The screen's semi-translucent material permits viewing from either side. Coupled with the slowed action of the film, it allows and encourages careful scrutiny of both image and object. Katrina Brown describes these conditions as a prompt for 'a physical involvement that only strengthens the way in which the viewer is implicated . . . [She can] see the projection from both sides and become aware of the manipulation to which the material has been subjected'.[38] While the hanging screen takes precedence in the exhibition history of *24 Hour Psycho*, it's the standing, leaning screen

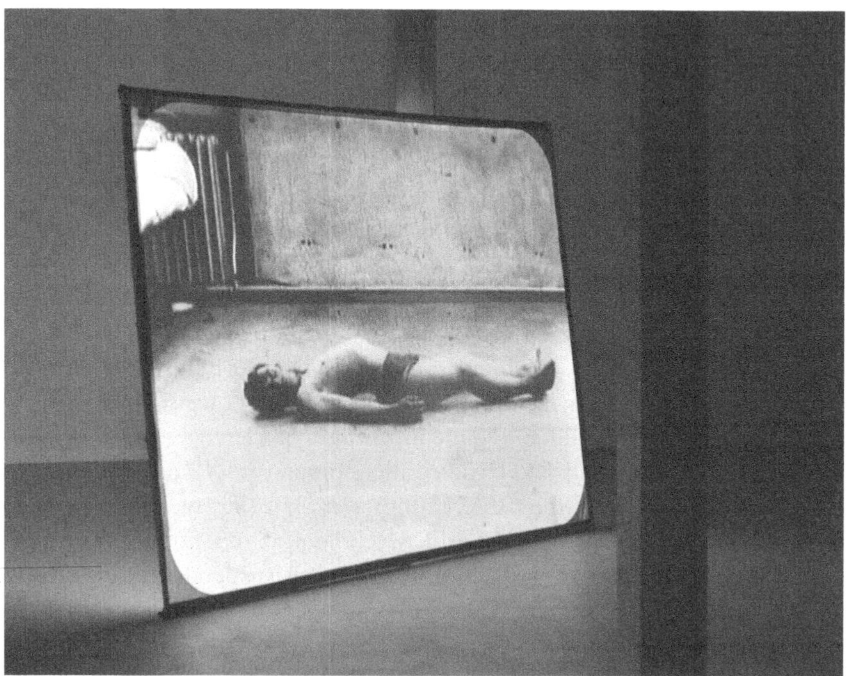

Figure 4.2 *Douglas Gordon, 10ms⁻¹, 1994. Video installation, dimensions variable. Courtesy Studio lost but found, Berlin. Installation view 'Blood, Sweat and Tears', Dox Prague, 2009, courtesy Studio lost but found, Berlin. © Studio lost but found / VG Bild-Kunst, Bonn 2015, © Douglas Gordon / SODRAC (2015), photo Studio lost but found / Frederik Pedersen*

that distinguishes Gordon's moving-image installations throughout the 1990s, becoming 'as much his trademark as the archetype of cinema revealing itself', according to Françoise Parfait.[39] With slight variations, this mode of display repeats across several works. In *10ms⁻¹* (1994), the screen is placed against a column (either pre-existing in the room's architecture or installed for the exhibition) situated at the centre of the room (Figure 4.2). The screen bears the decelerated black-and-white footage of a World War I medical film depicting a patient apparently suffering neurological damage who falls to the floor and struggles repeatedly to rise to his feet. *Remote Viewing 13.05.94 (Horror Movie)* (1995) presents a scene inspired by the film *Leave Her to Heaven* (John M. Stahl, 1945) on a leaning screen placed in the midst of a red room. In several other slowed projection pieces, Gordon appoints the gallery space with paired standing screens for double projections. The same image may appear on both screens, often inversed laterally or tonally on one screen, and the pair may be leaning on each other or on the surrounding architecture. *Hysterical* (1994–5), for example, presents on adjacent screens the same

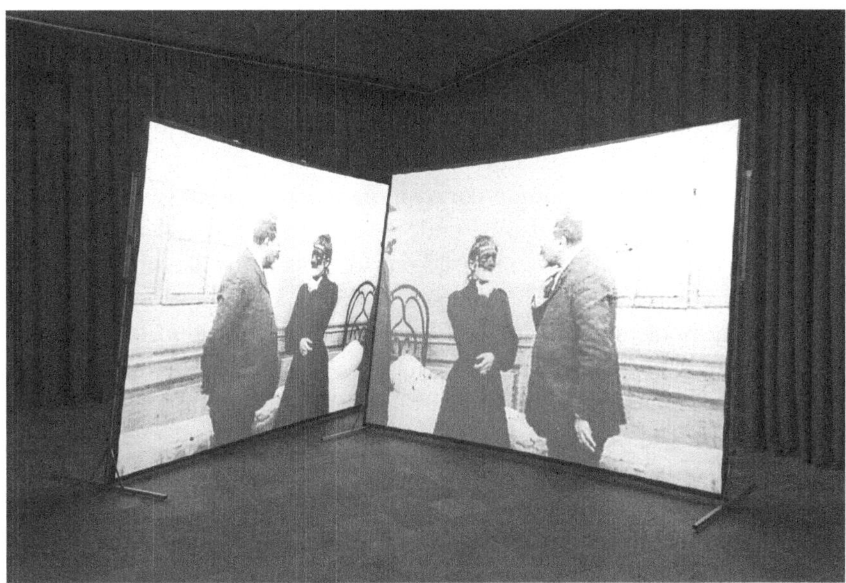

Figure 4.3   *Douglas Gordon,* Hysterical, *1995. Video installation, dimensions variable. Courtesy Studio lost but found, Berlin. © Studio lost but found / VG Bild-Kunst, Bonn 2014, © Douglas Gordon / SODRAC (2015), photo Studio lost but found / Frederik Pedersen*

silent-era found footage of a masked woman between two men beside a bed (Figure 4.3). As the men struggle to subdue the woman, as though they are doctors treating a case of hysteria, the image is projected at standard speed on one screen while appearing significantly slowed on the other. One of Gordon's earliest double projections, *Hysterical*'s two screens lean together at a slightly obtuse angle, their upper interior corners nearly touching. *Film Noir (Twins)* (1995) presents a close-up of a terrorised face on two screens placed at an angle – one resting horizontally, the other vertically – with the projected image turned to match the screen form. *Film Noir (Fly)* (1995) offers a close-up of a dying fly projected onto a screen that leans against a column. *Confessions of a Justified Sinner* (1995–6) presents in negative and positive a slowed excerpt from *Dr. Jekyll and Mr. Hyde* (Rouben Mamoulian, 1931) on two screens that lean against adjacent gallery walls or are situated like those in *Hysterical*. The 1996 work *Black and White (Babylon)* projects a 1950s peep-show striptease film onto a pair of screens of differing size placed against two walls, with the image projected upside-down on one.[40]

As Giorgio Verzotti explains, 'The fragments that are bound into [Gordon's] works . . . are all subjected to duplication, inversions, mirror-like redoubling, all in the service of an apparent sense of symmetry and, therefore, of equivalence, an impression of equality that only close observation reveals as fictitious'.[41] While Verzotti and others interpret these configurations in relation to dichotomy or psychological conditions such as schizophrenia or multiple personality disorder, this twinning produces a symmetry that also mimics architectural construction.[42] Gordon has claimed that his two-screen works derive from the common contemporary experience of watching multiple screens, but they can also be understood in terms of classical architectural symmetry, appearing as inversed pairs of elements, like broken pieces of a frieze reunited in the museum space. The colossal heads of *Film Noir (Twins)* or the nude torsos of *Black and White (Babylon)* contribute iconographically to such an interpretation (all the more so when one takes into account the historical reference of the latter's title).[43] With these works – unlike *24 Hour Psycho* – Gordon rescues film fragments from greater or lesser obscurity. Medical films, stag films, early-sound literary adaptations . . . all are artefacts previously buried under the onslaught of mass-produced imagery in the latter half of the twentieth century, only to be unearthed by Gordon at the dawn of the twenty-first.

THEATRICAL SCREENS

Once lowered to the ground and placed at an angle, the screens in Gordon's works lose all allusion to window or picture frame to become resolutely material to the spectator. 'If we accept now to see the work of art as an object, even when it is an idea, then one has to create as much space around it as possible', Gordon remarks. 'This social and psychological space is vital.'[44] In this regard, Gordon has claimed that his greatest aesthetic contribution lies less in altering the images he presents than in the simple act of bringing them into the gallery. 'In their nature, they have nothing to do with museums or galleries', he claims. 'Some of them are avant-garde films, others are regular films and should therefore be shown in genuine cinemas.'[45] Presented on screens leaning against walls and other structures, this film culture enters into dialogue with the neo-avant-garde's major post-war aesthetic turn toward the materiality of the object as means to foregrounding the spectator's temporal and spatial engagement with the work. The leaning screen becomes an object of manifest mass and weight, relying on gravity to remain in place, much like the leaning metal sheets or wooden planks of Minimalist sculptures by artists such as Richard Serra and John McCracken.

Robert Morris' influential 1966 essay, 'Notes on Sculpture', posits such presentations as integral to the artwork's function as they trigger new spatial relationships not only in the opposition between object and architecture but also in the new-found dynamics between object and spectator. Morris emphasises illusion and materiality as fundamental to the difference between painting and sculpture. 'An object hung on the wall does not confront gravity; it timidly resists it', he asserts.

> One of the conditions of knowing an object is supplied by the sensing of the gravitational force acting upon it in actual space. That is, space with three, not two coordinates. The ground plane, not the wall, is the necessary support for the maximum awareness of the object.[46]

Situating the object as a potential disruption within a room's volume forces new interactivity, inscribing spectators' presence more strongly within the grip of the work's phenomenological operation in ways that both recall, and fundamentally diverge from, Rauschenberg's 1953 Stable Gallery gesture. Thus, Gordon can claim, 'So when you're visiting my exhibitions, you have the opportunity to do something you were never allowed to do in the movie theatre – touching [sic] the screen. In the movie theatre usually you keep a distance.'[47] Of course, that opportunity for tactile interaction is present in some of the alternative cinema forms already considered in this book, such as with impromptu home-movie screens or the architecture of peep-show screens and booths. In studying the Minimalist art that led to Morris' aesthetic claims, Michael Fried calls such potential visitor interaction with the work 'theatricality'. For Fried, the mere intersection of two media within a work (e.g. film and sculpture) immediately casts it as theatre. 'The concepts of quality and value – and to the extent that these are central to art, the concept of art itself – are meaningful, or wholly meaningful, only within the individual arts. What lies between the arts is theater', he explains in his well-known 1967 rejoinder to Morris, 'Art and Objecthood'.[48]

Reacting to both Morris and Fried, Rosalind Krauss offers a path that teases out the architectural and artefactual dimensions of these experiences, opening a route into the potential meanings of Gordon's screen configurations. Writing about the possible placements of a column, Krauss explains that 'Upright, the column seems light and thin, its erectness unburdened by the downward pressure of weight. It seems fluid, linear, and without mass.' However, 'in a prone position, the column changes *in kind*. It appears massive, constricted and heavy; it seems to be *about* weight. The import of the column is, then, not that it is the same throughout "any variation of that form", but that it is different.' Krauss concludes by pointing out that 'this difference strikes at the heart of the idea that the meaning of shape is to be found in its abstractness, or separability, in its detachment from an actual situation, in the possibility that we can transfer it intact from one place and orientation to another'.[49] From the upright to the prone position, then, the free-standing column can appear compromised, bringing about an entirely different reading of its presence and potential role. The object can shift from utility to superfluity, from activity to passivity, from integrality to supplementality, and from architecture to artefact.

Drawing on these possibilities, a leaning screen not only beckons the acknowledgement of materiality suggested by Morris, but also unleashes new readings of displacement as it is literally lowered from its expected situation as a suspended object representing a transparent window to the status of an earthbound mechanical or technological artefact. Indeed, by retaining the basic physical properties of the movie screen while bearing images of 'salvaged' films considered ancient by the standards of twenty-first-century visual culture, Gordon's leaning screens come close in form and function to the fragment of a ruin or monument.[50]

The extremely slow, often worn, archival images in Gordon's presentations verge on a stillness that places his screens on the register of recovered artefacts, despite their flawless surfaces. The hint of fragility and instability produced by the screen's inclined placement, coupled with the use of projected images broken away from their original contexts, uses and narrative import, fuses material and image in the performance of the archaeological. Just as the image is 'detached', according to Gordon, or 'fossilized', according to Mulvey, the installation encourages readings of the cinema as being in ruins, which sustains Gordon's views on the medium's demise while reflecting his enduring fascination with British Romanticism.[51] The collapsed or broken architectural element, propped against the remains of surviving structures, was a primary iconographic and literary trope in the aesthetic of ruins in eighteenth- and nineteenth-century Europe. Such artefactual elements regularly appear in the paintings of classical ruins by Hubert Robert and others that became fashionable in the late eighteenth century (Figure 4.4), not to mention the thousands of archaeological photographs taken in the latter half of the nineteenth century. Giovanni Battista Piranesi's celebrated archaeological engravings of ancient Roman sites abound with such compositions. Just as Gordon's screens appear to find refuge in the clean, stable environment of the gallery, Piranesi's engravings include depictions of the re-siting and arrangement of archaeological fragments for display and further study.

In her theorisation of 'ruin time', Florence Hetzler defines the ruin in two ways that distinguish it from the artefact. First, the ruin retains its original unity of structure despite the impact of time and Nature. A castle in ruins may be structurally compromised, but it still retains the basic properties of a castle. Once those are gone, all that is left is rubble. Second, a ruin must remain in the location that made it a ruin. When a ruin – or any part thereof – is moved to, say, a museum, it becomes an artefact.[52] This distinction is important,

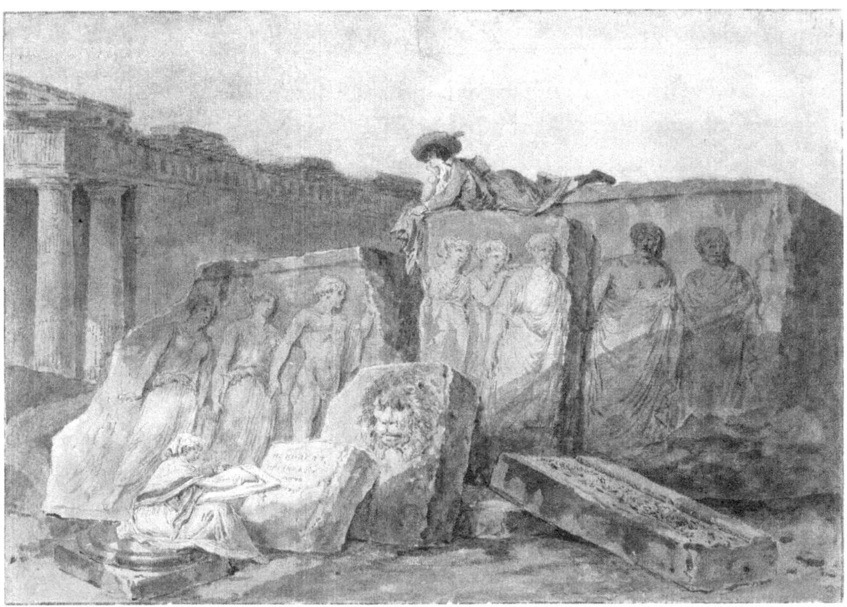

Figure 4.4   *Hubert Robert,* An Artist amongst Ancient Ruins, *1796, pen, ink, pencil and watercolour on paper. State Hermitage Museum, St. Petersburg*

since such recontextualisation estranges the fragment at two levels. First, the fragment loses its original architectural purpose, no longer serving as a physical support but rather requiring support from an outside structure or object (the plinth, the base). Second, the fragment is alienated from its prior cultural purpose. While it may offer clues to the past, the story is usually incomplete, requiring the archaeologist's eye and historical knowledge to situate the fragment within a cohesive narrative. Similarly, *24 Hour Psycho* may strike the viewer as a puzzle piece of images caught in an unstable object, stripped of narrative progression. '*24 Hour Psycho* exploits our memory of the film and the myths that surround it', Katrina Brown surmises, 'as much [as it does] the film itself'.[53] In essence, the installation does not display the film as story, but rather the film as a medium – made of fragments – perceived by some to be on the verge of collapse by 1993. In the journey from *24 Hour Psycho*'s presentation at Tramway to *5 Year Drive-By*'s appearance in the Mojave desert, Gordon would capitalise on that perception by revisiting one of cinema's nearly extinct forms – the drive-in – to expose the cracks in the single-model myths of film-making and viewing that still stalked the history of the moving image. This journey would shift the role of the projection screen from that of modern artefact to one of modern ruin.

DRIVE-IN RUINS

Ruins have been a recurrent theme in the critical response to projected moving-image art since the 1990s. British artist Tacita Dean's works on and about film as a historical object – often comprised of 16- and 35-mm celluloid loops and projectors placed in the gallery space – have been considered an exercise in the subject, presenting 'ruins of various sorts through the ruined medium of film' or embodying 'ruination gone wrong (repeated ruination, exacerbated ruination, ruination that turns temporal passing into a spectral remnant)'.[54] Others have argued for a consideration of cinema more generally as a ruin medium.[55] While the ruin developed as both object and metaphor during the Enlightenment and became an essential component of Romantic thought, it has taken on new significance in contemporary theories of post-modernism and post-industrialism where a major twentieth-century phenomenon such as cinema can be an easy target. Andreas Huyssen identifies a millennial 'ruin craze' in northern trans-Atlantic cultures that not only includes increased conversion of ancient 'authentic' ruins into sanitised tourist destinations but also the transformation of modern industrial sites into multi-purpose cultural and commercial centres. This interest in ruins, Huyssen claims, bears a troubling nostalgia for modernity in spite of the political, humanitarian and environmental catastrophes of the last century. 'This contemporary obsession with ruins hides a nostalgia for an earlier age that had not yet lost its power to imagine other futures', Huyssen states. 'Our imaginary of ruins can be read as a palimpsest of multiple historical events and representations.'[56] In other words, the ruin acts as a screen-like surface for projecting desire. This makes the film projection screen of modernity a particularly powerful ruin, capable of harbouring these projections while also invoking the projections (both literal and figurative) of a modernist past. The screen ruin reaches its most powerful representation in the twentieth-century drive-in, a cinema form that peaked at the start of the period covered in this book, and which has left the ruins of cinema scattered across the topography of several continents.[57]

In its celebrity, *24 Hour Psycho* has taken on numerous forms in recent years, adapting both to Gordon's evolving career, which includes *Zidane, A 21st Century Portrait*, a feature-length documentary for theatrical release that was co-directed with Philippe Parreno in 2006, and contemporary curatorial strategies that privilege unorthodox exhibition spaces.[58] One of its more extraordinary iterations was a 'drive-in' screening as part of British artist Phil Collins' *Auto-kino!* exhibition in Berlin in 2010. Collins devised a drive-in movie theatre at the Temporäre Kunsthalle by parking a dozen or so second-hand cars in a hall, all facing a large screen where he projected German films from the 1920s to 1940s along with video works by contemporary artists.

Collins chose *24 Hour Psycho* to open the cycle. As the press release claimed, *Auto-kino!* sought to explore 'the simultaneous erection and abolition of cinema's visual pleasures [that] lie at the heart of significant parts of both contemporary filmmaking and visual arts' through the 'nearly obsolete' viewing context of the drive-in.[59] Although Gordon appears never to have imagined *24 Hour Psycho* as a drive-in experience, this 'post-mortem' exploration of the visual and temporal vulnerabilities of the film body that previously passed through the dissecting device of video recorders finds a potentially compelling physical construction in the drive-in format. While movie theatres still abound – at least in multiplex form – today the drive-in is prone to 're-creations' and 'simulations' like *Auto-kino!*, suggesting a moribund practice to be resuscitated in institutional contexts.

Despite its demise, the drive-in may represent the apogee of film as the dominant mass medium of much of the twentieth century. The drive-in marks the moment when cinema transcended both movie theatre and home entertainment models to become a prominent fixture across the landscape, most prominently in the US. The image and screen were literally embedded in the environment, as accessible to birds in the air as people on the ground. In the US, the drive-in neatly united the commodified image with American ideals of the outdoors. The simultaneous popularity of drive-ins and westerns in 1950s America may indicate a collective national psyche envisioning middle-class suburban exodus and automobile culture as the logical – even inevitable – legacy of earlier Manifest Destiny expansionism and subjugation of indigenous populations. In watching Hollywood wagon trains and cowboy heroes arduously lay trail and claim lands across the Plains and Rockies, post-war families snug in their station wagons at roadside drive-ins saw the triumphant beginnings of their prosperous society. From *River of No Return* (Otto Preminger, 1954) to *How the West Was Won* (John Ford, Henry Hathaway and George Marshall, 1962), western watching at the drive-in was like peering through a magic window onto the history of the surrounding land to see the white settlers' first encounters with the landscape that their moviegoing descendants now enjoyed. 'In the iconography of the classic Western', notes Linnie Blake, 'we can see Hollywood providing Americans with a visual means for making sense of their "manifest destiny", whilst erasing any alternative claims to competing visions of American identity, or competing claims to the land'.[60]

Peter Cowie suggests that director John Ford's cinematic obsession with Monument Valley across several westerns constitutes a coherent mythology of national growth in even the most formidable terrain by establishing a sequence of narratives presenting the multiple phases of US settlement. With Ford's first Monument Valley film, *Stagecoach* (1939), Cowie detects 'an image of the West as a hostile environment, vast and ungovernable, so intimidating that the stagecoach must dash across the floor of Monument Valley from one settlement to another'. Ten years later, in *She Wore a Yellow Ribbon* (1949), the valley had been settled, however sparsely, and the film's protagonist, US Calvary Captain Nathan Brittles, 'clearly regards [the valley] as home', Cowie contends.[61]

Gordon appears to deliver on Ford's promise of the land ceding to and serving civilisation in his California presentation of *5 Year Drive-By*. By projecting the western in a context recalling the drive-in, Gordon foregrounded the relationship of both to ideologies of adventure and settlement within the American imaginary. As Philip Monk has said, 'Ideally set in the grandeur of the desert, Gordon's projection is a memorial to the site and to the grand obsession of the story set there. Given the extravagance of its proposal, we should rather conceive it as a monument to time.'[62] Of Gordon's numerous projected works, therefore, it may not be *24 Hour Psycho* – born as a bedroom video experiment – that most convincingly engages the monumentality of film as a twentieth-century mass medium. By offering a screen seemingly exiled in the desert like a ruined drive-in, Gordon created a monument that, as an interface between the natural surroundings and the slowly changing Technicolor landscapes projected on the screen surface, stands at the intersection of the historical, the mythological, the geological and the archaeological. Surrounded by Joshua Tree National Park to the south, the San Bernardino National Forest to the west, the Mojave National Preserve to the north and the Havasu National Wildlife Refuge to the east, *5 Year Drive-By* becomes – like the western and drive-in – the centre point of a modern topographical narrative of Euro-American nationalism and colonisation. This is all the more significant when one considers that Monument Valley, where Gordon had hoped to place his work, is also a national park – not of the United States, however, but of the Navajo nation.

The long, improbable journey of *5 Year Drive-By* to the Mojave desert began in Scotland in the early 1970s, when a school-age Gordon first saw *The Searchers* on television. The film follows Civil War veteran Ethan (played by John Wayne) as he scours the American desert for five years to find his niece, kidnapped by a Comanche chief. From the film's minimal plot Gordon claims to have gleaned only that 'five whole years was a very long time, especially in relation to my short life'. The film's unusual narrative and structure continued to haunt him until he saw the film again in the mid-1990s. 'Now I realize what I thought to be the problem; and it's quite simply a question of time', he told Thierry Pratt, the director of the Lyon Biennale, in 1995. 'How can anyone even try to sum up 5 miserable years in only 113 minutes?' From that question of narrativity's problematic desire to compress time in transmitting events and constructing history, Gordon developed an installation involving the film as 'something of a companion piece to *24 Hour Psycho* but [that] may appear to be a little more extreme in some ways'.[63]

Beyond the central issue of time and temporal dilation as narrative strategy, Gordon has understood *The Searchers* as also accommodating and even emphasising absence in the spatiality of its visual rhetoric. 'Nothing happens in the movie' he claims, pointing out that the film's desert landscape 'obviously is a metaphor for nothingness, no growth, and a spiritual wilderness'.[64] Shortly before Ford began shooting the film in 1955, he confided to French film historian Jean Mitry that *The Searchers* would be 'A very simple story as I like them. A strange adventure in the setting of the Rocky Mountains.'[65] Perhaps more than any of his previous westerns, *The Searchers* demonstrates Ford's belief in the genre as inherently monumental and timeless. 'When I make a Western', he claimed a decade later, 'all I have to do is to film a documentary on the West, just as it was: epic. And from the moment that one is epic, one can't go wrong. It's the reality, outside time, that one records on the negative.'[66]

Working with emptiness and the imperceptible passage of time in a plot that troubles the linear progression of action in the classical Hollywood narrative, Gordon proposed to Pratt in 1995 a projection of *The Searchers* at an exponentially slowed speed. The twenty-four frames of one second of normal film time would now require 6.46 hours to play out, thereby extending a single screening of the film into an epic endeavour equivalent to the full, five-year duration of Ethan's quest. As the three-month Lyon Biennale permitted only a fraction of the work to be screened, Gordon projected an excerpt there under the title *Proposal for Public Art Work: Reconstituting John Ford and* The Searchers.[67] Conforming to his screen practices of that period, the excerpt was shown on a leaning screen.

The project would stretch well beyond the limits of its initial presentation in Lyon, both in temporal and spatial terms. While the slowed rate of one frame every sixteen minutes would remain constant, subsequent incarnations offered new exhibition durations under varied physical parameters. To cite Gordon's description, the process of bringing the work to fruition in its intended form required six years of 'talk[ing] about it, and occasionally present[ing] the idea in proposal form' in different gallery exhibitions. After unveiling his 'proposal' in Lyon, Gordon hoped next to show it in an underground parking garage at Skulptur Projekte Münster in 1997. Anticipating the structure would be adaptable to 'the big projection', upon inspection of Münster's garages he realised that accumulated car exhaust would prohibit visitors from staying long enough to experience the work effectively.[68] Instead, he presented a one-night, outdoor version at the Kunstverein

Hannover, projected onto a standing, inclined screen with the title *Overnight #1*.[69] It would emerge again at the Neue Nationalgalerie in Berlin during the 1999 Berlin Film Festival. Alongside Gordon's *Bootleg (Empire)* (1997) in the glass-walled spaces of the gallery's Mies van der Rohe building, the juxtaposition of architecture and installation crossed the clean 'perfection' of modernism with the 'rough' aspect of Gordon's projection pieces. The architecture also assured that the screen image was scarcely visible during daylight hours, a crucial component of Gordon's conception of the work as a long-term outdoor installation.[70]

Considering the limitations that gallery spaces and exhibition schedules impose on such a work, Nancy Spector suggested to Gordon in 1997 that perhaps the project was meant to remain an idea rather than a physical entity. 'Given the monumentality of such a project, it seems more to be about the search itself for you. It embodies the great quest', she reasoned in a conversation with the artist, asking him 'Can this piece exist only in the mind or is it critical to actualize it in tangible form?' Gordon tactfully responded 'Sure, this piece need not be made', while nevertheless resisting that thought. 'The struggle necessary to realize it and situate it where I want it runs parallel to the narrative of the original film', he told Spector, implying a confrontation with the desert as the only satisfactory outcome.[71] 'I would like to make it as a drive-by cinema', he explained, 'ideally situated in, or nearby[,] Monument Valley in southern Utah. I like the idea of a physical monument to the idea of the search – and if this is the case, then the potential viewer has to be involved in some kind of physical journey in order to see the work. This is a real parallel with the original story.'[72] In Gordon's mind, the temporal monument that is the journey or *search* would reach its end at the foot of the physical monument of the screen erected among the geological wonders of the desert. Exactly as the film's slowing to a frame every quarter-hour represents a significant protraction of movement from the two frames a second of *24 Hour Psycho*, to turn the decelerated film into a series of fixed (or fossilised) images, the physical exertion necessary to complete the pilgrimage to the work would set in motion a 'theatricality' of the art work far beyond the scale imagined in Fried's earlier engagement with Minimalism.[73]

DRIVE-IN MONUMENTS

Barely surviving into the twenty-first century, the drive-in movie theatre remains fixed in American cultural memory as a product and symbol of post-World War II economic development and prosperity. It represents the unprecedented incorporation into consumer culture of theretofore untouched or under-utilised zones outside cities and towns, as well as a

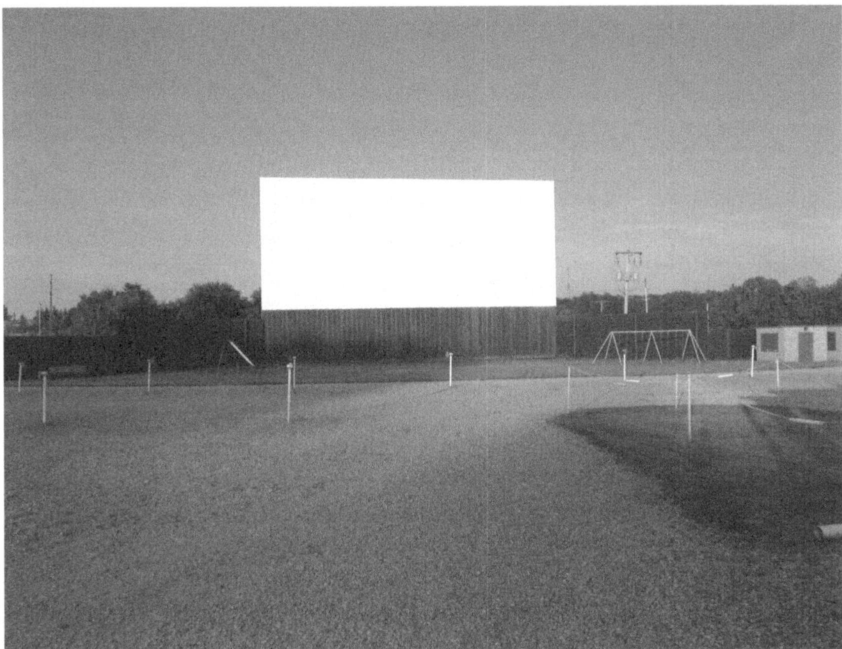

Figure 4.5   *Magic City Drive-in Theatre, opened in 1953 in Barberton, Ohio, 2012. Photo courtesy Andrew Borgen, Creative Commons Attribution-NoDerivs 2.0 licence*

penetration of mass-produced imagery into the landscape. While television or radio would broadcast mass entertainment across considerable distances into the home, the drive-in (like the billboard that preceded it) became a highly visible sign of the mass media's infiltration of the countryside (Figure 4.5). The movies tamed the land through the drive-in, just as the cowboys and cavalry did time and again in countless westerns projected across the screen. After frontier conquests and the rise of cities in the nineteenth century, the consolidation of the twentieth century involved the development of such spaces existing on the fringes of established or burgeoning communities. 'Out in the open spaces, in potato field and prairie, cars were being parked by the thousand, bumper to bumper, in drive-in theatres', *Life* magazine observed of the phenomenon in 1952.[74]

Film exhibition has been linked to the outdoors since the early days of cinema, when programmes of short films were screened at fairs, beer gardens, city squares and other open-air gatherings. Although tapering off in the 1910s, outdoor exhibition continued through the development of the first drive-in theatre in Camden, New Jersey, in 1933. That event marked a critical step in the progression of exhibition and consumption models by crossing cinema with other commodities and retail strategies that would eventually include strip malls, condominium developments, enclosed malls and 'big-box' stores, as well as multiplex movie-theatre chains. After World War II, the outdoor theatre, where viewers could remain in their cars and watch the screen through the frame of the windshield, benefited from a sharp increase in car ownership alongside retailers' cultivation of the post-war baby boom's teenage population as a new consumer class. The mid-1950s represented the peak of the drive-in's popularity in America. Inversely proportional to the downward trajectory of American movie-theatre attendance discussed in Chapter 1, drive-ins grew from less than 300 at the end of 1947 to over 3,500 by 1953, the year Hollywood heralded widescreen formats as the possible saviour of traditional indoor theatres.[75] At the time of *The Searchers'* release in March 1956 about 4,000 drive-ins existed in America – accounting for a quarter of all movie theatres.[76]

An amalgamation of diverse social and consumer spaces, drive-ins (sometimes known as 'ozoners') brought together the parking lot, the take-out counter, the playground and the movie theatre in a single entertainment experience. Catering to baby-boom families, exhibitors provided laundry and baby-bottle services, nurseries, kiddie rides, miniature golf and driving ranges to accommodate a wider spectrum of moviegoers than were likely to attend urban indoor theatres. Located on the outskirts of towns, cities and tract-housing developments created to house returning veterans and their families, the drive-in became an escape from the city, the suburbs and the farm. In less-populated areas, the drive-in might be the only place to see movies in fifty miles or more.[77] They were outdoor spots meant for social interaction. 'People went to the drive-in for many reasons but, unlike patrons at indoor shows, the film itself was hardly ever a major priority', claims Kerry Segrave. 'They went to drive-ins to let their kids play, to have sex, to party, to spend time with their kids, to be outdoors, to enjoy the various amenities available at most ozoners, to be with their cars, and so on.'[78]

The projection screen was a drive-in's most conspicuous visual element, not only for those attending the show, but also for those passing by the theatre, day and night. A monumental structure with a projection surface averaging 40 x 80 feet, the screen tower distinguished a drive-in from what might otherwise be a parking lot or field (Figure 4.6).[79] From the screen's base the audience fanned out into the landscape in rows of parking spots intersected by lines of speaker stands. Early drive-in screen towers were art deco buildings sheathed in stone, concrete or stucco and skirted by carefully pruned shrubbery.[80] Later, lighter versions could contain multiple materials, including plywood, asbestos, aluminium, galvanised iron, steel and transite. For the typical American drive-in of the 1950s, building and maintaining the

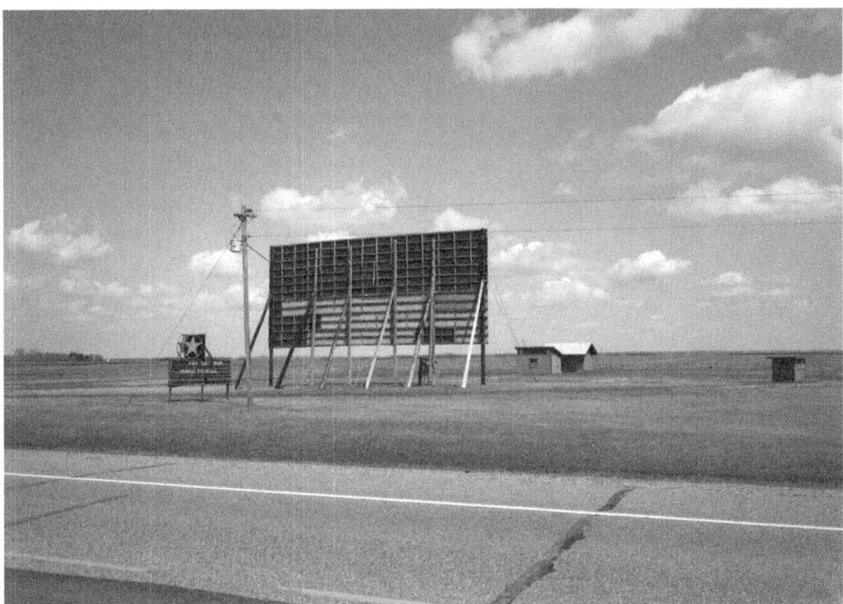

Figure 4.6   *Mahnomen City Drive-in Movie Theatre, Mahnomen, Minnesota, May 1990. Library of Congress, Prints & Photographs Division, Historic American Buildings Survey, HABS MN-121-1*

screen might cost as much as, or more than, the entire projection and sound system. It might require up to six coats of white paint to achieve adequate reflectivity in an outdoor setting, and would normally require repainting every one to two years.

These monuments of modern popular culture often referenced their regional surroundings with colourful murals, installed on the back of the tower in neon and paint, representing scenes of history, folklore or wildlife. For example, screen towers in Texas – a state with hundreds of drive-ins by the mid-1950s – were decorated with cattle, cowboys, Native Americans, wagon trains and moonlit prairies (Figure 4.7).[81] In the case of westerns, such images – seen as one entered the drive-in – augured a continuity between the surrounding landscape and the images produced by the screen. As drive-ins 'mushroom[ed] out of the open prairie', according to a 1956 report, relating the screen to the surrounding environment through these visual cues transformed it into a time-bending window onto the landscape.[82]

The growth of the drive-in in the 1950s paralleled increases in population migration out of eastern industrial cities to the surrounding suburbs or less-congested, auto-centric western cities. In the months that *The Searchers* played on screens across America, drive-in theatre construction outpaced

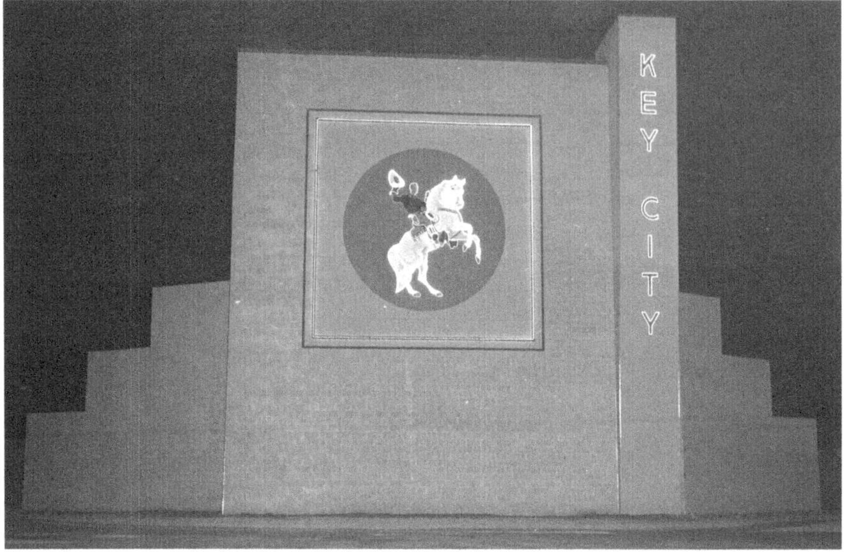

Figure 4.7   *Key City Drive-in Theatre tower, Abilene, Texas, 1954. Abilene Photograph Collection, Hardin-Simmons University, Abilene, Texas*

that of indoor theatres nearly four to one. 'The Western states, with 39 new drive-ins, are the leading construction area in the outdoor field . . . reflecting the tremendous population growth experienced by that region in the postwar years', reported one industry journal.[83] As on-screen wagon trains mirrored the population shift of loaded cars and trailers on newly-constructed inter-state freeways, the pioneer myth of the western seemed to justify the reality of twentieth-century car culture. 'The wide expanses of land, the free move-ment of men on horses', Robert Warshow pointed out at the height of the western in 1954, 'the physical freedom they represent belongs to the moral "openness" of the West'.[84] Families who sought the individualistic myth of re-conquering the wilderness, however, also held tight to the acquired com-forts of industrial production and modern living. As Todd Gitlin puts it,

> For growing numbers [in the 1950s], daily life was delivered from the cramp of the city, lifted out to the half-wide, half-open spaces, where the long-sought and long-feared American wilderness could be trimmed back and made habitable. The prairie became the lawn; the ranch, the ranch house; the saloon, the Formica bar. And the six-shooter became the point-and-shoot home movie camera.[85]

The drive-in fitted perfectly into this mind-set, with amenities that created thoroughly safe, sanitised renditions of the on-screen settlers' experiences crossing the American wilderness. Beyond playgrounds and golf, it offered

picnic grounds, canoe ponds, carousels and pony rides. Some drive-in operators modelled their entire operation on a western theme. The Cow Town
Drive-In in St. Joseph, Missouri, for example, honoured the city's 'important
role in building the west [sic]' by creating a ranch-like setting with buildings
in brick and redwood, fencing in cedar, and scattered wagon wheels and oxen
yokes. 'We are constantly being held up by little buckaroos with cap pistols',
the owner joked in a 1954 *Boxoffice* article that encouraged operators to 'Give
It the Rustic Touch'.[86] Theatre suppliers tapped into this trend, as with the
Fence Company of America's promotion of 'hand-peeled' and 'knife-peeled'
rail fence and line posts to 'create atmosphere that fits into [the] natural surroundings of the outdoor theatre'.[87]

At least one drive-in had a miniature train ride that circled the screen
through 'a landscaped region of small evergreens and shrubs' and passed
through a tunnel built into the back of the tower. Such offerings tied the
cinema to landscape in particularly important ways, recalling early 'cinema
of attractions' films such as *Going Through the Tunnel* (1898) from Thomas
Edison's 'Southern Pacific Company Series' of films shot in the West.[88] In
referencing (deliberately or not) these early films of commercial cinema,
drive-ins also opened up new ground for amateur film-making. Pony rides,
miniature trains and canoe rentals became prime occasions to load the camera
and shoot one's little 'pioneers' in action. Commercial and vernacular cinema
intersected and fed each other at the drive-in.

The life cycle of the drive-in was less than that of the western, however,
lasting little more than thirty years. By the early 1980s slightly more than two
thousand still remained, but that number dropped to less than a thousand
by 1987.[89] 'In much of the U.S., it may not survive the end of the decade',
intoned *Time* magazine in 1983, quoting popular historian Oscar Handlin's
claim that 'Their decline is a sign that a certain stage in American life is
over'.[90] Many factors contributed to this demise. Drive-ins built on previously
undeveloped expanses of land in the 1940s and 1950s had been enveloped by
residential or commercial building by the 1970s and 1980s, raising property
values and making the land too valuable for seasonal use. The development
of multiplexes – often on land occupied by, or near, drive-ins – transformed
the indoor movie theatre into an entertainment complex offering expanded
food concessions, game arcades, ample parking and other features previously
found only at the drive-in. Advances in projection and audio technology,
like Dolby surround-sound systems, widened the already existing quality
gap between indoor and outdoor exhibition. Shifts in teen culture and lib-
eralised sexual mores made dark lots and car backseats far less appealing for
high-school trysts. More than all of these reasons, however, the advent of
shopping malls may have delivered the sharpest blow to drive-in cinemas.

The indoor mall united shopping, dining and entertainment in a single, enormous complex. Anne Friedberg notes that the movies are a key component to this commercial model, with theatres often placed at the far end of malls as anchors allowing and encouraging multiple consumer and social activities en route to a screening.[91] This retail strategy reduces movie watching to one activity among many for the mall moviegoer, ironically returning the cinema to its roots as an activity centred in shopping districts.

As drive-ins died out, they were sometimes sold to commercial developers building condominiums or shopping centres. Others were converted to different purposes, such as self-storage businesses, where the vestiges of the site's cinematic past, including the screen tower, might be left intact. Sites lacking any significant commercial appeal were simply abandoned to the elements. After anything of value, such as projectors and kitchen equipment, was sold, what remained would rot, rust and eventually collapse. By the time Gordon projected *5 Year Drive-By* at Twentynine Palms on a weekend in 2001, dilapidated drive-ins and their weathered screens had long dotted the American landscape as reminders of a lost twentieth-century popular imaginary (Figure 4.8).

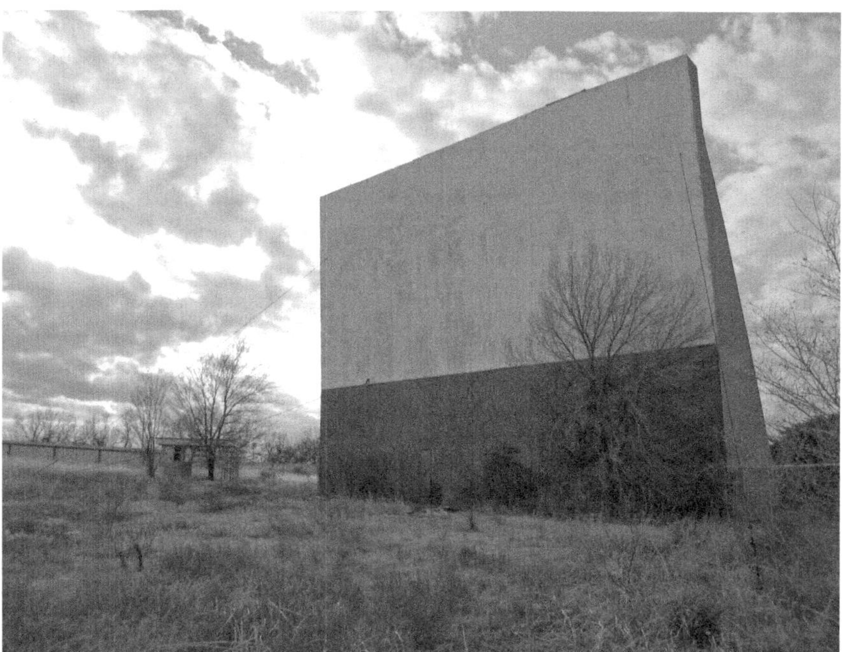

Figure 4.8   *The abandoned Chief Drive-in Movie Theatre in Quanah, Texas, 2006. The drive-in's name likely references Quanah Parker, a nineteenth-century chief of the Comanche nation. Photo courtesy Josh Berglund, Creative Commons Attribution 2.0 Generic licence*

If the drive-in theatre had become the cinema ruin par excellence, it is important to acknowledge that even at its height it embodied elements of ruin and archaeology. Indoor theatres always retained first-run rights for films, so drive-ins regularly projected second- and third-run prints. By the time a film arrived at the local drive-in, it might be scratched, grimy and full of ellipses where torn celluloid had been cut out and the filmstrip re-spliced. What projectors did not wear down, nature would. Using fabric for the projection surface might produce a 'lofty flapping canvas screen [that] made the movie lovers look pretty grotesque when the wind blew', according to one observer.[92] Manufacturers of pre-fabricated metal screens in the 1950s emphasised their product's durability against wind pressure of thirty pounds (or more) per square foot; paint companies devised outdoor plastic screen coatings meant to last up to eight years.[93] From one season to the next, the drive-in's exposure to the elements placed it at risk of significant damage to equipment, structures and materials. 'A Drive-in that is completely closed for the winter deteriorates rapidly', observed one theatre executive in 1956.[94] In both the worn prints it projected and its susceptibility to natural elements, the drive-in was always bound to evoke the unremitting entropic effects of time's passage, potentially triggering ideas of loss, memory and nostalgia in the spectator, even as the experience lent itself to engaging social interactions.

American Landscapes and the Cinematic Imaginary

When Douglas Gordon first visited Los Angeles in the mid-1990s, he discovered an anomaly of time that mirrored the drive-in's simultaneous evocation of the contemporary, commodified image and the irretrievable past. 'All we have to look at there is a city built around a film industry, around Hollywood, which is nothing, it's not even existed for a hundred years', he would remark. 'And then before that . . . there is no trace of anything except for the dinosaurs, so you've got this gigantic gap.'[95] In Gordon's description, the global capital of film entertainment is the spot where modern mass media projects onto the pre-historic fossil, collapsing in a stark, frightening way the vastly different temporalities of twentieth-century society and the Mesozoic era of 245 to 65 million years ago. It was on this trip to Hollywood that Gordon first visited Twentynine Palms 'to see the landscape', and it may have then that his idea for a time-based, desert film installation was conceived.[96]

The sedimentary rock of Monument Valley is even older than Hollywood's dinosaurs, formed during the Palaeozoic era nearly 300 million years ago. In *The Searchers* and Ford's six other westerns shot there from 1939 to 1964, the stratified mesas and buttes of siltstone, sandstone and shale rising a thousand feet or more from the desert floor offer the film spectator a visual metaphor for the immensity of time stretching back beyond comprehension. The abraded surfaces and irregular profiles of these stone outcroppings recall the damaged forms of ruined architecture that give the valley its name. The cinematic grandiosity of this landscape reaches its apex in *The Searchers*' subdued action and long takes, as movie reviewers noted on the film's premiere. 'The VistaVision-Technicolor photographic excursion through the southwest – presenting in bold and colorful outline the arid country and area of buttes and giant rock formations – is eyefilling and impressive', remarked Ronald Holloway in *Variety*.[97] When Gordon finally had his chance to present *5 Year Drive-By* under conditions approximating his ideal by placing it in the empty expanses of Joshua Tree National Park on 22–23 September 2001 (just days after the events of 9/11, when ruins and monuments were very much on people's minds), the film's images of these distinctive geological forms resonated with the parched, stony landscape surrounding the screen. This confrontation between screen and landscape produced an echo effect between object and representation, geographic space and filmic space, and the pro-filmic and the filmic. 'As the landscape disappears, the image of the landscape starts to come out', Gordon explains of his work, an effect that produces a rhythmic passage from one landscape to another, mediated by the interface of the screen monument. Even in close-ups of John Wayne (which were indeed shown during the installation's run in Twentynine Palms) or shots of other characters, objects and actions, the obstinate stone-stillness of the image harmonised its forms with the petrified backdrop.[98]

Erected in an open area of gravel and sand surrounded by sage and cactus, the 'specially constructed, scaled-down drive-in screen'[99] rose from the valley floor like an outcropping amid the sparse, hardy vegetation (see Figure 4.1). Large stones arranged in a line alongside it (reminiscent of ancient worship grounds but likely placed there to demarcate a property line or parking area), telephone lines running behind it, and settlements in the distance all signalled the encroachment of civilisation. The screen was a fraction of the size of the largest drive-in screens and lacked the stone-and-brick shells or wood-and-steel scaffolding that supported such screens. Yet by arranging a special screening of *The Searchers* at a local drive-in in tandem with *5 Year Drive-By*, Gordon directly invoked the correspondence between his desert screen and that form of cinema exhibition.[100] His installation appeared to be more fragile than a typical drive-in screen tower, unlikely to last even the five years of the work's title.

Visitors' accounts of the installation provide valuable insights into the interaction between natural environment and film projection. According to Gordon,

> The notion of so-called 'real time' [in *5 Year Drive-By*] is dependent on whether you're sitting outside or inside, whether you feel the wind or don't feel the wind. Who you're with and who you're not with . . . if you're waiting for something or remembering, those bring about different modes of perceiving time.[101]

David Harding, one of Gordon's instructors from his student days at the Glasgow School of Art, flew to California for the event and was overwhelmed by the experience. 'Nothing had prepared me for this. It was dark as we walked up to the huge screen set in the desert scrub some way behind the inn. It was stunning', Harding claims. 'I stood mesmerised and soaked in the detail. The intricate weave of Wayne's cowboy hat, the fine check on his shirt, his neckerchief, his staring, steel-blue eyes, the gnarled, chiselled, confrontational expression on his face.' Harding returned the next day to find that 'The film was playing but the screen was still white and showed no image'. He explains, 'Slowly, against a clear, pale blue sky and a diagonal ridge of mountains behind the screen, cutting it in two, John Wayne appeared – virtually the same image as the night before. At one frame every 20 minutes, the only change in an hour of viewing was the slightest movement at the end of his neckerchief.'[102] Philip Monk describes the way the work entered into the rhythms of the landscape sweeping around it. 'Environmental light and weather, the flight of birds or the call of coyotes ply our perception of the work and play uncannily upon motifs and scenes in *The Searchers*. At any one moment, the image is static but the screening enters into a dynamic with its setting.'[103]

Exile

By compounding the screen's resemblance to a drive-in screen with its placement in a desert flat along a line of large stones and the projection of a film shot in the desert but projected at a frame-rate slow enough to produce a series of imperceptibly changing still images, *5 Year Drive-By* unites the archaeology of a ruined drive-in culture with the slow and hardly detectable (but constant) processes of nature. Harding and Monk both emphasise a close, almost 'natural' relationship between the installation and the desert environment in their observations. Against the unchanging profile of the mountains, the image emerged 'virtually the same' from one day to the next. The movements and sounds of wildlife, like the wind, placed this comparatively 'still', silent film, along with its fixed screen, on the same kinetic and temporal register as the mountains and desert floor. '[In] the static images of *5 Year Drive-By*', Monk points out, 'the concatenation of past, present, and future is rendered null in the perpetual, it seems, present of the image'.[104] The time of the image entered the temporal register of natural processes.

Upon seeing Gordon's installations at the Turner Prize exhibition in 1996, critic Adrian Searle claimed 'For Gordon, and many others of his generation, film is simply a part of the shared modern landscape of the imagination'.[105] *5 Year Drive-By* represents drive-in movies as a bygone culture, inscribed within the fading culture of movie exhibition itself, folding back into the landscape it references in the imaginary of both its film narratives and its exhibition conditions. In Gordon's staging, film dimples the landscape like a healing scar that slowly returns the commodified space of cultural discourse that one drives *in*, to the undifferentiated and undeveloped natural landscape that one drives *by*. This provocatively situates the legacy of cinema and drive-in theatres in relationship to history, memory and identity as the three relate to the land.[106]

In its construction, *5 Year Drive-By* unearths stratified memories of obsolete technologies like film projection, obsolete economic models like the Hollywood studio system, obsolete narrative forms like the classic western, and obsolete exhibition models like the drive-in theatre. Situating the piece in the desert in 2001 placed that stratification in relief against the opposing ideas of continuity of time and physical impermanence and the inevitability of change on a scale of millennia, ages and epochs. In underscoring the certainty and swiftness of change in narrative forms and media technologies within a lifetime, it established the idea of the ruin as a structural, accelerating condition of contemporary living, where the 'death' of cinema is more generally the 'death' of medium specificity and hegemonic models, whether inside or outside the art world.

Since Gordon's 2001 presentation of *5 Year Drive-By*, excerpts have been shown in alternative formats in multiple exhibitions of his work.[107] The example of the piece in the collection of Norwegian telecommunications company Telenor has achieved the work's temporal potential, having been screened in its full, five-year version from 2002 to 2007. The projection took place over five years on a screen hung in the smart, glassed-in atrium of Telenor's corporate headquarters outside Oslo, however, rather than on a screen abandoned to the American desert. The work's 'retirement' to a decorative role in the lobby of a mobile telecommunications company aptly reflects the changes in media of the past half-century that have profoundly transformed film and cinema, as well as art.

Notes

1. In the wake of the 11 September attacks on the World Trade Center and Pentagon only days before, it is likely a sense of modernity in ruins was already in the minds of many visitors to this installation.

2. Michael Witt, 'The Death(s) of Cinema According to Godard', *Screen* 40:3 (Fall 1999): 331–46, p. 331.

3. See for example Paolo Cerchi Usai, *The Death of Cinema: History, Cultural Memory and the Digital Dark Age* (London: BFI, 2001); Stefan Jovanovic, 'The Ending(s) of Cinema: Notes on the Recurrent Demise of the Seventh Art, Part 1', *Offscreen*, 7:4 (April 2003), see http://offscreen.com/view/seventh_art1 (accessed 1 September 2015).

4. Anne Friedberg, 'Les Flâneurs du Mal(l): Cinema and the Postmodern Condition', *PMLA* 106:3 (May 1991): 419–31, p. 428. See also Laura Mulvey, *Death 24x a Second: Stillness and the Moving Image* (London: Reaktion Books, 2006).

5. These changes had a similar effect on film studies. Within film theory, the realisation of the possible demise of analogue production and movie-theatre exhibition prompted a reconsideration of the role of time within the medium. Among other things, technologies from the cassette to DVD produced new interactions between viewer and film by offering audiences fresh possibilities for slowing, replaying and pausing the image. The issue of temporality as the essence of cinema came under scrutiny with Gilles Deleuze's Bergsonian study *Cinema 1: The Movement-Image* (Minneapolis: University of Minnesota Press, 1986).

6. Malcolm Turvey, Hal Foster, Chrissie Iles, George Baker, Matthew Buckingham and Anthony McCall, 'Round Table: The Projected Image in Contemporary Art', *October* 104 (Spring 2003): 71–96, p. 74. Even as late as 2007 Mary Ann Doane would remark that 'the cinema-we-once-knew is dead or dying'. Mary Ann Doane, 'Laura Mulvey, *Death 24x a Second: Stillness and the Moving Image*', *Screen* 48:1 (Spring 2007): 113–18, p. 114.

7. For example, with the 2010 Cannes Film Festival's Palme d'Or award to *Uncle Boonmee Who Can Recall His Past Lives* (Apichatpong Weerasethakul, 2010), a film conceived as part of an installation, Colin MacCabe observed, 'If it can seem that art cinema is dying in the multiplexes, it is nevertheless finding new life in galleries and museums where the moving image has become more and more dominant'. Colin MacCabe, 'An Amorous Catfish', *Film Quarterly* 64:1 (Fall 2010): 59–61, p. 60.

8. Yann Beauvais, 'Speed Reeling', in *3e Biennale d'art contemporain de Lyon: installation, cinéma, vidéo, informatique* (Paris: Réunion des Musées Nationaux, 1995), pp. 65–6.

9. Kerry Brougher, *Hall of Mirrors: Art and Film Since 1945* (Los Angeles: Museum of Contemporary Art/Monacelli Press, 1996) p. 23.

10. Beauvais, 'Speed Reeling', in *3e Biennale d'art contemporain de Lyon*, p. 67.

11. For an alternative view drawing links between recent film installations and

Expanded Cinema, see Jonathan Walley, '"Not an Image of the Death of Film": Contemporary Expanded Cinema and Experimental Film', in A. L. Rees, Duncan White, Steven Ball and David Curtis (eds), *Expanded Cinema: Art, Performance, Film* (London: Tate Publishing, 2011), pp. 241–51.

12. Gordon, as quoted in Nancy Spector, 'This is all True, and Contradictory, if not Hysterical', in Douglas Gordon, *Déjà-Vu: Questions and Answers, Volume 2, 1997–1998* (Paris: Musée d'Art Moderne de la Ville de Paris, 2000), p. 76.

13. Ibid. p. 70. In a conversation with Russell Gordon on 27 December 1995 – the eve of the centenary of the Lumière Brothers first public cinema screening – Gordon claimed of the cinema 'If it's not dead already, it's dying for sure. So we are afforded this distance, where you can make an analysis of it and enjoy it at the same time'. Russell Ferguson, 'Divided Self', *Parkett* 49 (1997): 59–63, p. 60.

14. In addition to building a reputation for privileging extreme slow motion with appropriated films (*24 Hour Psycho, 5 Year Drive-By*), Gordon has also created films in near-real time in his original film productions (*Feature Film* (1999), *Zidane: A 21st Century Portrait* (2006)). Johannes von Moltke has identified a 'ruin aesthetic' in film production and reception that contains some of the properties of Gordon's interventions within the film document itself. He counts among these 'Slow, ostentatious camera movements, long takes, [and] contemplative viewing'. Johannes von Moltke, 'Ruin Cinema', in Julia Hell and Andrea Schönle (eds), *Ruins of Modernity* (Durham, NC: Duke University Press, 2010), p. 414.

15. Gordon, as quoted in Spector, 'This is all True, and Contradictory, if not Hysterical', in Gordon, *Déjà-Vu*, vol. 2, p. 80.

16. Jerry Saltz, 'Up and Down', *Village Voice* (30 March 1999), 141, reprinted in Jerry Saltz, *Seeing Out Loud: Village Voice Art Columns, Fall 1998–Winter 2003* (Great Barrington: The Figures, 2003), p. 370.

17. Spector, 'This is all True, and Contradictory, if not Hysterical', in Gordon, *Déjà-Vu*, vol. 2, p. 67. Specter prefaces her important 1997 interview with Gordon with the admission that 'I had only been able to view a couple of his video installations – and only a few more documentary tapes – over the last two or three years. Thus I was destined to make comments and ask questions based on my own fantasies of what *Psycho* must look like when slowed down to near stasis'.

18. Douglas Gordon *et al.*, 'Artist Questionnaire: 21 Responses', *October* 100 (Spring 2002): 6–97, p. 46.

19. Simon Sheikh, 'Art is Merely an Excuse for Communication', in Gordon, *Déjà-Vu*, vol. 2, p. 17. One of Gordon's earliest works is a text-based piece, installed in a rotunda at University College, London, entitled *Meaning and Location* (1990).

20. Gordon, as quoted in Jan Debbaut, 'Excerpt: . . . in conversation: Jan Debbaut and Douglas Gordon', in Gordon, *Déjà-Vu*, vol. 2, p. 113.

21. Gordon, as quoted in David Sylvester, 'Interview of Douglas Gordon', in Russell Ferguson (ed.), *Douglas Gordon* (Cambridge, MA: MIT Press, 2001), p. 153.

22. The work has even inspired a novella, Don Delillo's *Omega Point*. See Charles

McGrath, 'Don Delillo, a Writer by Accident Whose Course is Deliberate', *New York Times* (4 February 2010) p. C1.

23. Gordon, as quoted in Scarlet Cheng, 'He Tweaks the Language of Hollywood: Douglas Gordon's Video Installations Cast Such Famous Films as *Psycho* and *Taxi Driver* in an Unfamiliar Light', *Los Angeles Times* (16 September 2001), p. 1. In a variation on this idea, artist Jim Campbell scanned every frame of the film in *Illuminated Average #1: Hitchcock's* Psycho (2000) to produce a lightbox image of a textured haze.

24. Richard Flood, '24 Hour Psycho', *Parkett* 49 (May 1997): 37–9, pp. 38–9.

25. Gordon, as quoted in Amine Haase, 'On the Other Side of the Mirror', in Douglas Gordon, *Déjà-Vu: Questions and Answers, Volume 3, 1999–2000* (Paris: Musée d'Art Moderne de la Ville de Paris, 2000), p. 141. 'The viewer is catapulted back into the past by his recollection of the original [film], and at the same time he is drawn into the future by his expectations of an already familiar narrative', Gordon says of this exercise. 'A slowly changing present forces itself in between [the two].' See Russell Ferguson, 'Trust Me', in Ferguson (ed.), *Douglas Gordon*, p. 16.

26. Michael Newman, 'Moving Image in the Gallery since the 1990s', in Stuart Comer (ed.), *Film and Video Art* (London: Tate Publishing, 2009), p. 91.

27. Gordon, as quoted in Haase, 'On the Other Side of the Mirror', in Gordon, *Déjà-Vu*, vol. 3, p. 140.

28. Mulvey, *Death 24x a Second*, p. 102.

29. André Bazin, *What Is Cinema?*, vol. 1, trans. Hugh Gray (Berkeley: University of California Press, 2005), p. 15.

30. Eric Mézil, 'Douglas Scissorhands', in Eric Mézil (ed.), *Douglas Gordon: Où se trouvent les clefs?* (Paris: Éditions Gallimard/Collection Lambert en Avignon, 2008), p. 90, and Flood, '24 Hour Psycho', p. 38.

31. Graham Fagen, 'The Exact Vague History', in Gordon, *Déjà-Vu*, vol. 3, p. 83. In fact, user-generated recreations of the work occasionally have appeared on on-line video-sharing sites.

32. Gordon, as quoted in ibid. p. 110.

33. Gordon, as quoted in ibid. p. 80.

34. Gordon, as quoted in Cheng, 'He Tweaks the Language of Hollywood', p. 1.

35. See illustrations in Douglas Gordon, Mirta D'Argenzio and Giorgio Verzotti, *. . . prettymucheverywordwritten, spoken, heard, overheard from 1989 . . .: Voyage in Italy* (Milan: Skira, 2006), pp. 86–8, and Newman, 'Moving Image in the Gallery Since the 1990s', in Comer, *Film and Video Art*, p. 92.

36. Curator Klaus Biesenbach explains of the 1993 Kunste-Werke configuration, 'Gordon and [curator Charles] Esche had brought a ten-by-fourteen-foot translucent screen that we leaned against one of the pillars for support'. Klaus Biesenbach, 'Sympathy for the Devil', in Douglas Gordon and Klaus Peter Biesenbach, *Douglas Gordon: Timeline* (New York: Museum of Modern Art, 2006), p. 13. See illustrations in Gordon, D'Argenzio and Verzotti, *. . . prettymucheverywordwritten, spoken, heard, overheard from 1989 . . .*, pp. 27 and 89.

37. Gordon, as quoted in Spector, 'This is all True, and Contradictory, if not Hysterical', in Gordon, *Déjà-Vu*, vol. 2, p. 75.

38. Katrina Brown, *DG: Douglas Gordon* (London: Tate Publishing, 2004), p. 26.

39. 'Tant sa marque de fabrique que l'archétype d'un cinéma qui s'expose.' Françoise Parfait, *Vidéo: un art contemporain* (Paris: Éditions du Regard, 2001), p. 156. My translation.

40. For examples of these works in these configurations, see *10ms^{-1}* (1994) illustrated in Brown, *Douglas Gordon*, pp. 44–5; *Remote Viewing 13.05.94 (Horror Movie)* (1995) in *Wild Walls* at the Stedelijk Museum, Amsterdam, 1995, illustrated in ibid. p. 52; *Hysterical* (1994–5) in *Propositions* at the Musée départmental d'art contemporain de Rochechouart, 1996, illustrated in ibid. p. 46; *Film Noir (Twins)* (1995) illustrated in ibid. p. 50; *Film Noir (Fly)* (1995) illustrated in Douglas Gordon, *Douglas Gordon: Kidnapping* (Eindhoven: Stedelijk Van Abbemuseum, 1998), p. 72, both from *Entr'Acte 3, Douglas Gordon* at the Stedelijk Van Abbemuseum, Eindhoven, 1995; *Confessions of a Justified Sinner* (1995–6) against adjacent walls in the 1996 Turner Prize exhibition, Tate Britain, and side-by-side in *By Night* at the Fondation Cartier, Paris, 1996, illustrated in ibid. pp. 76–9; *Black and White (Babylon)* (1996) at Galerie Micheline Szwajcer, Antwerp, 1997, illustrated in ibid. pp. 154–7. Even *24 Hour Psycho* has undergone this doubling effect in the two-screen projection *24 Hour Psycho Back and Forth and to and fro* (2008), which presents the original version of the work beside a version played in reverse.

41. Gordon, D'Argenzio and Verzotti, . . . *prettymucheverywordwritten, spoken, heard, overheard from 1989 . . .*, p. 18.

42. For a consideration of dichotomy and the divided self in Gordon's work, see Brown, *Douglas Gordon*, pp. 65–70.

43. As Brown says of *Black and White (Babylon)*, 'Increasing the scale from the intended intimate, domestic to the monumental . . . effectively strip[s] the work of its erotic potential. Brown, *Douglas Gordon*, p. 51.

44. Gordon, as quoted in Sheikh, 'Art is Merely an Excuse for Communication', in Gordon, *Déjà-Vu*, vol. 2, p. 23.

45. Gordon, as quoted in ibid. p. 21.

46. Robert Morris, 'Notes on Sculpture, Part 1', *Artforum* 4:6 (February 1966): 42–4, reprinted in Robert Morris, *Continuous Project Altered Daily* (Cambridge, MA: MIT Press, 1993), p. 4.

47. Gordon, as quoted in Haase, 'On the Other Side of the Mirror', in Gordon, *Déjà-Vu*, vol. 3, p. 143.

48. Michael Fried, 'Art and Objecthood', in Michael Fried, *Art and Objecthood* (Chicago: University of Chicago, 1998), p. 164. Of particular importance in the current context is Fried's difficulty in reconciling the modernist fascination with cinema with his argument for the atemporal object. Although he claimed film is not theatre, he also believed it cannot be called modern art.

49. Rosalind Krauss, *Passages in Modern Sculpture* (Cambridge, MA: MIT Press, 1977), pp. 238–9; emphasis in text.

50. As Friedrich Meschede has pointed out, the elimination of sound in *24 Hour Psycho* (due to its slowed image rate) tends to make Gordon's source material seem older than it is, as well as 'more monumental and timeless'. This effect extends to his other projected works. Friedrich Meschede, 'Lessness: Phenomena of Time in the Work of Douglas Gordon', in Douglas Gordon and Eckhard Schneider, *Douglas Gordon* (Hannover: Kunstverein Hannover, 1998), unpaged.
51. This is evinced most directly in his series of works related to James Hogg's 1824 Gothic novel, *Private Memoirs and Confessions of a Justified Sinner*. The novel inspired not only the projection-installation *Confessions of a Justified Sinner*, but also served as the source for *Fog* (2002) and *Black Star* (2002).
52. Florence M. Hetzler, 'Causality: Ruin Time and Ruins', *Leonardo*, 21:1 (1988): 51–5, pp. 51–2.
53. Brown, *DG*, p. 22.
54. Erika Balsom, *Exhibiting Cinema in Contemporary Art* (Amsterdam: Amsterdam University Press, 2013), p. 95; Christine Ross, *The Past is the Present; It's the Future Too: The Temporal Turn in Contemporary Art* (New York: Continuum, 2012), p. 171.
55. von Moltke, 'Ruin Cinema', in Hell and Schönle (eds), *Ruins of Modernity*.
56. *Andreas Huyssen*, 'Nostalgia for Ruins', *Grey Room* 23 (Spring 2006): 6–21, p. 7. See also Hell and Schönle (eds), *Ruins of Modernity*; Brian Dillon (ed.), *Ruins* (Cambridge, MA: MIT Press/Whitechapel Gallery, 2011).
57. In addition to North America, drive-in movie theatres have operated (and in some cases continue to operate) in South America, Europe, Africa, Asia and Australia.
58. In 2008 Gordon showed the double-screen diptych version, *24 Hour Psycho Back and Forth and To and Fro* (2008) as part of the 'theanyspacewhatever' exhibition at the Solomon R. Guggenheim Museum. In this expanded version, one screen exhibits the film transfer of *Psycho* as it appears in *24 Hour Psycho*, while the other displays it played in reverse, as though being slowly rewound.
59. 'Auto-Kino!', see http://www.e-flux.com/announcements/auto-kino/ (accessed 1 September 2015).
60. Linnie Blake, 'New Genre Forms in "New Hollywood" Film', in David Holloway and John Beck (eds), *American Visual Cultures* (London and New York: Continuum, 2005), p. 217.
61. Peter Cowie, *John Ford and the American West* (New York: Harry N. Abrams, Inc., 2004), pp. 166–8, 172.
62. Philip Monk, *Double-Cross: The Hollywood Films of Douglas Gordon* (Toronto: The Power Plant/Art Gallery of York University, 2003), p. 81.
63. Douglas Gordon in *3e Biennale d'art contemporain de Lyon: installation, cinéma, vidéo, informatique*, pp. 371–2, reprinted in Gordon, *Douglas Gordon: Kidnapping*, pp. 137–8.
64. Gordon, as quoted in David Sylvester, 'Interview of Douglas Gordon', in Ferguson, *Douglas Gordon*, p. 167.
65. Ford, as quoted in Jean Mitry, 'John Ford Accords an Exclusive Interview

to *Cinémonde*', in Gerald Peary and Jenny Lefcourt (eds), *John Ford: Interviews* (Jackson: University Press of Mississippi, 2001), p. 31.

66. Ford, as quoted in Eric Leguèbe, 'John Ford', in Peary and Lefcourt (eds), *John Ford: Interviews*, pp. 73–4.

67. Douglas Gordon in *3e Biennale d'art contemporain de Lyon: installation, cinéma, vidéo, informatique*, reprinted in Gordon, *Douglas Gordon: Kidnapping*, p. 139. For a photograph of the installation, see Parfait, *Vidéo: un art contemporain*, p. 309.

68. Gordon, as quoted in Debbaut, 'Excerpt: . . . in conversation: Jan Debbaut and Douglas Gordon', in Gordon, *Déjà-Vu*, vol. 2, p. 106; and Fagen, 'The Exact Vague History', in Gordon, *Déjà-Vu*, vol. 3, p. 116.

69. Gordon, *Douglas Gordon: Kidnapping*, p. 136.

70. Haase, 'On the Other Side of the Mirror', in Gordon, *Déjà-Vu*, vol. 3, p. 147. One critic recommended the works be seen at night, from outside the building. See Dominic Eichler, 'Berlin Art Diary', artnet (20 April 1999), http://www.artnet.com/magazine_pre2000/reviews/eichler/eichler4-20-99.asp (accessed 1 September 2015).

71. Gordon, as quoted in Spector, 'This is all True, and Contradictory, if not Hysterical', in Gordon, *Déjà-Vu*, vol. 2, p. 72.

72. Gordon, as quoted in ibid. p. 72.

73. In creating a long-duration outdoor film event designed to inspire pilgrimage to a spectacular setting, *5 Year Drive-By* has affinities with *Eniaios* (1947–91), Gregory J. Markopoulo's monumental, eighty-hour film, ten-hour segments of which have been projected since 2004 over three nights, every four years, in the Peloponnesian mountain village of Lyssaraia.

74. 'Drive-in Film Business Burns up the Prairies', *Life* (24 September 1952): 105–6, 108, p. 105.

75. *Life* reported only 295 drive-ins at the start of 1948, and estimated 3,580 for 1953. Ibid. p. 105.

76. Between 1954 and 1958, drive-in theatres rose from 3,775 to 4,063 in the US, compared to a drop from 14,716 to 12,291 indoor movie theatres over the same period. At least 196 drive-ins were built in 1956 alone. See Segrave, *Drive-in Theaters, a History from their Inception in 1933* (Jefferson: McFarland & Co., 1992), pp. 235–6; Phil Hannum, '$51,809,395 for 250 New Theatres in 1956', *Boxoffice* (4 August 1956): 18–20, p. 18.

77. Frank J. Taylor, 'Big Boom in Outdoor Movies', *Saturday Evening Post* 229 (15 September 1956): 31, 100–2, reprinted in Gregory A. Waller (ed.), *Moviegoing in America: A Sourcebook in the History of Film Exhibition* (Malden, MA: Blackwell Publishers, 2002), p. 248.

78. Segrave, *Drive-in Theaters*, p. 199.

79. These dimensions correspond to the average widescreen drive-in of the 1950s. For comparison, the CinemaScope screen installed at the Roxy Theater for the 1953 premiere of *The Robe* was smaller by fifteen feet both in height and width. Wesley Trout, 'Those Special Projection Problems at the Drive-In Theatre', *Boxoffice* (4 February 1956), *The Modern Theatre Section*: 8–9, 74, 76, 78–82, p. 78.

80. See the illustration of Los Angeles' first drive-in in Segrave, *Drive-in Theaters*, p. 20.

81. See additional examples in Don and Susan Sanders, *The American Drive-In Movie Theatre* (Osceola: Motorbooks International, 1997), pp. 36, 54, 59.

82. Frank J. Taylor, 'Big Boom in Outdoor Movies', p. 248. Of course, in addition to these enormous, unique screens, there also were unadorned white screens erected on scaffolding, which Gordon's Twentynine Palms installation more closely resembled.

83. In the first six months of 1956, 196 new drive-in theatres were built, compared to 54 indoor theatres. Hannum, '$51,809,395 for 250 new theatres in 1956', p. 20.

84. Robert Warshow, 'Movie Chronicle: The Westerner', in Gerald Mast and Marshall Cohen (eds), *Film Theory and Criticism*, 2nd edn (Oxford and New York: Oxford University Press, 1979), p. 473.

85. Todd Gitlin, *The Sixties: Years of Hope, Days of Rage* (New York: Bantam Books, 1987), p. 14.

86. 'Give it the Rustic Touch', *Boxoffice* (4 February 1956), *The Modern Theatre Section*: 14.

87. Fence Company of America advertisement reprinted in Sanders and Sanders, *The American Drive-In Movie Theatre*, p. 56.

88. Phil Hannum, 'The Family is 'Target' of New Drive-In', *Boxoffice* (4 August 1956): 38–40, pp. 38–9; Nanna Verhoeff, *The West in Early Cinema: After the Beginning* (Amsterdam: Amsterdam University Press, 2006), p. 200.

89. In 1982, there were 2,129 drive-in theatres still in operation, but only 999 in 1987. Segrave, *Drive-in Theaters*, pp. 235–6.

90. Gerald Clarke and Denise Worrell, 'Dark Clouds over the Drive-ins', *Time* 122:6 (8 August 1983): 74–5, p. 74.

91. Anne Friedberg. 'Les Flâneurs du Mal(l)', p. 425.

92. Taylor, 'Big Boom in Outdoor Movies', p. 247.

93. See advertisements for Selby Wide Ratio Towers, *Boxoffice* (20 January 1954), p. 43, and Raytone Screen Corporation's Cinemaplastic screen coating, *Boxoffice* (4 February 1956), *The Modern Theatre Section*, p. 83.

94. Phil Hannum, 'In Unwrapping Your Drive-in, Remember . . .', *Boxoffice* (4 February 1956), *The Modern Theatre Section*: 33–4, p. 33.

95. Gordon, as quoted in Fagen, 'The Exact Vague History', in Gordon, *Déjà-Vu*, vol. 3, p. 95.

96. Gordon recalled in 2001, 'I had wanted to make that piece in a desert environment. First time I came to Los Angeles was in 1995 or 1996, and some friends took me to Twentynine Palms to see the landscape'. Cheng, 'He Tweaks the Language of Hollywood', p. 1.

97. Ronald Holloway, 'The Searchers', *Variety* (14 March 1956), p. 6.

98. Gordon, as quoted in Cheng, 'He Tweaks the Language of Hollywood', p. 1.

99. This is Monk's assessment of what he saw. Monk, *Double-Cross*, p. 93.

100. Philip Monk, *Spirit Hunter: the Haunting of American Culture by Myths of Violence:*

Speculations on Jeremy Blake's Winchester Trilogy (Toronto: Art Gallery of York University, 2005), p. 9.

101. Gordon, as quoted in Ruth Rosengarten, 'He Loves You', *Déjà-Vu*, vol. 3, pp. 17–18.

102. David Harding, '*5-Year Dive-By*: Douglas Gordon in 29 Palms', http://www.davidharding.net/?page_id=3 (accessed 1 September 2015).

103. Monk, *Double-Cross*, pp. 81, 93.

104. Ibid. p. 86.

105. Adrian Searle, 'Winning Game of Good and Evil', *The Guardian* (29 November 1996): 3.

106. In this regard, Gordon's installation is also in dialogue with the ideological and material legacy of Land art, an important aspect of the work that extends beyond the scope of this study. Gordon's piece forms a twenty-first-century response to Robert Smithson's work on urban and industrial archaeology, the relationship between cinema and the landscape, and the ruin and monument as site or nonsite. Take for example Smithson's comments on cinema and theatres in 'Entropy and the New Monuments' and 'A Cinematic Atopia', and his unrealised plans for a film bunker at his Salt Lake earthwork, *Spiral Jetty* (1970). See Robert Smithson, 'Entropy and the New Monuments', *Artforum* 5:10 (June 1966): 26–31; Robert Smithson, 'A Cinematic Atopia', *Artforum* 10:1 (September 1971): 53–5.

107. For example, the piece was included in a two-work Gordon exhibition at the University of Quebec-Montreal in 2007 and *Print the Legend: The Myth of the West*, a 2008 group show at The Fruitmarket Gallery in Edinburgh. See http://www.uqam.ca/nouvelles/2007/07-264.htm (accessed 1 September 2015) and http://www.fruitmarket.co.uk/wp-content/uploads/2014/03/PTL_report_web.pdf (accessed 1 September 2015).

Conclusion

There is nothing new about screened images in art spaces today. And why should there be when screens have become a part of nearly every contemporary device and setting, from automobiles and looms to classrooms and bus stands? Nevertheless, this proliferation of screens continues to impact and shape our understanding of art. Some theorists, including Rosalind Krauss, Lev Manovich and Peter Weibel, have claimed that contemporary culture – perhaps especially art – has moved beyond past constraints of medium.[1] Proclamations of a 'post-media' era build on corollary discussions such as that of the 'post-cinema' in emphasising the difficulty of establishing and maintaining stable boundaries between forms and methods of expression that once seemed autonomous and distinct. Amid these claims of the withering meaning of 'medium' at a time when music, film, television, animated games and other content may be accessed through a single device, it must be remembered that the screen remains at the centre of such activity as the most common site of interface for these transactions. To measure the significance of this medium that is the screen, it is important to consider the role that screens and screened images have played for over a century as places of physical, social and ideological interface in diverse cultural contexts.

The relationship between the development of cinema's many forms and the history of modern and contemporary art presents a privileged path in this process. As competing and intersecting realms of visual practice since the late nineteenth century, cinema and art have borne the traits of convergence, hybridity and adaptability often ascribed to today's media culture, long before these became common ways of conceptualising or describing visual media. Indeed, the history of modern art can be regarded as a long struggle to dissolve the often arbitrary and ideological boundaries that had been imposed on varied practices of visual expression while also testing imposed divisions of sensory experience. Space and contingency – both fundamental to cinema – became key points of access in this transformation. Many of the most significant and lasting works in contemporary art have grown out of the cracks opened up by that process. This is the case with the artists considered here. Despite important differences in their beliefs and aims concerning art, media and social engagement, Robert Rauschenberg, Andy Warhol, Mona Hatoum and Douglas Gordon all have shared the fundamental need to break down divisions between specific material practices, spatial contexts and social norms. One means of accomplishing this goal has been recognising and incorporating a range of culturally popular film- and cinema-related activities into their works and exhibition choices. This exposes the close – but often neglected – overlap between spaces and methods for art production and reception and those found in wider visual culture, while also demonstrating the broad range of practices that fell under the heading of 'cinema'. If the culture of cinema has been not only the corner movie theatre and the scenes on its screen, but also a variety of other circumstances that have crossed film (and later video) narratives with different populations and spaces, then art could – and should – similarly reflect greater diversity in its forms and circumstances. This conviction aligns these four artists with many others working today. It also suggests that gaining durable insights into recent developments in communicative technologies and their application in (and as) art requires greater knowledge of the historical interdependence of art and popular forms of expression, even when these would appear to be at odds.

Note

1. Rosalind Krauss, *A Voyage on the North Sea: Art in the Age of the Post-Medium Condition* (London: Thames and Hudson, 1999); Lev Manovich, 'Post-Media Aesthetics' (2001), available at http://manovich.net/index.php/projects/post-media-aesthetics (accessed 1 September 2015); Peter Weibel, 'The Post-Media Condition', in AAVV, *Postmedia Condition* (Madrid: Centro Cultural Conde Duque, 2006). Félix Guattari had spoken and written on several occasions in the 1980s about an on-coming post-media era. See, for example, Félix Guattari, 'L'impasse post-moderne', *La Quinzaine littéraire* (1–15 February 1986): 20–1.

EU Authorised Representative:

Easy Access System Europe Mustamäe tee 50, 10621 Tallinn, Estonia

gpsr.requests@easproject.com

Printed and bound by CPI Group (UK) Ltd, Croydon, CR0 4YY

10/03/2026

02068781-0004